KU-695-328

Explorations in Sociology

British Sociological Association conference volume series

Sami Zubaida (*editor*) 1 *Race and Racism*
Richard Brown (*editor*) 2 *Knowledge, Education and Cultural Exchange*
Paul Rock and Mary McIntosh (*editors*) 3 *Deviance and Social Control*
Emmanuel de Kadt and Gavin Williams (*editors*) 4 *Sociology and Development*
Frank Parkin (*editor*) 5 *The Social Analysis of Class Structure*
Diana Leonard Barker and Sheila Allen (*editors*) 6 *Sexual Divisions and Society*
Diana Leonard Barker and Sheila Allen (*editors*) 7 *Dependence and Exploitation in Work and Marriage*
Richard Scase (*editor*) 8 *Industrial Society*
Robert Dingwall, Christian Heath, Margaret Reid and Margaret Stacey (*editors*) 9 *Health Care and Health Knowledge*
Robert Dingwall, Christian Heath, Margaret Reid and Margaret Stacey (*editors*) 10 *Health and the Division of Labour*
Gary Littlejohn, Barry Smart, John Wakeford and Nira Yuval-Davis (*editors*) 11 *Power and the State*
Michèle Barrett, Philip Corrigan, Annette Kuhn and Janet Wolff (*editors*) 12 *Ideology and Cultural Production*
Bob Fryer, Allan Hunt, Doreen MacBarnet and Bert Moorhouse (*editors*) 13 *Law, State and Society*
Philip Abrams, Rosemary Deem, Janet Finch and Paul Rock (*editors*) 14 *Practice and Progress*
Graham Day, Lesley Caldwell, Karen Jones, David Robbins and Hilary Rose (*editors*) 15 *Diversity and Decomposition in the Labour Market*
David Robbins, Lesley Caldwell, Graham Day, Karen Jones and Hilary Rose (*editors*) 16 *Rethinking Social Inequality*
Eva Gamarnikow, David Morgan, June Purvis and Daphne Taylorson (*editors*) 17 *The Public and the Private*
Eva Gamarnikow, David Morgan, June Purvis and Daphne Taylorson (*editors*) 18 *Gender, Class and Work*
Gareth Rees, Janet Bujra, Paul Littlewood, Howard Newby and Teresa L. Rees (*editors*) 19 *Political Action and Social Identity*
Howard Newby, Janet Bujra, Paul Littlewood, Gareth Rees and Teresa L. Rees (*editors*) 20 *Restructuring Capital*
Sheila Allen, Kate Purcell, Alan Waton and Stephen Wood (*editors*) 21 *The Experience of Unemployment*
Kate Purcell, Stephen Wood, Alan Waton and Sheila Allen (*editors*) 22 *The Changing Experience of Employment*
Jalna Hanmer and Mary Maynard (*editors*) 23 *Women, Violence and Social Control*
Colin Creighton and Martin Shaw (*editors*) 24 *Sociology of War and Peace*
Alan Bryman, Bill Bytheway, Patricia Allatt and Teresa Keil (*editors*) 25 *Rethinking the Life Cycle*
Patricia Allatt, Teresa Keil, Alan Bryman and Bill Bytheway (*editors*) 26 *Women and the Life Cycle*

Editors	No.	Title
Ian Varcoe, Maureen McNeil and Steven Yearley (*editors*)	27	*Deciphering Science and Technology*
Maureen McNeil, Ian Varcoe and Steven Yearley (*editors*)	28	*The New Reproductive Technologies*
David McCrone, Stephen Kendrick and Pat Straw (*editors*)	29	*The Making of Scotland*
Stephen Kendrick, Pat Straw and David McCrone (*editors*)	30	*Interpreting the Past, Understanding the Present*
Lynn Jamieson and Helen Corr (*editors*)	31	*State, Private Life and Political Change*
Helen Corr and Lynn Jamieson (*editors*)	32	*Politics of Everyday Life*
Geoff Payne and Malcolm Cross (*editors*)	33	*Sociology in Action*
Pamela Abbott and Claire Wallace (*editors*)	34	*Gender, Power and Sexuality*
Robert Reiner and Malcolm Cross (*editors*)	35	*Beyond Law and Order*
Pamela Abbott and Geoff Payne (*editors*)	36	*New Directions in the Sociology of Health and Illness*
Claire Wallace and Malcolm Cross (*editors*)	37	*Youth in Transition*
Malcolm Cross and Geoff Payne (*editors*)	38	*Work and the Enterprise Culture*
Sara Arber and Nigel Gilbert (*editors*)	39	*Women and Working Lives*
Roger Burrows and Catherine Marsh (*editors*)	40	*Consumption and Class*
Nigel Gilbert, Roger Burrows and Anna Pollert (*editors*)	41	*Fordism and Flexibility*
Catherine Marsh and Sara Arber (*editors*)	42	*Families and Households*
Lydia Morris and E. Stina Lyon (*editors*)	43	*Gender Relations in Public and Private*
Colin Samson and Nigel South (*editors*)	44	*The Social Construction of Social Policy*
Joan Busfield and E. Stina Lyon (*editors*)	45	*Methodological Imaginations*
Janet Holland and Lisa Adkins (*editors*)	46	*Sex, Sensibility and the Gendered Body*
Lisa Adkins and Vicki Merchant (*editors*)	47	*Sexualizing the Social*
Jeffrey Weeks and Janet Holland (*editors*)	48	*Sexual Cultures*
Sallie Westwood and John Williams (*editors*)	49	*Imagining Cities*
Nick Jewson and Suzanne MacGregor (*editors*)	50	*Transforming Cities*
Kevin Brehony and Nazima Rassool (*editors*)	51	*Nationalisms Old and New*
Avtar Brah, Mary J. Hickman and Máirtín Mac an Ghaill (*editors*)	52	*Thinking Identities*
Avtar Brah, Mary J. Hickman and Máirtín Mac an Ghaill (*editors*)	53	*Global Futures*
Paul Bagguley and Jeff Hearn (*editors*)	54	*Transforming Politics*
Jeff Hearn and Sasha Roseneil (*editors*)	55	*Consuming Cultures*
Sasha Roseneil and Julie Seymour (*editors*)	56	*Practising Identities*
Julie Seymour and Paul Bagguley (*editors*)	57	*Relating Intimacies*
Linda McKie and Nick Watson (*editors*)	58	*Organizing Bodies*
Kathryn Backett-Milburn and Linda McKie (*editors*)	59	*Constructing Gendered Bodies*
Nick Watson and Sarah Cunningham-Burley (*editors*)	60	*Reframing the Body*
Sarah Cunningham-Burley and Kathryn Backett-Milburn (*editors*)	61	*Exploring the Body*

Exploring the Body

Edited by

Sarah Cunningham-Burley
Reader, Department of Community Health Sciences
University of Edinburgh

and

Kathryn Backett-Milburn
Senior Research Fellow, Research Unit in Health, Behaviour and Change
University of Edinburgh

Review Editors:

John Holmwood
Professor of Sociology
University of Sussex

Odette Parry
Senior Research Fellow, Research Unit in Health, Behaviour and Change
University of Edinburgh

and

Edwin R. van Teijlingen
Lecturer in Public Health
University of Aberdeen

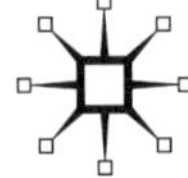

First published 2001 by
PALGRAVE
Houndmills, Basingstoke, Hampshire RG21 6XS and
175 Fifth Avenue, New York, N. Y. 10010
Companies and representatives throughout the world

PALGRAVE is the new global academic imprint of St. Martin's Press LLC Scholarly and Reference Division and Palgrave Publishers Ltd (formerly Macmillan Press Ltd).

ISBN 0–333–77595–3

This book is printed on paper suitable for recycling and made from fully managed and sustained forest sources.

A catalogue record for this book is available from the British Library.

Library of Congress Cataloging-in-Publication Data
Exploring the body / edited by Sarah Cunningham-Burley and Kathryn Backett-Milburn.
p. cm. — (Explorations in sociology.)
Includes bibliographical references and index.
ISBN 0–333–77595–3
1. Body, Human—Social aspects—Congresses. 2. Body, Human—Research—Congresses. I. Cunningham-Burley, Sarah. II. Backett-Milburn, Kathryn, 1948– III. Series.

HM636 .E96 2001
306.4—dc21

2001032729

10 9 8 7 6 5 4 3 2 1
10 09 08 07 06 05 04 03 02 01

Printed and bound in Great Britain by
Antony Rowe Ltd, Chippenham, Wiltshire

Contents

Notes on the Contributors

Kathryn A. Burnett is a Lecturer in Sociology at the University of Paisley. Her main interests are rural identity constructions, the negotiated nature of claims to belonging, home and localness, and the cultural heritage of Scotland.

Pia Christensen is a Lecturer in Anthropology and Co-Director of the Centre for the Social Study of Childhood, University of Hull. Her main interests and publications are in the anthropological study of children's everyday lives and of children's health, family and rural communities. Her current research is a comparative study of Danish children's understandings and use of time. This project is funded by the Danish Research Council's 'Children and Welfare Programme'. Her most recent publication is *Research with Children. Perspectives and Practices* (edited with A. James, 2000).

Brian Heaphy is a Senior Lecturer in Sociology at Nottingham Trent University. He has researched and published in the areas of non-heterosexual relationships, sexual identities and AIDS/HIV. He has recently completed (with Catherine Donovan and Jeffrey Weeks) a book on non-heterosexual patterns of relating, and is currently writing a book on the 'everyday politics' of living with HIV.

Mary Holmes is a Lecturer in Sociology at the University of Aberdeen whose research interests include cultural and political representation, gender and bodies.

Allison James is Reader in Applied Anthropology at the University of Hull and currently Director of the Centre for the Social Study of Childhood. Her main research interests are in childhood, ageing and the life course. Recent publications include *Childhood Identities* (1993); *Growing Up and Growing Old* (with J. Hockey, 1993); and *Theorising Childhood* (with C. Jenks and A. Prout, 1998). Her recent research is on children's perception and understandings of time (with Pia Christensen and Chris Jenks).

Chris Jenks is Professor of Sociology and Pro-Warden (Research) at Goldsmiths' College, University of London. He has worked for a number of years on the sociology of childhood and the sociology of culture.

His most recent major publications are *Childhood* (1996); *Core Sociological Dichotomies* (1998); *Theorizing Childhood* (with Allison James and Alan Prout, 1998); and *Images of Community: Durkheim and the Sociology of Art* (with J. Smith, 2000).

Joost van Loon is a Senior Lecturer in Social Theory at the Department of English and Media Studies, Nottingham Trent University and is associated with the Theory, Culture & Society Centre. He has published extensively in the areas of culture, poststructuralism, mass media, technology and risk, including *The Risk Society and Beyond: Critical Issues for Social Theory* (co-editor with Barbara Adam and Ulrich Beck, 2000). He is also co-editor of *Space and Culture*. His current research interests are focused on the issues of risks, infectious disease and embodiment.

Mike Michael teaches sociology at Goldsmiths' College, University of London. He has published extensively in a number of fields, including the public understanding of science, critical social psychological theory, and the animal experimentation controversy. More recently his interests have turned to the role of mundane technologies in social ordering and disordering. He is author of *Constructing Identities* (1996) and *Reconnecting Culture, Technology and Nature: From Society to Heterogeneity* (2001).

Kevin Paterson is a research student in the School of Social Sciences at Glasgow Caledonian University. His main research interests are the body and disability. He is actively involved with the Centre for Independent Living in Glasgow.

Gerald Pillsbury is Associate Professor of Educational Studies at Western Michigan University. His primary research interests are the role of the self and the body in education and the development of their social dimensions. He is currently working on a discourse analysis project at Western and writing a book on the opportunities for understanding human relationships that chronic disease offers. Previous publications include 'Creating the Plural Self: Athletic Teams' Use of Members' Bodies', *International Journal of Qualitative Studies in Education* (1996); 'Achieving Vision of the Social Construction of Self' in *Encounter: Education for Meaning and Social Justice* (1998); and 'First-Person Singular and Plural: Strategies for Managing Ego- and Sociocentrism in Four Basketball Teams', in *Contemporary Ethnography* (1998).

Hannah Rockwell is Associate Professor of Communication and Director of Peace Studies at Loyola University Chicago. She has published several essays on gender and language processes, and is working on *The Life of Voices: Embodied Subjectivity and Dialogue.*

Anne Scott is a Lecturer in the Department of Sociology and Anthropology, University of Canterbury, New Zealand. She has recently completed a research project on feminist alternative medicine, and is now studying gender issues relating to science and technology. She is particularly interested in women's embodied experiences of 'electronic' activism, and is looking at the use of information technology within transnational women's politics.

Clive Seale is Professor of Medical Sociology at Goldsmiths' College, University of London, and has been involved in research concerning the experience of dying and bereavement over the past fifteen years. His recent publications include *Constructing Death: The Sociology of Dying and Bereavement* (1998) and *The Quality of Qualitative Research* (1999). He is currently working on a study of media representations of people with cancer.

Greg Smith is Senior Lecturer in Sociology at the University of Salford. His teaching and research interests are in ethnographic and interaction sociology and sociological and cultural theory. He is co-author of *Analyzing Visual Data* (1992) and *Introducing Cultural Studies* (1999). He has published on the sociology of Erving Goffman, most recently as editor of *Goffman and Social Organization: Studies in a Sociological Legacy* (1999).

Paul Sweetman is a Lecturer in Sociology at the University of Southampton. His recent publications include work on body modification, fashion and subcultural formations, while his research interests centre on issues of the body, identity, fashion and consumption.

Simon J. Williams is a Reader in Sociology in the Department of Sociology at the University of Warwick, and Co-Director of the Centre for Research in Health, Medicine and Society. His current research interests centre on the relationship between social theory and the sociology of health and illness, with particular reference to issues emotions and embodiment. Recent publications include *The Lived Body: Sociological Themes, Embodied Issues* (with G. Bendelow, 1998); *Emotions in Social Life: Critical Themes and Contemporary Issues* (with G. Bendelow 1998); *Emotions and Social Theory: Corporeal Reflections on the (Ir)rational* (2001); *Health, Medicine and Society, Key Theories, Future Agendas* (with J. Gabe and M. Calnan 2000); and *Emotion and Social Theory* (2000).

Preface and Acknowledgements

This is one of four books comprising chapters originally presented as papers at the annual conference of the British Sociological Association (BSA), held at the University of Edinburgh, 6–9 April 1998. The theme of that conference was 'Making Sense of the Body: Theory, Research and Practice'. This book incorporates some of the many high-quality papers delivered on the theme of the sociology of the body and embodiment. The companion volumes are: *Constructing Gendered Bodies*, edited by Kathryn Backett-Milburn and Linda McKie, *Organising Bodies: Policy, Institutions and Work*, edited by Linda McKie and Nick Watson, and *Reframing the Body*, edited by Nick Watson and Sarah Cunningham-Burley.

The editors of these books formed the organizing committee for the 1998 BSA conference and our call for papers was rewarded with a conference embracing nearly 300 presentations with over 500 participants. The rich conference programme was organized into 21 streams and these were coordinated by members of BSA study groups and interested individuals. Through this format we were able to involve many sociologists, at differing stages of their careers, in the process of developing and running the conference. At the end of the conference there were over 180 papers submitted for consideration by the organizing committee for inclusion in the four books. The editors of the books have had an extremely difficult task in selecting papers to be revised into the format of chapters. We were greatly assisted in this task by review editors who had previously acted as coordinators of relevant streams at the conference.

The conference and these books would not have been possible without the input of many people. We would like to thank the staff of the British Sociological Association and University of Edinburgh for their support in the organization of the conference. Many members of the BSA assisted in numerous ways with the academic content of the conference and we would like to thank them for their ongoing support. The editors are also grateful to their colleagues at the University of Aberdeen and the University of Edinburgh. We would especially like to thank Carolyn MacDougall for her help preparing this typescript. Families and friends helped out in practical and emotional ways; we owe them a personal debt.

We dedicate this and the other three books to the stream coordinators for the 1998 Annual BSA conference. Their enthusiastic support for our goal of running a welcoming, egalitarian and participative conference was much appreciated, and together, we hope to have achieved this.

Introduction

Sarah Cunningham-Burley and Kathryn Backett-Milburn

From being under-researched and theorized, the body has now become central to the sociological project. We have moved from what Freund (1988: 839) described as a 'curiously disembodied view of human beings' to one in which '[b]odies are in, in academic as well as in popular culture' (Frank 1990: 131). This interest in the body as a site of sociological analysis has in part been driven by the influence of feminism (Martin 1987; Grosz 1996), in part by the work of Michael Foucault (Foucault 1981) and developments in social theory, especially in postmodernism (Frank 1991). We all have bodies, but how we use bodies and what meaning is ascribed to a body are the products of social relations (Hurst and Woolley 1982); the body has provided the focus for situated, historical analysis. In addition, Freund (1988: 840), amongst others, notes that there is increasing recognition amongst sociologists that 'the social actors that populate their theories have bodies that are integral to human existence and thus a central consideration in any theory'.

Bryan Turner (1984) was one of the first to bring the body into the mainstream of sociological theory, although the pioneering work of Goffman (1969) should not be forgotten. Turner noted that in contrast to sociology, the 'human body has been accorded a place of importance in anthropology since the nineteenth century' (Turner 1991: 1). The work of a number of anthropologists (for example, Douglas 1970, 1973; Caplan 1987) has informed the development of a sociological theory of the body. Subsequent work by, for example, Freund (1988), Frank (1990), the edited collection by Featherstone et al. (1991), Shilling (1993), Falk (1994) and Crossley (1996) all served to ensure that the body remained in the foreground of sociological theory. The launch of *Body and Society* in 1995 signalled the establishment of sociology of the body as an area of sociological work in its own right. Anybody doubting the upsurge of sociological interest in the body and its consequent relevance to modern day social theory should try typing in 'body' as a key word in any social science search index.

There is, however, no single sociology of the body. In the same way that postmodernism rejects the metanarrative, so sociology of the body incorporates a plurality of theories and empirical work. It has synthesized a number of developments in sociological theory in the last 20 years (Davis 1997; Shilling 1997). In summary, these include:

- challenges to concerns that some sociology was replicating the mind/body dualism of Cartesian thought (Frank 1991; Turner 1991; Leder 1992);
- Foucault's conceptualization of power through the exploration of surveillance and control of the body and sexuality (Foucault 1981);
- feminist theorists and researchers whose examination of identity and everyday embodied experiences gave renewed impetus to debates on gender, sexuality and identity (Martin 1987; Butler 1990; Grosz 1996; Lindemann 1997);
- the critique of the medical model through sociological explanations of health and illness and social action (Goffman 1969; Fox 1993; Annandale 1998);
- the blurring of boundaries for bodies and identities, focusing on the body as a site for shifting notions of consumption (Boyne 1991; Shilling 1993; Jagger 1998); and
- the impact of social and economic changes upon the body in global policies to enhance development and to tackle environmental concerns (Connell 2000).

Contributors to this book draw upon a range of sociological theories and research to enhance the distinctive development of the sociology of the body. Their chapters demonstrate how the sociology of the body provides an opportunity to study the body as integral to social action and social being, and thus further the discipline of sociology.

This book is specifically concerned with the range of ways in which sociologists are exploring the body and embodiment. It brings together chapters with diverse subject matter, but with the common aim of expanding the fields of research and broadening the scope of theory. Many of the chapters draw on empirical work, for example, interview accounts, participant observation and autobiography; a few select under-researched areas for detailed theoretical and conceptual treatment.

The book is divided into three parts. In Part I, 'Theorizing Embodied Practice: Metaphor and Methods', the chapters explore different ways in which embodied practice, whether with homeopathy, organizational change, chronic illness or scar stories, can be both accessed empirically and conceptualized using different metaphorical and theoretical strategies. Part II, 'Neglected Bodies and Everyday Life', brings together chapters on neglected areas within the sociology of the body: living with mortality, death as cultural practice, bodies in sleep, and the phenomenology of disability. Again, a range of methods are used to explore these areas. Then, in Part III, 'Exploring Bodies: Time, Space and Leisure', contributions focus on running, tattooing and piercing, childhood and socio-technological relations. In its own way, each considers the social relations of embodiment in time and space, and takes seriously the way in which human agency creates embodied practice, as well as being constrained by structures and artefacts.

Theorizing embodied practice: metaphor and methods

Part I begins with an elegant exploration by Anne Scott of the contradictions and ambiguities which are inherent in daily embodied experience. She discusses the limits of dualism and the creative potential of ambiguity. Drawing on a range of writing, but especially the work of Anzaldúa, Scott focuses on how the body can be conceptualized as a crossroads or Borderlands. This challenges the view of the body as object which characterizes western biomedicine, but finds voice in alternative medicine, especially homeopathy. Using some of her own data, Scott considers how homeopathy establishes a 'commonplace' in which the patient's body, the therapeutic relationship, the social and physical environment, the remedies used and the patient's consciousness begin collaborating to materialize a biographical narrative. Storyteller, metaphor and trope all offer ways of being and understanding the body.

Kathryn Burnett and Mary Holmes consider further the potential for theorizing from empirical work and offer a fascinating exploration of the body as a heritage site in Chapter 2. They examine the construction of scar stories as narratives which locate the body in time and space. This is a moral activity, and suggests that such selective storytelling creates the opportunity to refashion the body's history in a way that serves present needs: 'Telling stories about the embodied self is a way of selectively revealing one's socially situated history'. Like Scott, Burnett and Holmes transcend the stark dualism which separates mind and body, and show how scar stories can accomplish this blurred exposition. The metaphor of heritage allows the body to be understood as something that is valued and cared for, but where the past is reformulated, with the appearance of authenticity, for the present.

Using as a starting point an insightful moment, when one of the authors was involved as a consultant/researcher during a process of cultural engineering in a large company, Joost van Loon and Hannah Rockwell explore how the concept of performativity, introduced by

Butler, can be developed to allow an empirical exploration of bodies and embodiment. They argue that embodiment must be an integrated feature of method. They propose using method (an essential component of the sociological endeavour) as a way of exploring the complexity of performativity, moving through issues of spatialization, resonances and shadows to do this. They develop the concept of choreography as a metaphor for understanding the social, thus challenging the structure/agency divide. Choreography involves both dissonant as well as consonant elements. So, rather than abandoning method in the wake of poststructuralism, van Loon and Rockwell argue for its centrality: 'methods in social and cultural research are always performative, and hence engage in processes of embodiment and spatialization'.

Gerald Pillsbury concludes Part I with a direct and intimate challenge to the vast body of sociological work as well as common-sense discourse, which depicts chronic disease as 'uncompromisingly' negative. His chapter changes the metaphors that structure the experience of disease: his thought-experiment challenges taken for granted assumptions and framings; his personal experience leads him to frame the disease as a form of play. In this way he asks: 'What can chronic disease reveal about the social dimension of self?' Language, he argues, is the primary tool in the construction of our experience, and play is a perspective created through words. He takes a phenomenological approach and develops what he terms a playful perspective towards his own experience. By analysing his experience of the social interaction of restricted roles, he reveals how relationships are bounded by the ambiguities of social interaction. Language as metaphor for experience is better than literal description, but none the less remains limited, thus preventing holistic understanding. Pillsbury demonstrates that a truly embodied sociology requires reflexive sociologists, able to reflect on and incorporate their own experience – a theme taken up in Parts II and III of this volume.

Neglected bodies and everyday life

Part II brings together four contributions which, in different ways, examine bodies and aspects of embodiment often neglected in social theory and empirical work. Kevin Paterson persuasively attempts to counter the disablism inherent in phenomenology and disability studies' disembodied view of disability, by developing a highly socialized phenomenological approach to the impaired body. As is the case with other contributors to this volume, Paterson transgresses Cartesian dualism. He argues that phenomenology can become a political discourse, thus contributing to the agenda of disability studies. Paterson neatly explores how such a project can be achieved first through an exploration of pain and, second, through a focus on speech impairment, when he draws on autobiographical experience. Developing the work of Leder, he demonstrates how bodily dys-appearance suggests the way in which carnality informs all aspects of social experience, whether this be physical and spatial barriers or communicative norms of 'time to talk'. 'Norms, values, conventions, buildings, even time and space are carnally informed, shaped and structured by bodily activity. However, the information that is imprinted onto the world is dominated by non-disabled bodies, by a specific hegemonic form of carnality which excludes as it constructs.' The pursuit of a sociology of impairment thus advances a more radicalized disability studies.

In Chapter 6 Clive Seale, argues that a sociological analysis of the body must account for the way in which the fact of death underpins cultural practices. In so doing, he responds to the underdevelopment of contemporary sociology of the body, and contributes to current social theory. As with many of the other chapters, he challenges the nature/culture divide, offering a truly embodied account of everyday life. After reviewing the contributions of key social theorists, Seale finds himself still requiring more before he can tackle the questions he has posed himself, namely how the turning away from death underpins social and cultural activity. Like Paterson, Seale has to tackle the long-standing problematic of adequately theorizing both structure and agency. Seale turns to conversational analysis to provide a route to understanding daily discourse as constitutive of and constructing our social lives. He develops three key concepts – imagined community, revivalism and resurrective practice – to assist our understanding of the body and death. He then illustrates his theorizing with an apposite case study of a confessional death: the last TV interview with the playwright Dennis Potter, who died of cancer. Seale explores how Potter's special authority as someone touched by death is rhetorically achieved, and how this provides insight into the way in which social and cultural life can 'be considered as a human construction in the face of death'.

In the next chapter, Brian Heaphy uses the personal narratives of those living with HIV and AIDS to explore how they incorporate mortality into everyday life. Following Plummer, he stresses the power of such stories. He draws on narratives of testing, reskilling and relating, each showing the dynamics and imperatives underlying the 'possibilities' and 'impossibilities' of living as PWA. Stories of reskilling show the position of the clinic as central to the moral and medical management of AIDS and PWA, confirming the declining and dying body, as well as promoting strategies of silence and invisibility in relation to disclosure. Testing introduces the real possibility of death into life. Counselling and therapy, although focusing on living, reinforce 'the assumed impossibility of incorporating an acute awareness of death into everyday living'. The interviews in this study, through their narratives of relating, also show how these interactions support silence with respect to the intimacy of illness and death. Heaphy argues that the incentives to silence and invisibility present in expert resources and PWAs' own understandings must be understood within the wider context of power and the management of the problematic body. The personal and political challenge is to ensure that the reality of death and the voice of the dying are not rendered invisible in everyday life.

In Chapter 8 Simon Williams argues that, like death, sleep is a central aspect of social life, and so brings a much needed sociological discussion of this neglected area. He makes a strong case for the sociological importance of sleep: sleep is fundamental to society, its institutions and its embodied agents. The sociological focus must be on the 'doing of sleep'. In this chapter, we find that sleep, though a biological imperative, is a socially organized practice which cannot be explained in physiological terms. Following Mauss, Williams reiterates that sleep is a 'technique of the body'; it 'bears the imprint of tie and marks of culture'. To demonstrate this, Williams draws on the work of Elias to trace 'the historical changes in sleep behaviour, from its earlier public organisation to the increasing private affair it is today'. He also draws on the example of the modern hospital as a microcosm of the sleeping society, demonstrating the multifaceted nature of sleep; the control of sleepers; and the relationship between social organization and sleep routines. As with other contributors to this volume, Williams' discussion of sleep can help sociology transcend the many entrenched dichotomies of western thought which hinder our understanding of embodied social life.

Exploring bodies: time, space and leisure

In the opening chapter of Part III, Greg Smith provides a stimulating contribution to how we can explore the body, by combining theoretical explanation with ethnographic elaboration. Smith draws on interviews with adult runners and race walkers, and his own participation in these activities. Abuse commentary is a common threat to runners.

The norm of civil inattention, so often attended to in public places, is often transgressed as runners experience comments from passers-by. Smith examines his interview data, elaborating on Matza's techniques of neutralization. Whilst runners' interview accounts suggest that they neutralize the import of street remarks – for example, through the denial of injury – an embodied analysis must link this to runners' body management techniques: ignoring 'ignorance'; avoiding 'trouble'; talking back; hitting back. Such techniques were often gendered, and indeed, running can be seen to magnify aspects of gendered experience in public places. Smith's analysis shows 'that an adequate sociological analysis of the body management techniques of publicly harassed runners requires attention to both the details of bodily enactment and to the practical reasoning informing that enactment'.

In the next chapter Paul Sweetman considers the problems with the textual and semiotic approach to understanding subcultures. He draws on his own research on the process of becoming tattooed, before addressing more recent developments in subcultural studies and wider theoretical and methodological issues. The early attempts to theorize subcultures, he argues, neglected the way in which stylistic devices might construct rather than just express embodied subjectivity. Like Smith, Sweetman was, to some extent, a participant observer, as someone who has himself been tattooed or pierced. He argues that the process of becoming tattooed or pierced – or writing the self as text – is central rather than peripheral to many contemporary body modifiers' motivations and experience. It is the experiential aspects of this that Sweetman seeks to understand in his study. This makes the tattooed body much more than symbol or text, and its study brings the affectual dimensions into understanding subcultural experience. This strongly suggests that the subcultural body is not reducible to textual or semiotic analysis. As with many of the other chapters in this volume, Sweetman's contribution raises methodological issues. As he himself asks: 'Can standard methods of data collection really capture the affectual dimensions of experience?' He suggests that this may be one area where the researcher's own direct experience is important in developing final understanding and interpretation.

Pia Christensen, Allison James and Chris Jenks explore the ways in which the body incorporates both time and temporality. Time and being, in relation to the body, predominate in children's everyday lives at school. They focus on the different ways in which children come to understand the qualitative passing of time, especially in their everyday lives at school. They explore three aspects. First, the ways in which children come to understand the time and temporality of everyday life through their bodily habituation to social routines in the social context of the school. Second, the understanding children have of the ageing body in relation to the accomplishment of these everyday social practices. Third, how children engage with issues of timing – 'what to say, what to do and when' – for a successful social performance as a schooled child. Classical social theory has primarily paid attention to the spatiality of codes and rules of bodily behaviour; this chapter stresses the importance of their underlying temporality. Bodily discipline is most obviously structured by teachers; however, children are able to liberate themselves from these constraints, as this contribution demonstrates.

Mike Michael's fascinating chapter deals with the important relationship between the body and technology; the merging of human and non-human forms and the social practice within which this is embedded. Michael problematizes Latour's analysis of hybridizations by focusing on the television remote control and the couch potato. Dreams of disembodiment, evident in the development of technological artefacts which replace human labour, also result in the return of the body, adapting to new routines. The remote control demands certain bodily components, yet it is also tied to domestic power relations. The 'working-ness' of this technology rests on relations of power between a number of potential users-in-interaction, yet the remote control is not an innocent in this struggle, it also mediates – symbolizes, crystallizes and materially affects – these relations. Michael sees the way in which popular cultures shape the hybrid, through an examination of the discourses of the couch potato. This discussion challenges Latour's assertion of modernist disinterest in hybrids. Michael is able to demonstrate the involvement of human and material factors, coincidence and unintended effects, by analysing the process of 'losing' the remote control. Finally, he suggests that hybrids themselves practise surveillance, and it is the examination of this to which sociology should now turn if it is to explore the social, corporeal and technological.

These diverse contributions challenge our taken for granted thinking about many aspects of the body and embodiment; they also pose difficult questions for sociologists striving to develop more sophisticated but grounded understandings of diverse bodies and practices. The strong empirical focus of some of the contributions suggests that much further research, imaginatively using a range of methods, could usefully be conducted. This will further refine existing ways of conceptualizing the body, and will help link theoretical and empirical work in this area.

References

Annandale, E. 1998. *The Sociology of Health and Medicine*. Cambridge: Polity.

Bowlby, J. 1988. *A Secure Base: Clinical Applications of Attachment Theory*. London: Routledge.

Boyne, R. 1991. 'The Art of the Body in the Discourse of Postmodernity', pp. 281–96, in M. Featherstone, M. Hepworth, B.S. Turner (eds.) *The Body. Social Process and Cultural Theory*. London: Sage.

Butler, J. 1990 *Gender Trouble: Feminism and the Subversion of Identity*. New York: Routledge.

Caplan, P. (ed.) 1987. *The Cultural Construction of Sexuality*. London: Tavistock.

Connell, R.W. 2000. 'Bodies, Intellectuals and World Society', in N. Watson and S. Cunningham-Burley (eds.) *Reframing the Body*. Basingstoke: Macmillan – now Palgrave.

Crossley, N. 1996. *Intersubjectivity: The Fabric of Social Becoming*. London: Sage.

Davis, K. (ed.) 1997. *Embodied Practices. Feminist Perspectives on the Body*. London: Sage.

Douglas, M. 1970. *Purity and Danger: An Analysis of Concepts of Pollution and Taboo*. Harmondsworth: Penguin Books.

Douglas, M. 1973. *Natural Symbols: Explorations in Cosmology*. Harmondsworth: Penguin Books.

Elias, N. 1978. *The History of Manners: The Civilising Process. Volume 1*. New York: Pantheon.

Falk, P. 1994. *The Consuming Body*. London: Sage.

Featherstone, M., Hepworth, M. and Turner, B.S. 1991. *The Body. Social Process and Cultural Theory*. London: Sage.

Foucault, M. 1981. *The History of Sexuality. Volume 1: An Introduction*. Harmondsworth: Penguin Books.

Fox, N. 1993. *Postmodernism, Sociology and Health*. Buckingham: Open University Press.

Frank, A. 1990. 'Bringing Bodies Back in: A Decade Review'. *Theory, Culture and Society*, 7: 131–62.

Frank, A. 1991. 'For a Sociology of the Body: An Analytical Review', pp. 36–102, in M. Featherstone, M. Hepworth and B.S. Turner (eds.) *The Body. Social Process and Cultural Theory*. London: Sage.

Freund, P. 1988. 'Bringing Society into the Body', *Theory and Society*, 17: 839–64.

Goffman, I. 1969. *The Presentation of Self in Everyday Life*. Harmondsworth: Penguin Books.

Grosz, E. 1996. *Space, Time and Perversion. Essays on the Politics of the Body*. New York: Routledge.

Hurst, P. and Woolley, P. 1982. *Social Relations and Human Attributes*. London: Tavistock.

Jagger, E. 1988. 'Marketing the Self, Buying an Other: Dating in a Post Modern, Consumer Society', *Sociology*, 32(4): 795–814.

Leder, D. 1992. 'A Tale of Two Bodies: the Cartesian Corpse and the Lived Body', in D. Welton (ed.) *Body and Flesh: A Philosophical Reader*. Oxford: Blackwell.
Lindemann, G. 1997. 'The Body of Difference', pp. 73–92, in K. Davis (ed.) *Embodied Practices. Feminist Perspectives on the Body*. London: Sage.
Martin, E. 1987. *The Woman in the Body*. Milton Keynes: Open University Press.
Shilling, C. 1993. *The Body and Social Theory*. London: Sage.
Shilling, C. 1997. 'The Undersocialised Conception of the (Embodied) Agent in Modern Sociology', *Sociology*, 31 (4): 737–54.
Turner, B.S. 1984. *The Body and Society: Explorations in Social Theory*. Oxford: Blackwell.
Turner, B.S. 1991. 'Recent Developments in the Theory of the Body', pp. 1–35, *The Body. Social Process and Cultural Theory*. London: Sage.

Part I

Theorizing Embodied Practice: Metaphor and Methods

1

The Storyteller's Paradox: Homeopathy in the Borderlands

Anne Scott

Introduction: the problem of dualism

> 1,950 mile-long open wound
> dividing a *pueblo*, a culture,
> running down the length of my body,
> staking rods in my flesh,
> splits me splits me
> *me raja me raja*
> This is my home
> this thin edge of
> barbwire.
> (Gloria Anzaldúa 1987: 2–3)

Dualism has been a key theme in feminist theory over the past 20–30 years. In one of their earliest insights, second-wave feminists noted that western thought is structured by an interweaving network of radical, hierarchical, fixed dichotomies, and that women have generally found themselves on the wrong side of these divides. Feminist analyses have demonstrated that seemingly neutral concepts such as 'rationality', 'individuality', 'secularism', 'objectivity' and 'citizenship' are, in fact, premised on assumptions of dualism.[1] Feminist theory has itself contributed to the dualistic world-view. Recently, some feminist theorists have pointed out that, with its split between 'sex' and 'gender', a dualistic division between biological and social realities has been central to the second-wave feminist project (Kirby 1991; Nicholson 1994). Some contemporary ecofeminists have argued that the dualistic divisions which ground the oppressions of race, gender, class and species are connected, by means of a network of linking postulates, to each other and to a basic dualistic division between reason and nature within western culture (King 1989; Plumwood 1993: 44–5).

Feminist philosophers have analysed the logical structure of dualism in a series of discussions over the past 20 years. Nancy Jay (1981) notes that the two terms of the dualism are not in a symmetrical relationship; the structure is, rather, one of inclusion and exclusion. The secondary term of the dualism is perceived only as an infinite, homogeneous background against which the primary term is defined. It is, as Simone de Beauvoir (1949) famously put it, 'the Other'. Val Plumwood describes the structure of dualistic thinking as 'the logic of colonisation' (1993: 41). Her analysis draws on Karen Warren's (1990) distinction between contingent dichotomies, which exist within every conceptual system, and dualisms, which play a role in some socially oppressive conceptual systems. Plumwood describes a dualism as 'an intense, established and developed cultural expression of such a hierarchical relationship, constructing central cultural concepts and identities so as to make equality and mutuality literally unthinkable' (1993: 47). Dualisms, she claims, are conceptual structures created by hierarchical and oppressive social relationships. They construct identities which are unitary, fixed and oppositional.

Both Jay's and Plumwood's discussions of the logical structure of dualism point to the centrality of the self–other relationship within western ontology; 'the Other' is a background against which the western individual defines his or her subjectivity. For the master consciousness, more than social power is at stake in the maintenance of a dualistic relationship; a very *identity* seems to hang in the balance. Jessica Benjamin (1988), a feminist object relations theorist, has drawn on psychoanalytic and Hegelian theory to explore the development of these intersubjective relationships of domination. She identifies an inevitable tension for the developing child between psychological needs to assert the self and to receive the recognition of others. The modern, western 'self' wants to be established as an absolute and independent agent. In order to achieve this, however, he or she must be recognized as such by another independent agent; this need to cede agency to another acts to limit the absolute agency of the self. The tension thus generated may seem intolerable:

> In a world construed of codifiable rules alone, the Other loomed on the outside of the self as a mystifying, but above all a confusingly ambivalent presence: the potential anchorage of the self's identity, yet simultaneously an obstacle, a resistance to the ego's self-assertion.

> In modern ethics, the Other was the contradiction incarnate and the most awesome of stumbling-blocks on the self's march to fulfilment. (Bauman 1993: 84)

The tension can be addressed by fixing the relationship as one characterized by dominance and submission; one actor becomes primary, while the other takes on a reflecting role, as his or her 'Other'. The logic of dualism is played out on a personal scale.

Benjamin argues, however, that the ideal resolution of this tension is *no* resolution. The tension between sameness and difference must be maintained if a capacity for egalitarian relationships is to be created. This experience of paradox – of ambiguity and contradiction – is a creative one. Benjamin's analysis points towards the need to aim for a different sort of life – a life lived on the Borderlands. In addressing the many dualisms which structure western society, the continual overcoming or assimilation of difference is neither necessary nor desirable. Many feminists have argued that the social oppressions of gender, class, race, ethnicity, sexuality and disability cannot be addressed without an acceptance that some degree of paradox, conflict and ambiguity is inevitable. It is my contention, however, that the tension between the mind and the body – as well as that between spirituality and everyday life – can be equally productive. The creative power of ambiguity is also embedded in the body.

This chapter uses Gloria Anzaldúa's exploration of life within the *Aztlán* (The US Southwest) Borderlands as a starting point for a discussion that ranges across several sorts of dualisms. I will begin by exploring the concept of the Borderlands, or the crossroads, as it has been developed by a number of postcolonial, feminist and ecological theorists. I will then focus on the human body as a specific type of crossroads arguing that, from this perspective, the biomedical model of the body as 'object' makes little or no sense. I will briefly sketch in a new model of the body which is, I will argue, drawn on by the alternative medical therapies in general, and by homeopathy in particular. These therapies, I will suggest, may be more adequate for understanding bodily experience in the Borderlands.

The Borderlands

In her exploration of the process by which *Aztlán*'s mixed race people deal with the everyday collisions of Anglo, Native American and Spanish culture, Gloria Anzaldúa writes, 'The new *mestiza* copes by developing a tolerance for contradictions, a tolerance for ambiguity' (1987: 79):

> I am an act of kneading, of uniting and joining that not only has produced both a creature of darkness and a creature of light, but also a creature that questions the definitions of light and dark and gives them new meanings. We are the people who leap in the dark; we are the people on the knees of the gods. In our very flesh, (r)evolution works out the clash of cultures. It makes us crazy constantly, but if the centre holds, we've made some kind of evolutionary step forward. (Anzaldúa 1987: 81)

This concept of a crossroads, or a Borderlands, where we can *hold* ambiguity and contradiction rather than trying to assimilate it, collapse it or push it into a dualistic opposition, has become a powerful metaphor within the work of an emerging group of ecofeminists, poststructuralists, artists and feminist science theorists. The Vietnamese-American filmmaker Trinh Minh-ha's (1989) concept of the 'inappropriate/d other' has become a part of this project. These are the people who seem inauthentic, or even oxymoronic; they don't 'fit'. They do not belong within the conceptual categories we have constructed to contain them (Haraway 1992a). The 'inappropriate/d other' is a trickster, wearing a number of masks; beneath the masks, however, there is no authentic, essential, unitary subject. Rather, the shifting disguises *are* his or her essence. Within this vision of humanity, a division between appearance and reality cannot be maintained. The Borderlands are not a transitional location for the inappropriate/d other; they are a 'natural' state.

The stories of coyote, themselves products of the *Aztlán* Borderlands, have emerged as another figuration within this new feminist project (Cheney 1989: 319; Haraway 1991b; 1991c; Phelan 1996). Coyote is a trickster, a shape shifter. Coyotes are not noble creatures. They are not beautiful, virtuous or altruistic. Complex and ambivalent, full of desire and ambition, coyote is a mythic survivor, and he achieves this survival through camouflage, sneakiness and cunning. As Shane Phelan notes, 'Tricksters are noted for their ability to die and then show up again; even dismemberment and decomposition do not spell the end' (1996: 134). Coyotes have no divine plan, but they are adept at devising solutions to the specific problems they face in their lives. In the process they, like human beings, create the world.

One problem with these tropes is that they have become associated with a postmodern sensibility which can be uncongenial to spiritual considerations. Another dualistic division, that between surface and depth, is relevant here; in the western world-view, spirituality has been associated with depth, with essence and with authenticity; it has been considered inimical to the shifting manifestations of surface life. As Bauman (1992: 194) notes, the body is seen as the material substratum – the sole constancy – within a constant flux of self-constituting identities. A postmodern sensibility which is seduced by 'the body' thus learns to ignore its own corporeality. Vicky Kirby has noted:

> the pervasive yet unpalatable belief that the anatomical body is indeed the unarguably real body, the literal body, the body whose immovable and immobilizing substance must be secured outside the discussion. This improper body is quarantined for fear that its ineluctable immediacy will leave us no space for change, no chance to be otherwise... (Kirby 1991: 8)

Postmodern discussions of identity and of the body have tended to concentrate on consumption, appearance, body-sculpting and other phenomena, which are generally considered to be opposed to 'spirituality'. This problem is grounded in the western assumption that authenticity and spirituality require essence, fixity and depth. Language is spirituality's 'other', and it is the practice of language which generates, as its very *alter ego*, ambiguity (Bauman 1991: 1).[2] These beliefs are culturally-specific to the modernist and postmodernist traditions. The coyote stories, for example, closely connected with spiritual concerns within the Native American tradition (Cheney 1994), do not make this assumption. Donna Haraway's discussion (1992a) of Jesus Christ and Sojourner Truth as trickster figures indicates that, even within western culture, the association of spirituality with fixity is not inevitable.

The Borderlands are not a comfortable place. Living within them may catalyse a state of corporealized psychic unrest which is, Anzaldúa writes:

> like a cactus needle embedded in the flesh. It worries itself deeper and deeper, and I keep aggravating it by poking at it. When it begins to fester I have to do something to put an end to the aggravation and to figure out why I have it. I get deep down into the place where it's rooted in my skin and pluck away at it, playing it like a musical instrument – the fingers pressing, making the pain worse before it can get better. (1987: 73)

The Borderlands are essentially a location for matter 'out of place' and, as Mary Douglas (1966) has noted in her often cited study of the concepts of purity and pollution, taboos are often erected to guard against these crossover points. Jay argues (1981) that the concepts of purity and pollution play a central role within dualistic thinking. Because the primary term depends on the absolute exclusion of its 'other' in order to maintain its identity, any contact between the two terms of a dualism becomes a source of potential pollution. A hyper-separation between the dualized opposites must be maintained. The Borderlands are a place where this separation cannot hold. As Donna Haraway (1991c: 21) notes, boundary creatures do not fit neatly into previously constructed *taxa*; they are, literally, monsters. A borderland, Anzaldúa states, 'is a vague and undetermined place created by the emotional residue of an unnatural boundary. It is in a constant state of transition. The prohibited and forbidden are its inhabitants' (1987: 3).

The human body as a Borderlands

The human body is itself such a crossroads. Most people, most of the time, can identify with their conscious, willed, reasoning selves, using their bodies as reliable instruments and ignoring the hidden shadows of their own beings. In this, to some degree, they can remain congruent with the western concept of 'individuality', which keeps the body in an *external* relationship to the 'self'.[3] Their self remains in a stable, dualistic relationship with their body; their identity is secure. But when illness, pain, disability or trauma strikes, this stability is undermined; the body may enter its own Borderlands. It suddenly seems to be an alien or dysfunctional object (Williams 1996). As Kleinman describes the ill body: 'It menaces. It erupts. It is out of control. One damned thing follows another...' (quoted in Frank 1991: 87). Cathy Winkler describes the experience of rape trauma similarly: 'This trauma surfaces as a feeling of separation between the mind and the body; this separation is trauma felt viscerally and unexplained mentally' (1994: 248). The onset of pain or illness can thus generate an intense and uncomfortable experiential dualism in which the body demands attention, while seeming to be alienated from the self.

Biomedicine, the hegemonic medicine of modern western society, tends to treat the body as a thing – a fixed object (Gordon 1988; McKee 1988). This seemingly natural fact is, however, a specifically western figuration, as the experience of illness has made clear. The body, Carol

Bigwood argues, is an 'indeterminate constancy' (1991: 61), which is born together with a specific, historically constituted, intersubjective, environment. When it is in pain, it becomes impossible to maintain the illusion that the body is simply the instrument of the mind. The body turns on itself – it becomes both the object and the constitutive ground of perception (Jackson 1994):

> She is getting too close to the mouth of the abyss. She is teetering on the edge, trying to balance while she makes up her mind whether to jump in or to find a safer way down. That's why she makes herself sick – to postpone having to jump blindfolded into the abyss of her own being and there in the depths to confront her face, the face underneath the mask. (Anzaldúa 1987: 74)

The crisis the body is undergoing may catalyse a new attentiveness towards its agency; a new process of storytelling may commence. Gareth Williams (1984) argues that in this process of 'narrative reconstruction', patients may begin to account for their experience of illness. A new alignment of the body, the self and the social/environmental world may thus be negotiated.[4]

The Borderlands are a place where dualized oppositions are thrust together and yet are not assimilated. The tension they embody cannot be collapsed into a hierarchical relationship in which one agent is subsumed and instrumentalized by the other. In a state of both isomorphic sameness and irreconcilable difference, the borderland's inhabitants are inherently oxymoronic. Like tricksters they are, simultaneously, both themselves and something else entirely. When the body locates itself in this logic of metaphor, its reality is seen to be that of an overdetermined story, made up of many layers of figurations, displacements and variations on a theme. Freund (1990) draws on Johnson's work (1987) regarding the bodily basis of metaphor to argue that emotional states can be isomorphic, at the level of meaning, with the pattern and intensity of bodily movements.[5] He argues further that there are structural isomorphisms of meaning in our experience of physical and social objects in the world.

It seems that the production of bodily experience can be described as a creative action with a structure which is, perhaps, similar to that found within complex novels or films; the same themes appear, with variations, among the different actors and narratives which combine to make up the work as a whole. Crucially, however, this creation of bodily experience cannot be the act of an isolated individual. The narratives created are social narratives, interweaving wider social and environmental structures within individual bodily experience.

A medicine for the Borderlands

Drawing on a phenomenological anthropology, Thomas Csordas (1993) has described the alternative medical therapies as 'somatic modes of attention', or as 'culturally elaborated ways of attending to and with one's body in surroundings that include the embodied presence of others' (1993: 138). Alternatively, they might be described as 'communicative technologies' (Scott 1996: 190–1, 203–4), as techniques for translating between a practitioner, a patient's body, the social environment and the everyday consciousness of the patient.[6]

Lucy Goodison, an intuitive massage therapist, offers one account of the way in which alternative medical therapies may work as somatic modes of attention. She describes her work with one patient – a Jewish exile from Hitler's Germany who had also suffered childhood sexual abuse:

> When Peggy first came for massage, she described her body as 'in pieces': she experienced some parts as too numb to feel anything and others as too excruciatingly tender to bear being touched. She had chronic back trouble. She suffered from asthma, breathed shallowly, and was unusually troubled by her reaction to body smells like sweat. Living alone, she found it hard to cook adequately for herself. She was also anxious about penetration. (Goodison 1992: 208)

Goodison treated Peggy with a mixture of therapy and massage. Peggy would talk about the images and symbols which Goodison's touch brought up for her; they would then become subjects for more traditional therapy. Goodison describes how Peggy had internalized her oppression within her body: 'her [sexually abusive] brother in her right side, her father in her stomach and sexuality, the Holocaust in her sense of smell, the migration in her missing legs...' (1992: 222). Her asthma was linked to an association of breathing with her father's death, and to a fear of violation from anything entering her body. Her hatred of her own Jewishness had led to a revulsion for food, bodily odours and sexuality. Over the course of her treatment, Peggy

> gradually reached a state where there was power in a quiet place inside her which could reach in a positive way out into the world... I am

> hesitant ever to use the term 'cure', but this hard-won reclaiming of her inner landscape was accompanied by many concrete changes in her everyday living, all reflecting a growing ability to engage with human life; to stand up for herself and to move towards others. (1992: 224)

Goodison's use of massage therapy had enabled Peggy to turn her body from a simple object of pain into a teller of tales.

Western science draws a firm line between objects and stories. Objects are things; they are possessed of a stable, clear referentiality. The mechanisms of their operation can be observed, understood and manipulated. Ursula Sharma describes the western biomedical body as 'inner, penetrable, space' (1995: 36); it can be synchronically represented by a series of static diagrams. Storytelling and metaphor have no intrinsic place in this mode of perception. Donna Haraway calls this reification of the body a 'scientific fetishism' (1997: 134–7) and argues that it represents a basic epistemological error.

Recently, some feminist science theorists have begun conceptualizing nature as a 'high tension zone' (Star 1991: 53) which is self-created by a multitude of human and non-human actors operating within a wider, intersubjective milieu. Within this cyborg figuration, the firm division between human actors and non-human objects – whether natural or mechanical – becomes nonsensical (Haraway 1991a and 1992b; Franklin 1993; Law and Mol 1995). Donna Haraway has drawn on actor network theory (Latour 1993) to develop a notion of a 'social nature' (1992b: 309); she describes this nature as a 'commonplace' (1992b: 296), which is co-created through the dynamic inter-relationships of all its inhabitants:

> If organisms are natural objects, it is crucial to remember that organisms are not born; they are made in world-changing technoscientific practices by particular collective actors in particular times and places... The actors are not all 'us'. If the world exists for us as 'nature', this designates a kind of relationship, an achievement among many actors, not all of them human, not all of them organic, not all of them technological. In its scientific embodiments, as well as in other forms, nature is made, but not entirely by humans; it is a co-construction among humans and non-humans. (Haraway 1992b: 297)

In this conceptualization, nature as 'object' does not – indeed, cannot – exist. Nature is a diffuse and highly distributed storyteller. Its materialized agency works, in part, through displacement, metaphor, figuration and trope.

Michael Jackson has noted that 'metaphors are means of doing things and not merely ways of saying things' (1983: 138). Similarly, Jim Cheney (1994) uses Leopold's concept of 'storied residence' to include bio-regions within the moral community, thus extending the notion of narrative into the non-human world. Anzaldúa describes 'the ways metaphor and symbol concretize the spirit and etheralize the body' (1987: 75). She describes the process of writing, of storytelling, as requiring a 'blood sacrifice':

> For only through the body, through the pulling of flesh, can the human body be transformed. And for images, words, stories, to have this transformative power, they must arise from the human body – flesh and bone – and from the Earth's body – stone, sky, liquid, soil. (1987: 75)

The production of literature, too, can act as a somatic mode of attention.

Within the Borderlands, then, a different kind of medicine becomes both possible and necessary. It must understand the body as a cross-roads, where intersubjective relationships, the environment, individual history, wider social structures and its own somatic creativity combine to create a meaningful narrative in the form of a corporeal object. Homeopathy is one form of medicine which operates with such a notion of the body. As Ursula Sharma (1995) argues, homeopaths do not operate with a notion of the body as 'object'. They draw on a phenomenological body, characterized by symptoms, tendencies and preferences, all of which are mediated through a four-dimensional space–time by the patient's self-observation and conscious experience. Phillip Nicholls argues further that the homeopathic 'body' does not really exist at all. Instead of an abstract 'body', homeopaths perceive remedies which are, in effect, holistic body pictures (1995: 110). Just as there are many remedies (2,000–3,000 at the current time), there are many 'bodies' within the homeopathic worldview.

Jackson (1983) argues that metaphor can play an instrumental role within medicine, providing a means of moving amongst the various domains of being. Homeopathy deliberately uses metaphor in this way.[7] Each homeopathic remedy can be conceptualized as one node within a complex system of displacements and figurations. It represents a type of human being with a characteristic set of physical symptoms and ailments. Each remedy is associated with characteristic emotional states, dream images, food preferences, climatic responses, bodily events and belief structures. It is connected with a particular way of relating to other people. Its 'keynote' represents a particular 'way of being' in the world. It is, itself, a material substance of some sort; the remedies' raw substances have their own social and environmental histories, and play their own part in constructing our natural/social world. Most remedies belong to a remedy family; their positive and negative connections with other remedies extend into a broad network. Finally, according to Rajan Sankaran (1991, 1994), each homeopathic remedy is associated with a characteristic social or environmental situation; he claims that each remedy picture represents the best possible response to some set of social or environmental circumstances. When a patient is treated constitutionally with a particular remedy, then that patient is located within a multi-layered trope.

Homeopathic medical treatment thus draws on a cycling, interlocking set of metaphors and stories – each of which may become a source for the creation of biographical meaning.

> Quite often, people have quite serious chronic things and then you see them making improvements. You see they take a risk somewhere; they move some fear on in themselves. And then you see the body react to that. You cannot make a movement in yourself, at those deeper levels, without it, at some point, coming out in the body. And then again, that's disease working in reverse. (Homeopath A 1994)[8]

A 'commonplace' is established, in which the patient's body, the therapeutic relationship, the social and physical environment, the remedies used and the patient's consciousness begin collaborating to materialize a biographical narrative. 'There are interactions,' as one homeopath put it, 'between our energy and the environmental energy of air, and water, and mountains. And also there's that energy created by society... people's thoughts and attitudes have an energy of their own' (Homeopath B 1994). The remedy, although it is 'just' a material substance, becomes an actor in this process.

> I'm fascinated by the way the body will ask for a particular remedy, and if not given that remedy, it will just go on producing symptoms of the same remedy, until you go 'Oh! It's Arsenicum!'... That fascinates me about the vital force – moving the body in a particular way, sort of pushing towards the right remedy. (Homeopath C 1994)

The homeopathic remedies are thus located in a Borderlands – a landscape of crossroads and junctions. They are nodes within a complex, horizontally organized, intersubjective network, where 'imagined connections' between diverse parts of the natural and social worlds may be expressed:

> you take something from the world, be it from the animal kingdom, the mineral world, whatever. Say, gold. As a substance, gold is fairly inert. And you potentize it in a homeopathic remedy, and it has this *whole different energy*. But you can still see the connection between that energy and the substance gold. And then somebody comes along, who is *that*. And giving them a little bit of that allows them to move on... (Homeopath D 1994)

In this homeopath's world-view, the natural world is understood to be characterized by complex networks of identity and difference. The patient cannot be subsumed into the remedy, *Aurum metallicum*, or into the substance, gold. However, somebody has come along 'who is *that*'. There is an identity, but it is based on figuration. Its figurative character does not, however, make this identity less real, less natural or less effective in a practical sense; in clinical practice, the health of patients are regularly improved by the administration of homeopathic remedies.[9]

The contemporary world's engagement with the consequences of dualism is itself addressed by a homeopathic remedy. In her discussion of the remedy *Hypericum perforatum*, Katherine Boulderstone (1997) relates the actions and characteristics of the plant to its remedy picture. Noting that it tends to grow in coppices, on the borders of fields and meadows, along railway sidings, along roadsides and beside hedges – where it acts to knit divided pieces of land back together – Boulderstone argues that the plant's growing practices hold an important clue to the remedy's clinical action. 'In other words it often will appear where the land is rent in two, where there is a gaping cut or tear...' (1997: 678). *Hypericum* is Britain's great native woundwort, Boulderstone notes, and she argues that its healing action applies to more than superficial, physical, wounds. 'The core of it,' she claims, 'is the traumatic wounding, leading to dissociation or splitting of some kind. For those crushed or bruised physically, emotionally and in spirit' (1997: 680).

Boulderstone then draws out the symptoms associated with this remedy in the *materia medica*, noting an emphasis on trauma, pain and sadness, fear of physical pain, and dissociation from the body in both the physical and the mental symptoms of this remedy. She notes its clinical efficacy in treating people who have survived prolonged trauma, denial of self and oppression – particularly mentioning survivors of domestic violence, of civil war and of life under dictatorship. *Hypericum perforatum*, she argues, is a great healer of splits at any level – physical or mental, individual, social or political, in animals or even – in the action of the growing plant to reassociate two disconnected pieces of land – in the land itself. Perhaps, in order to make sense of homeopathic remedies such as *hypericum*, we need an ontology of the Borderlands, which can take account of the figurative identities which overlay structural diversity in the natural world.

Conclusion

Zygmunt Bauman eloquently argues that, in a postmodern ethics, 'the Other would be no more he who, at best, is the prey on which the self can feed to replenish its life-juices, and – at worst – thwarts and sabotages the self's constitution. Instead he will be the gatekeeper of moral life' (1993: 85). This embrace of irreconcilable difference, and of the tension and contradiction it engenders, may offer us an ethics for the Borderlands. It is the body, however, which is the original Other, and it is the female connection with bodily experience which has historically justified the social oppression of women (Ortner 1974; de Beauvoir 1949). Thus, to embrace the expression of the body, this 'measure between the beginnings of our sense of self and the chaos of our strongest feelings' (Lorde 1984: 54), is to accept that stability and containability are, ultimately, impossible. The ethics of difference must be a bodied ethics.

To acknowledge the inutterable *difference* of the body, and yet to accept it as equal collaborator in co-constructing our world is to chance a step beyond the seemingly solid division between external reality and the shadow world of the imagination. It is to accept Anzaldúa's claim that 'the spirit of the words moving in the body is as concrete as flesh and as palpable' (1987: 71). In this unaccustomed place, the dualistic categories that hold identity secure and naturalize social oppression begin to make less sense. The unitary subject has been fractured. The homogeneous background of 'the Other' has taken on a subtle and variegated texture. Powerful equivalences have appeared between people and phenomena that had previously seemed to be divided by a chasm. In this 'high-tension zone' of the contemporary world, where neither sameness nor difference can be taken for granted, new social and political possibilities may be emerging:

> And in rising from the depths I realize that down is up, and I rise up from and into the deep. And once again I recognize that the internal tension of oppositions can propel (if it doesn't tear apart) the *mestiza* writer out of the *metate* where she is being ground with corn and water, eject her out as *nahual*, an agent of transformation, able to modify and shape primordial energy and therefore able to change herself and others into turkey, coyote, tree or human. (Anzaldúa 1987: 74–5)

The senior homeopath who scandalized her colleagues by telling them that 'There are more important things to think about than health' (Homeopath E 1994) was drawing on a medical tradition that has been all but lost in our contemporary health-related fixation on the maintenance and repair of the body as a 'thing'. The body *is* a material object, but it is also a narrative crossroads, a site for storied residence. It is, to borrow Castells' (1996) expression, a 'space of flows'. The human body, in its dense corporeality, is as much constructed by figuration and trope as by biochemistry and bones. That these incommensurables could occupy the same space – could materialize themselves as a single agent – seems impossible. Impossible – and yet in the Borderlands it seems to be reality. It is in this contradictory tension that our creative power may lie.

Notes

An earlier version of this paper was presented at the British Sociological Association's Annual Conference in Edinburgh (April 1998); I am grateful to the participants for their feedback. I would also like to thank Jane Brown, Pauline Storie, Dot Moss and Hilary Rose for their assistance and helpful comments on earlier versions of this article.

1. See Lloyd (1984) on rationality; Bordo (1987), Keller (1985) and Harding (1986) discuss objectivity. Elshtain (1981), Pateman (1988) and Flax (1992) discuss the concepts of individuality and citizenship; see Griffin (1978) and Hein (1989) on secularism. A common theme running through these analyses is that these, seemingly neutral, terms depend on the existence of almost invisible contrasting terms for their meaning, and these 'other' terms are heavily gendered as female.
2. Bauman, like many postmodern theorists, draws heavily on bodily metaphors. Note, for example, his discussion of the caress as a corporeal embracing of ambiguity (1993: 92–4). However, a gap remains. Although it is

inscribed by the caress in the process of intersubjective identity construction, the body *itself* remains passive in Bauman's account.

3. Pateman (1988) discusses the concept of 'property in the person' which is central to liberal political theory, and which treats the body as property, with the same relationship to the self as any other external and alienable property. See similar discussions by Scott (1996), Franklin (1993) and Flax (1992).
4. For example, Adrienne Rich had a severe allergic reaction to her first pregnancy. In her attempts to understand the meaning of this experience, she produced a powerful, critical analysis of the institution of motherhood (Rich 1977). She also changed life direction, eventually abandoning her life as a middle-class housewife, and emerging as a lesbian feminist theorist. See Kaufman-Osborn (1993). There is now a large literature on the process of narrative reconstruction – see Kelly and Field (1996), Williams (1996) and Johannessen (1996).
5. Similarly, a study conducted by Felicitas Goodman (1986) indicated that particular bodily postures can be correlated, when subjects enter an altered state of consciousness, with particular sets of experiences.
6. See Johannessen (1996), Holst (1994) and Thornquist (1995) on the process of diagnosis within several forms of alternative medical therapy. In these examples, the therapies seem to be playing a translatory, or communicative, role. The common conceptual opposition between 'technological' and 'natural' forms of medicine has obscured the fact that the unconventional medical therapies are also technologies; they are techniques which have been socially developed for use within the political economies of historically specific health care systems. Very few of these therapies use entirely 'natural' resources; their medicines and other accoutrements have been technologically selected and refined.
7. See Vithoulkas (1986) for an in-depth introduction to homeopathic medical theory. Grossinger (1990) places homeopathy within a wider context, analysing a number of metaphoric systems of medicine.
8. Homeopath quotes come from a series of interviews conducted as part of a project on feminist alternative medicine. See Scott (1996 and 1998).
9. See Kleijnen et al.'s (1991) review of several studies regarding the clinical effectiveness of homeopathy.

References

Anzaldúa, G. 1987. *Borderlands/ la Frontera: The New Mestiza*. San Francisco: Aunt Lute Books.

Bauman, Z. 1991. *Modernity and Ambivalence*. Cambridge: Polity.

Bauman, Z. 1992. *Intimations of Postmodernity*. London: Routledge.

Bauman, Z. 1993. *Postmodern Ethics*. Oxford: Blackwell.

Benjamin, J. 1988. *The Bonds of Love: Psychoanalysis, Feminism and the Problem of Domination*. London: Virago.

Bigwood, C. 1991. 'Renaturalizing the Body (with the help of Merleau-Ponty)', *Hypatia*, 6 (3): 54–73.

Bordo, S. 1987. *The Flight to Objectivity: Essays on Cartesianism and Culture*. Albany: SUNY Press.

Boulderstone, K. 1997. '*Hypericum perforatum*', *The Homeopath*, 64: 677–81.
Castells, M. 1996. *The Rise of the Network Society*. Oxford: Blackwell.
Cheney, J. 1989. 'The Neo-stoicism of Radical Environmentalism', *Environmental Ethics*, 11 (4): 293–325.
Cheney, J. 1994. 'Nature/Theory/Difference: Ecofeminism and the Construction of Environmental Ethics', in K. Warren (ed.) *Ecological Feminism*. London: Routledge.
Csordas, T. 1993. 'Somatic Modes of Attention', *Cultural Anthropology*, 8 (2): 135–56.
De Beauvoir, S. 1949; 1972. *The Second Sex*. Harmondsworth: Penguin Books.
Douglas, M. 1966. *Purity and Danger: An Analysis of the Concepts of Pollution and Taboo*. London: Routledge & Kegan Paul.
Elshtain, J.B. 1981. *Public Man, Private Woman: Women in Social and Political Thought*. Oxford: Martin Robertson.
Flax, J. 1992. 'Is Enlightenment Emancipatory? A Feminist Reading of "What is Enlightenment?"', in F. Barker et al. (eds.) *Post-modernism and the Re-reading of Modernity*. Manchester: Manchester University Press.
Frank, A. 1991. 'For a Sociology of the Body: An Analytical Review', in M. Featherstone et al. (eds.) *The Body: Social Process and Cultural Theory*. London: Sage.
Franklin, S. 1993. 'Postmodern Procreation: Representing Reproductive Practice', *Science as Culture*, 3 (4): 522–61.
Freund, P. 1990. 'The Expressive Body: A Common Ground for the Sociology of Emotions and Health and Illness', *Sociology of Health and Illness*, 12 (4): 452–77.
Goodison, L. 1992. *Moving Heaven and Earth: Sexuality, Spirituality and Social Change*. London: Pandora.
Goodman, F. 1986. Body Postures and the Religious Altered State of Consciousness: An Experimental Investigation', *Journal of Humanistic Psychology*, 26: 81–118.
Gordon, D. 1988. 'Tenacious Assumptions in Western Medicine', In M. Lock and D. Gordon (eds.) *Biomedicine Examined*. London: Kluwer.
Griffin, S. 1978. *Woman and Nature: The Roaring inside Her*. New York: Harper and Row.
Grossinger, R. 1990. *Planet Medicine: From Stone Age Shamanism to Post-Industrial Healing*. 5th edition. Berkeley, CA: North Atlantic Books.
Haraway, D. [1985] 1991a. 'A Cyborg Manifesto: Science, Technology and Socialist-Feminism in the Late Twentieth Century', in D. Haraway, *Simians, Cyborgs, and Women: The Reinvention of Nature*. London: Free Association Books.
Haraway, D. [1988] 1991b. 'Situated Knowledges: The Science Question in Feminism and the Privilege of Partial Perspective', in D. Haraway, *Simians, Cyborgs, and Women: The Reinvention of Nature*. London: Free Association Books.
Haraway, D. 1991c. 'The Actors are Cyborg, Nature is Coyote, and the Geography is Elsewhere: Postscript to "Cyborgs at Large"', in C. Penley and A. Ross (eds.) *Technoculture*. Minneapolis: University of Minnesota Press.
Haraway, D. 1992a. 'Ecce Homo, Ain't (ar'n't) I a Woman, and Inappropriate/d Others: The Human in a Post-humanist Landscape', in J. Butler and J. Scott (eds.) *Feminists Theorize the Political*. London: Routledge.

Haraway, D. 1992b. 'The Promises of Monsters: A Regenerative Politics for Inappropriate/d Others', in L. Grossberg, C. Nelson and P. Treichler (eds.) *Cultural Studies*. London: Routledge.

Haraway, D. 1997. *Modest-Witness@Second-Millenium. FemaleMan©-Meets-OncoMouse™*. London: Routledge.

Harding, S. 1986. *The Science Question in Feminism*. Milton Keynes: Open University Press.

Hein, H. 1992. 'Liberating Philosophy: An End to the Dichotomy of Spirit and Matter', in A. Garry and M. Pearsall (eds.) *Women, Knowledge, and Reality: Explorations in Feminist Philosophy*. London: Routledge.

Holst, T. 1994. 'In the Name of Rosen – on the Rosen Method and its Application in Sweden', in H. Johannessen, et al. (eds.) *Studies in Alternative Therapy 1: Contributions from the Nordic Countries*. Odense: Odense University Press.

Jackson, J. 1994. 'Chronic Pain and the Tension between the Body as Subject and Object', in T. Csordas (ed.) *Embodiment and Experience: The Existential Ground of Culture and Self*. Cambridge: Cambridge University Press.

Jackson, M. 1983. 'Thinking through the Body: An Essay on Understanding Metaphor', *Social Analysis*, 14: 127–49.

Jay, N. 1981. 'Gender and Dichotomy', *Feminist Studies*, 7 (1): 38–56.

Johannssen, H. 1996. 'Individualized Knowledge: Reflexologists, Biopaths and Kinesiologists in Denmark', in S. Cant and U. Sharma (eds.) *Complementary and Alternative Medicines: Knowledge in Practice*. London: Free Association Books.

Johnson, M. 1987. *The Body in the Mind: The Bodily Basis of Meaning and Imagination and Reason*. London: University of Chicago Press.

Kaufmann-Osborn, T. 1993. 'Teasing Feminist Sense from Experience', *Hypatia*, 8 (2): 124–44.

Keller, E.F. 1985. *Reflections on Gender and Science*. New Haven: Yale University Press.

Kelly, M. and Field, D. 1996. 'Medical Sociology, Chronic Illness and the Body', *Sociology of Health and Illness*, 18 (2): 241–57.

King, Y. 1989. 'Healing the Wounds: Feminism, Ecology, and Nature/Culture Dualism', in A. Jaggar and S. Bordo (eds.) *Gender/Body/Knowledge: Feminist Reconstructions of Being and Knowing*. London: Rutgers University Press.

Kirby, V. 1991. 'Corporeal Habits: Addressing Essentialism Differently', *Hypatia*, 6 (3): 4–24.

Kleijnen, J. et al. 1991. 'Clinical Trials of Homeopathy', *British Medical Journal*, 302: 316–23.

Latour, B. 1993. *We Have Never Been Modern*. Cambridge, MA: Harvard University Press.

Law, J. and Mol, A. 1995. 'Notes on Materiality and Sociality', *The Sociological Review*, 43 (2): 274–94.

Lloyd, G. 1984. *The Man of Reason: 'Male' and 'Female' in Western Philosophy*. Minneapolis: University of Minnesota Press.

Lorde, A. 1984. *Sister Outsider*. Freedom, CA: Crossing Press.

McKee, J. 1988. 'Holistic Health and the Critique of Western Medicine', *Social Science and Medicine* 26 (8): 775–84.

Minh-Ha, T. 1989. *Woman, Native, Other: Writing, Postcoloniality and Feminism*. Bloomington, IN: Indiana University Press.

Nicholls, P. 1995. 'The Homeopathy Discussion Group', in H. Johannessen, S. Gosvig Olesen and J. Østergård Anderson (eds.) *Studies in Alternative Therapy 2: Body and Nature*. Odense: Odense University Press.

Nicholson, L. 1994. 'Interpreting Gender'. *Signs*, 20 (1): 79–105.

Ortner, S. 1974. 'Is Female to Male as Nature is to Culture?', in M. Rosaldo and L. Lamphere (eds.) *Woman, Culture, Society*. Stanford: Stanford University Press.

Pateman, C. 1988. *The Sexual Contract*. Cambridge: Polity Press.

Phelan, S. 1996. 'Coyote Politics: Trickster Tales and Feminist Futures', *Hypatia*, 11 (3): 130–49.

Plumwood, V. 1993. *Feminism and the Mastery of Nature*. London: Routledge.

Rich, A. 1977. *Of Woman Born: Motherhood as Experience and Institution*. London: Virago.

Sankaran, R. 1991. *The Spirit of Homeopathy*. Bombay: privately published.

Sankaran, R. 1994. *The Substance of Homeopathy*. Bombay: Homeopathic Medical Publishers.

Scott, A. 1996. 'Embodied Politics: Emancipatory Epistemologies and Vitalistic Ontologies within Feminist Alternative Medicine', University of Bradford: PhD thesis.

Scott, A. 1998. 'Homeopathy as a Feminist Form of Medicine', *Sociology of Health and Illness*, 20 (2): 191–214.

Sharma, U. 1995. 'The Homeopathic Body: "Reification" and the Homeopathic "Gaze" ', in H. Johannessen, S. Gosvig Olesen and J. Østergård Anderson (eds.) *Studies in Alternative Therapy 2: Body and Nature*. Odense: Odense University Press.

Star, S.L. 1991. 'Power, Technology and the Phenomenology of Conventions: On Being Allergic to Onions', in J. Law (ed.) *A Sociology of Monsters: Essays on Power, Technology and Domination*. London: Routledge.

Thornquist, E. 1995. 'Musculoskeletal Suffering: Diagnosis and a Variant View', *Sociology of Health and Illness*, 17 (2): 166–92.

Vithoulkas, G. 1986. *The Science of Homeopathy*. Wellingborough: Thorsons.

Warren, K. 1990. 'The Power and the Promise of Ecological Feminism', *Environmental Ethics*, 15 (2): 125–46.

Williams, G.H. 1984. 'The Genesis of Chronic Illness: Narrative Reconstruction', *Sociology of Health and Illness*, 6: 175–200.

Williams, S. 1996. 'The Vicissitudes of Embodiment across the Chronic Illness Trajectory', *Body & Society*, 2 (2): 23–47.

Winkler, C. (with Wininger, K.). 1994. 'Rape Trauma: Contexts of Meaning', in T. Csordas (ed.) *Embodiment and Experience: The Existential Ground of Culture and Self*. Cambridge: Cambridge University Press.

2

Bodies, Battlefields and Biographies: Scars and the Construction of the Body as Heritage

Kathryn A. Burnett and Mary Holmes

Introduction: the body as a heritage site

There is a sense in which the body is considered as an historical entity with an 'age' and a 'past'. If it can be considered in historical terms why can it not also be reflected upon in heritage terms, as a site of interpretation and re-representation which is not necessarily 'true' nor 'accurate', but may be considered as 'meaningful' and/or 'authentic' (Walsh 1992; McCrone et al. 1995; Urry 1996)? Relating heritage to history is, according to Brett (1996: 155), a struggle between two kinds of time: one is the real, concrete time and the other mythic time. It is our suggestion that scars of the body are sites of the struggle between making sense of what is real or mythic in one's past and indeed one's present. To remember a scar, and the process by which it was gained, is to interpret selectively one's actions, relationships and emotions. The retelling of the scarring process allows individuals to recount what was meaningful about the event concerned and presents an opportunity to display or reveal to others what has been acquired by the engagement. The physical manifestation of a scar is bound in with mythic qualities as to its symbolic significance. In this sense we argue that the scar is akin to battlefields, castles, old ships or railway lines – the object is imbued with both real and mythic aspects which, through interpretation and sharing with others, constitute meaningful qualities of existence.

There are three ways in which we seek to explore the idea of the body as a heritage site. Our first approach refers to our concern with the protection and conservation of the body as an historical entity. The body's historicized past is viewed as heritage in a traditional sense – something to value and to be guardian of. The body can be considered, in the sense of heritage, as *patrimoine* or a cultural legacy of inheritance. There is a clear moral underpinning to such a view of the body as heritage: we have a duty to take care of and preserve it. We can borrow from McCrone et al. (1995: 160) the following perspective to illuminate this further: 'it's important to learn lessons from the past. Heritage is about how we have developed, the sense of continuity'. Yet our body betrays us; it reveals our failure to take good care of it by its marks, its lines and its disfigurements. Scars to the body as a result of accidental damage are visible proof of a person's misfortune or laxitude; the body has been wounded in some way. It is our suggestion that through the examination of scar accounts we can understand how a scar provokes in us a sense of moral duty as guardians of our body. Through recounting scar incidents, individuals appear first to recognize, and then respect, the scar as an opportunity for meaningful reflection. The reflective interpretations that might follow a scarring incident are an example of what Foucault (1988) calls a 'concern for self'. This forms the basis of our first main discussion theme.

As our second discussion theme we consider the body as an historical entity which can be selectively interpreted and accounted for. In doing this we draw parallels for a second time with the concept of heritage. Heritage is increasingly understood as a process by which discourses and representations must compete and struggle for favour; the past is commodified and packaged, and the emphasis is on what constitutes a 'good' or 'worthwhile' story. In drawing on our heritage site metaphor we are interested in the promotional opportunities scar accounts provide for the self. In this respect we argue that the scar is a resource to be exploited in the competitive environment of presenting interesting aspects of self.

Lastly, we suggest that the body can be viewed as a heritage site constituted by *meaningful interpretation of* physical marks or traces; the person can literally use the visible scar to locate themselves in time and space and thus use the scar as an *aide mémoire* to one's past situated self. This third discussion theme is linked to the idea that heritage sites provide individuals with an opportunity to locate the self in relation to past time and space constructions. The scars are objects for display which can 'trigger' memories which locate the self in particular environments and within memorable social relationships. Following Grosz (1995: 35), we suggest that scars provide a medium by which the body 'speaks' through its coded and signified aspects; bodies speak 'social codes' and are therefore 'intextuated' and 'narrativized'.

Whilst we recognize that our heritage metaphor has certain limitations – people rarely, if ever, refer to their bodies as 'heritage sites' – yet our discourses of our 'bodies through time', 'promoting self' and 'care of self' do have parallels with how society more generally accounts for past events and histories. The idea that particular events or objects can be isolated from the mundane in certain ways and promoted for consumption and reflection informs our research. The scar itself may be rather uninteresting in its physical characteristics and location on the body, yet it can be transformed into something 'worth knowing' through the account and this invites comparison with how heritage promotes the ordinary aspects of past into something extraordinary.

'Taking care': guarding the embodied self

Foucault (1988: 29) notes that practices of caring for the self were historically oriented towards the soul, but that there was an 'ambiguity about the body in this cultivation of self'. Some practices involved denial of the body (abstinence), others involved forms of indulgence (such as Epicurean), others again were concerned with using the body to show what or who you were (the symbolic actions of the penitent). Gradually, in the West, a particular Christian version of concern for self came to dominate. Care of the self became based on the idea of 'hidden' aspects within the self. Individuals were thought to construct self-illusions and therefore needed to confess their thoughts to an external 'judge'. In such a discourse, bodies remained ambiguous. Bodies may be what lead us into 'temptation' and the instrument with which we 'sin', and may therefore be the cause and site of moral problems. Bodies (or control of them) might also be the means to shaping a better self (Turner 1991). In order for self-caring to contribute to knowledge of oneself, it is necessary to recount what has been done; in a confessional society such as ours this function is performed by verbalizing (and sometimes writing down) one's thoughts, intentions and actions. So, representation is crucial in practices of self-care (Foucault 1988: 30–7).

We turn now to consider the embodied self and how we represent our care for self by examining accounts of unintentionally gained scars.[1] We begin our accounts with some of our own experiences. Our first example comes from Mary:

> There is one scar story I can tell ... the 'trigger' is not so much a mark as a dent, barely noticeable now. It is on the outside of my

> right thigh and marks where a car hit me when I was fourteen. I remember exactly what I was wearing (my lace-up trainers flew off) and that I was on my way to meet my father to buy a birthday present for my mother. It must have been late shopping night – Thursday. The accident happened at the top of our street as I tried to cross the main road. There were buses at the bus stop and I did not see the car that came from behind them. I was probably day-dreaming and should have looked more carefully. Afterwards, I was sitting on the kerb telling everyone that I had to go and meet my father. I didn't want him to worry. Someone from the office building across the road saw the accident and came down to help. It was a friend and neighbour of ours and he went to get my mother. Later, I remember being grateful that I lived in a place where that could happen. People knew me, and others outside my family would help watch out for me. I amazingly suffered very slight injuries and I decided I was quite hardy. However, for some years afterwards my leg would ache when the weather was cold and I would be reminded of my good fortune in having emerged relatively unscathed from such an accident.

Scar accounts are interesting because they can potentially combine a use of the body to show and to tell good stories about the self, including moral lessons learned (cf. Foucault 1988). The scar itself can be read as a mark upon the body (cf. Grosz 1995: 34), but this reading becomes incorporated into a representation of the self. Such representations have to account for a lapse in self-care of which a scar is usually evidence. In Mary's case she was 'probably day-dreaming' when the car hit her and this is presented by her as a fault and as a lapse in her own self-care. Yet, Mary notes that her injuries were slight and therefore she emerged from the whole incident with a degree of triumph. For Mary, the dent in her leg, and the remembrance of the events which caused it, enable her to locate herself in relation to a significant time, place and set of relationships (see our later discussion). Mary learned that she was physically hardy, within limits, but that lapses in mental concentration could be dangerous and could mean letting people down. Mary reflects on the notion that she needed to 'take more care of myself', partly in order not to worry others. Mary realized that she was surrounded by people who would care for her, and although she would not have used the word at the time, that she belonged to a *community*. These are some of the meanings Mary extracted from relating the story of a scar to herself and to others. Mary imagines these meanings as 'authentically' representing her personal history. If it is a 'good story', it is because of this.

Our second example comes from Kathryn:

> I have a small scar on my right index finger, at the join with the knuckle. It's a distinctive V-shape. I got the scar as a result of a glass cut. I was working in a bar and one night when drying glasses a bit of the rim broke off and cut into my hand. Like most glass cuts, it wasn't sore but the cut was quite deep. When I look at this scar I always feel a little sick in the stomach ... it brings back memories of a painful relationship which I had with another person working at the bar. Really I should have had stitches but there was no way I could leave the bar, it was a busy night and it would just have proved too much hassle. I look at the scar now and I think about how foolish I was to have been working still in that bar and to have still been involved with that guy at that time. The scar really is a painful reminder of my own stupidity, but I do think of it as a mark of survival of a worse time in my life.

In both extracts we realize that we are revealing aspects of our own moral and physical histories: the 'confessional' aspect clearly figures, but what about other people's experiences? In talking to our informants we found that many individuals provide reference to their own stupidity or recklessness when accounting for scars. This is not surprising because most unintentional scars come about through 'accidents', often as a result of undertaking risky acts or not paying due care and attention. Most of our informants reported scars which resulted from falling off things – walls, bikes, chairs – whilst doing something forbidden. Alistair recalls how the scar above his eye was his 'own fault':

> I got stitches above my eye ... largely as a result of my own fault I think because I was crawling under big piles of chairs and I think I was really small ... about six or something like that, and the stacks came tumbling down on top of me and a leg caught me in the eye ... and I had to get extricated from out of all these chairs.

A scar marks the impingement of the external upon the body, thus signalling an individual's encounter with boundaries. These boundaries include physical bodily 'edges' and more abstract limitations. The reopening of old wounds on certain parts of the body such as knees was quite common and the informants' stories suggest a certain impatience with one's body failing to mend. David provides his 'knee story'. He cut open his knee after sliding on ice 'around Primary 6 or 7' and recalls how the small circular scar 'kept opening back up'. '*Astroturf*' scars were noted as being particularly annoying because they were prone to heal slowly and 'bits of fluff getting into them'.

In short, the scar is the visible reminder that we should take care of the body. If it is expected that people should care for themselves (and particularly their bodies), then it is likely that scar stories will be constructed to account for the lapse in care and to make meaningful the potentially threatening encounter with external boundaries. We are guardians of our own corporeality and we must somehow morally benefit from the scar through a careful reflection of how the scar came about and 'who's fault it was'. In each of our examples a lesson appears to have been learned about how the body does need to be cared for.

Telling good stories: promoting the embodied self

To begin, let us reflect a little on the recounting of history, first with reference to feminist desires to refashion political symbolic orders, and second, by looking at heritage as social process which excels at refashioning historical fact. Easton (1994: 57) has stated that body and history are bound together, and any attempt to 'write the body' must recognize this whether it be taking account of one's racial, ethnic, sexual or emotional histories: 'the route into a new space must be *through* both that body and that history, because one cannot write one without the other' (Easton 1994: 57). Easton takes issue with a 'common feminist assumption' that the symbolic order is monolithically unified. She argues that where a singularity of meaning is reinforced, this presents limitations for experience, and women's experience in particular. Easton presents the work of black feminist writers such as Grace Nichols and Lauretta Ngcobo, who provide careful reworkings of history through their personal interpretations and accounts, such as in their prose or poetry. According to Easton (1994: 59), in Nichols' accounts of black (women's) experience she celebrates the possibilities for individuals to re-enter or reinterpret the symbolic order so that 'remembrance, if enacted in a new way, may offer a certain kind of liberation'. History is subverted through accounts such as Nichols'.

Lowenthal (1996: 143) notes the relationship between heritage and autobiographical life history: 'as with heritage, life histories become coherent and credible only by continual invention and revision, often in defiance of known fact'. Heritage is equated with reliving the past but this is very often through 'improving' the past to suit our present needs: 'we contrive a heritage exclusive to and biased in favour of ourselves' (Lowenthal 1996: 142). Certainly, heritage as an industry requires marketable and attractive properties. The scarred body should not be viewed simply in such thinly disguised economic terms, however. Nor are we suggesting that all scar accounts are used to promote a sense of 'good' self – as we have already shown, many scar accounts reveal the self to be stupid, pig-headed, lazy, or just plain *thrawn*[2] – but we suggest here that our accounts are a 'refashioning' of the body's history and we do this to serve present needs about what is important to us. Individuals provide 'good stories' and these must be both 'romanced' but plausible.

Consumerism encourages individuals to believe that the body and thereby the self can be reshaped and improved through buying and using the 'correct' products. Featherstone (1991) suggests that in contemporary consumer society bodies are no longer vessels of sin but objects to be displayed. Featherstone's work implies that concern for self is now a matter of body maintenance involving consumption work. The body symbolically shows who the person is (morally and biographically). However, the extent and manner of participation in body maintenance varies between individuals, over time, in different places and depending on who is looking.[3] Consumerist discourse provides a frame within which individuals' self-reflections are then judged according to how marketable they are. 'Cheque-book journalism' and the fame gained by those volunteering to appear on television chat shows are examples of how 'good stories' are rewarded. Such standards of marketability are likely to affect even the telling of stories not directly intended for 'sale'.

We explore how telling stories about the embodied self is a way of selectively revealing one's socially situated history. By examining scar accounts in particular we look at how a person may choose to prioritize aspects of past events and experiences in the retelling of how a scar was come by. The body can be understood as a site of promotional artefacts – the scars are used to display aspects of one's self. A key element of 'good stories' is a sense of authenticity. A story does not necessarily have to be 'true', but it needs to be somehow acceptable (Walker 1997), 'accessible and engaging' (Dunow 1997: 1). We would argue that stories are appreciated if they seem to communicate something 'real' and significant. What is real and significant is obviously open to interpretation and depends on who is telling and who is told. It is interesting to note how Mary reflects on her body's scar history and the pressure to provide a 'good story' which is believable; in short, the story must be 'authentically' constructed:

> The scar across the veins on my left wrist is one I often notice, but I can never remember how I did it. It does not have a story attached. I could make up a tale about teenage *angst* and a failed suicide attempt, but I would not see any meaning or authenticity in this. I would imagine that any listeners who knew me would be unlikely to believe such a tale.

It might seem like it would make a 'good story', but to be convincing a story needs to accord with people's (including the story-teller's) perceptions of what is authentic about a set of events or characters (Brett 1996; Walker 1997). The meaningful interpretation of scarring incidents is a selective process and one reliant on memories. These memories may be unreliable, although this does not necessarily make them untrue. The interpretations of the incident may vary between those who were present. The scarred person's interpretation and representations of it may also alter slightly over time, or in different contexts. Representation of the self is an ongoing process and authenticity is important, but there is no linear narrative through which a 'true' self is discovered. What is 'authentic' to an individual's past and present self will be decided through comparison with others. It will also involve assessments about what is 'true' in certain times and places. This is not a neat process. Fragments of bodies and memories are used to construct stories that represent the individuals' past history in partially managed ways and the construction may contain 'inaccurate' and unconscious elements (Scott 1991; Smith 1993; Walker 1997).

People may use scar accounts to give particular impressions of themselves (cf. Goffman 1959; 1963). They do not always tell the 'truth' about their scars. Mary recalls a scar account provided by a male friend in response to her asking him how he had got a scar on his stomach. He told her that it was acquired through a knife fight at school when he was fourteen. This conjured up a range of not entirely positive impressions about rebelliousness and 'machismo'. Perhaps the story was designed to impress Mary ('we were eighteen'), perhaps he wanted to see if Mary would believe it. She did, but later he told her it was a joke. Really, he had fallen off his skim board[4] at the beach and cut himself on a shell. This version definitely made him seem less rebellious to Mary, but there was still a touch of bravado attached to skim boarding. The first story was part of a relatively convincing construction of himself as a bad boy who was not afraid of trouble or danger. It represents the scar as gained in a chosen 'battle'. The second story acknowledges himself as vulnerable to accidental injury resulting from a temporary loss of bodily control. This story, while more 'truthful', represents him as a cool dude beach boy taking on bodily challenges. It still allowed Mary to be impressed, although it was perhaps not such a 'good story'.

This example shows how individuals may selectively package scar stories in order to give particular impressions. Whatever the degree of 'truth' in the stories, the representation of the scarring event conveys particular impressions by locating the individual in time and place. Tellers and listeners will use such clues as a background against which to make sense of the scar stories (Dunow 1997: 11). Reactions are always somewhat unpredictable. Interpretations will vary, but there are shared sets of meanings amongst groups which coexist in time and place. There is some concurrence within such groups about what is appropriate to certain times, places and social actors. If you change the knife fight venue to a New York back street, or the age or gender of the skim boarder, interpretations will vary in more or less predictable ways. The 'false' story shows that the skim board scar victim is aware of how to package his account for consumption, and how to attempt to create certain presentations of his self (Goffman 1959).

Ed provided us with a good example of this when he revealed that he has 'two scars just above my waist' and his 'good story' is about the reaction which the scars provoked. Ed 'got the scar' from falling on stones whilst 'running... taking a short cut through some trees', but he can recall taking off the bandage and 'the thing... I remember most about it was my dad saying "Oh it looks like you've been shot" because it looked like that so I thought, "Oh cool"...'. This opportunity to character play with one's embodied self, especially as a small child with such a 'cool' prop as a gun-shot-like scar, as Ed notes, makes the scar more interesting.

The actual effect of a scar account upon particular audiences depends greatly on what sets of meanings they might share with the storyteller, and on judgements as to how good, or 'authentic', a story it is. Personal histories can therefore be understood as constructed and interpreted for an audience which includes the self. Time, place and bodies are important elements in this construction.

Remembered pasts: locating the embodied self

Brett (1996: 154) takes up White's (1978) suggestion that the past is a field that can be represented only if it is first 'prefigured in the imagination as a domain with possible representable features'. Heritage as a succession of popular histories can be viewed as a series of imaginative acts or 'prefigurations' which are, according to Brett (1996: 155), 'intrinsically unquestioned'. In speaking about the heritage of people, time and space, Brett argues that these imaginings or prefigurations 'exist prior to any notion of explanation, and they are not in principle grounded in critical reason, but in commitment'. With this in mind Brett goes on to argue that heritage can be viewed then as a celebration of the 'topics' of history rather than the activity of history.

These topics of history as prefigurations are constitutive of social relations with others and the construction of identity. It is our suggestion that scars can be viewed as 'topics' of a body's history. The scars of the body appear to operate as prefigurations or imaginings of history in so far as each scar and its story situates the individual and their body in a remembered time and place, doing memorable things. This remembering is an explanation process in some respects – the circumstances resulting in the scar are related – but what is clear is that with each explanation an individual makes a commitment to retain particular feelings and understandings as formed at the time of scarring and hold them as significant. Polly, for example, recounts how she was playing cards at her Gran's house when she was 'about four' and she fell back and hit her head on the corner of an old wardrobe. Despite this being sore and leaving her with a scar she can 'still play with' at the back of her head, Polly remembers being very happy 'because she won' the card game! There may be no rational underpinning as to why certain scars are remembered in particular ways, or even why some scars are noted and others ignored, but the opportunity which is taken up by many to reflect upon and account for their scars – either to themselves or to others – is a common enough practice and one that invites further sociological analysis.

In a sociological analysis it is important that space is understood as having a temporal aspect, or at the very least that there is a consideration of space as *in process* (Walsh 1992: 150). However, the locating of self in space and time is no easy task. Although he is referring largely to museums and the heritage industry more generally, Walsh provides us with a rather accessible framework for how we 'locate' ourselves in space and time:

> Places are constituted through subjective recognition of 'time marks' ... both humanly and naturally constructed. Such marks make time 'visible'. People gain a sense of place through a set of 'filters', a subjective engagement with these time marks. (1992: 152)

Similarly, with scar accounts one can see how the self is located within a spatial and temporal context, but beyond that the account defies linearity and is more akin to a site of related but competing aspects of self and social relations (Urry 1996: 47).

Nikki's account is a good example of remembering the geographies of her own past:

> I cut my knee practically down to the bone but I was too scared to go to hospital ... I did it when I was in first year at university at St. Andrew's and they had a really bizarre tradition – not surprisingly being St. Andrew's – on May morning you go for a dip in the sea at dawn, which I duly did ... at half past four in the morning and ... swimming to the end of the old swimming pool – it was a deep ... sea swimming pool which is just basically a hole in the rock – by the time I got out the other end I didn't even realize because it was so cold and I looked down and suddenly my knee's hanging open and there's blood everywhere ... I ended up walking back to my halls of residence which was a bit stupid because it was about half a mile away and of course every time I took a step it opened ... (much laughter) ... and so when I got back to my halls ... I went to the first aid woman there and she just tied it all up for me and ... well, I couldn't bend my knee for weeks ... and I really wish I'd got it stitched now because the scar is quite bad but ... it is quite a good story ...

Each part of one's scar account is a statement which has particular significance for certain aspects of the self's multiple identities and realities; these are the filters through which we engage subjectively with our pasts. Gender, age, ethnicity, hobby, work, relationships, *habitus* and so on, are selectively resourced to assist in the construction of the account. The account has to be meaningful to self, and in order to do this aspects of self must be identified and drawn in as important and valuable and then made legitimate through discourse. Nick cannot really point to any body marks, but he certainly recalls times when the body was scarred and disfigured for a time, even though the marks have faded with time. Nick recounts an accident where he badly grazed his knee which secured the attentions of his Gran, 'who was a nurse in the war', and this placed him in a situation of special attention and distinction from his twin brother. As short-lived as the time of the tending and caring for the damaged knee was, Nick recounts the story as a meaningful experience in his own self realization.

Somehow, providing an account of one's misfortune, stupidities and/or braveries in relation to an anchor point of a scar – a bodily disfigurement – is to reveal how one views the past in the present. This viewing is an imposed framework of meaningful significance, but it cannot be said to be an accurate reflection of what 'really' occurred for there is always information which has been excluded and transformed through the accounting process. We note that the remembering process is selective – we cannot be wholly sure of the facts, but we insist on certain time/space elements in the account. For example, a scar proudly displayed as the result of falling on a broken bottle when Kathryn was just four years old invites reflection and interpretation. In emotional terms the reflection is one where the pain was considerable, as was the fear at the volume of blood being lost, an unhappiness as one rather snazzy pink catsuit was ruined and all the time these imaginings are wrapped up in the recollection of a mother cleaning up the leg and offering words of condolence and assurance that things will be all right – the institution of the family would protect 'this body' from further harm.[5] Kathryn locates herself in time and place through the scar – pictures of the field where the bottle lay and the kitchen where she was cleaned up flit through her mind; she can recall the look of her mother – as a younger woman than now – and the way her brother first laughed and then looked afraid when he saw the blood on her leg. She remembers walking home crying, but what day was it? And was it spring or autumn? These things are unclear. She remembers that she had sugar on a spoon 'to make it better' but this was usually for split lips and bitten tongues – maybe she didn't have sugar on a spoon, just 'should have done'; she can't remember what her mother said to her exactly, but it was all going to be all right. How does her mother remember it all? Differently? All of these things come and go each time Kathryn catches sight of the scar on her leg; a little silvery snail track high on her shin.

Certainly by reflecting on the past we have to take account of an understanding of the body as ageing and transforming/being transformed through time. Scars which have been gained in early childhood are placed in relative temporality with those gained last year. Earlier we noted how the ageing body must be 'concerned for itself' we must learn through our experiences, and one way in which we suggest this is done is where scar accounts reveal the self as located in relation to meaningful social institutions such as family, school or work.

The scar accounts we have gathered all contain elements which link the individual to certain social institutional contexts: being patched up by parents – mothers and grandmothers in particular figured strongly – and the family as an institution of care is clearly reinforced. School also played a part in many childhood scar stories. Haydn reveals how his accident with a pair of scissors in the classroom whilst trying to get drawing pins out of 'one of those old desks' produced a rather small scar, but a rather traumatic memory. In Hayden's account he speaks of the teacher's role in cleaning the hand and generally taking control of the situation and the unfortunate pupil.

Scars as a result of falls as a child were common happenings for our informants and in each case time/space details assist in locating the embodied self in a historical past. Nikki, for example, recalls clearly the wall and the strange white paintmark above the school steps where she once fell as a child and procured her scarred chin. Adams (1990: 99) notes that ageing bodies are *associated with* the irreversible direction of time; but whilst the process direction is seen to be *given*, the process of ageing is signposted by socially marked stages and, following Weigert (1981), Adams notes 'how biographical development is symbolically transformed into biographical statuses' where individuals are viewed as being 'locked into' certain space/time defined institutional contexts.

Conclusion

We have suggested that one obvious aspect of the scar account being 'worth anything' or meaningful is its ability to be both credible and interesting. These aspects make for a 'good story' and the self is successfully commodified. But there also appears to be something important about the moral value of scar accounts. The 'good story' aspect also appears to rest on the reflective quality one brings to a story. The sharing with others of a 'lesson learned' or at the very least a recognition of the moral aspect to protecting one's self (and therefore others) through good social practice is embedded in all good scar stories.

The body is cognitively mapped (see Walsh 1992 on museum heritage as cognitive mapping) through discourses and through this process it is 'understood', yet these discourses only exist through practice or by being retained as 'memory traces' (Frank 1991: 48–9, following Giddens 1984: 337). Scars are offered up, often literally, to others as a display of an individual's consciousness of their body as a site of corporeality but also of survival and resistance: the scar is the result of the body having resisted another object, the body has suffered damage, but the human being remains to tell the tale. Scarring is a discourse of embodied consciousness (Frank 1991: 50). Each scar, as self-consciously reflected upon, is an embodiment of one's relationship with a concrete and real world, but a reality which becomes transformed and reified through representation as formed in the account of telling how the scar was acquired and its significance to an individual.

We are not clear to what extent we concur with the idea that there is such a thing as a 'true' or 'core' self. But there does seem to be a sense of having a deep understanding of one's embodied past through reflecting. Furthermore, we appear to be selective in what it is that we choose to remember and to tell regarding our embodied self's past. Do we seek to construct a meaningful framework about our current identity by the careful reification of past experiences and reflection on which memories are retained as exceptional and valid and those others which are left out and forgotten? There is something in this for we have scars which have stories, but we often have others which are without a story unless, as Mary notes, we choose to 'make one up'. 'Knowing' our own bodies and in particular our own scars (or lack of them) is an interpretative process which cannot be simply understood as a recounting of past events as accurate or even real. Just as the heritage of a nation has to contend with a culture of 'imagined past', so too our embodied selves struggle to promote or deny our own body history.

In this chapter we have suggested that scar accounts are meaningful interpretations of the scarring process and the memories invoked provide the self with a repository by which one's ageing, identity, knowledge (especially 'learning' concern for self) and relationships (for example, with 'institutions' such as family, school or community) can be reflected upon in ways that are highly personal and unique. We have touched on the idea that accounts of scars present the opportunity for the telling of 'good stories' and through this we have explored the idea that scar accounts offer the opportunity to view the body as a heritage site whereby the past is reimagined for present consumption. Where our bodies have been marked by past events or 'battles' we can view such markings as sedimented memories or 'time marks' which are sensuous, emotional and politically significant, and provide a sometimes neglected but nonetheless common resource for situating and reflecting on one's identity.

Acknowledgements

Both authors would like to thank friends and colleagues who supported them in the process of writing this chapter, in particular

Andrew Blaikie and Mike Hepworth, Department of Sociology, University of Aberdeen for their valuable advice and support.

Notes

1. Where appropriate we have distinguished whose account is being referred to (either Kathryn or Mary), and, in some cases, the accounts have been written up in the third person to assist in this distinction, but also to present a degree of reflective distance from the data.
2. Scots word for those who defy good advice.
3. Featherstone (1991: 92) points out that those who do not conform to standards of body maintenance must accept the negative consequences in social interaction.
4. A skim board is a flat round board you throw along the water's edge at the beach and jump onto to skim along the water and sand.
5. A scar is a physical manifestation of bodies in action, of social relationships and emotional expression. For Frank (1991: 49) bodies exist at the intersection of discourses, institutions and corporeality and we know this by considering how a scar is talked about and viewed in terms of its flesh and blood properties, as well as how it is situated as a manifestation of the body coming into a relationship with a particular institution.

References

Adams, B. 1990. *Time and Social Theory*. London: Polity Press.

Brett, D. 1996. *The Construction of Heritage*. Cork: Cork University Press.

Dunow, D. 1997. 'Literary Models: Theoretical Considerations', in *Models of Narrative: Theory and Practice*. Basingstoke: Macmillan – now Palgrave.

Easton, A. 1994. 'The Body as History and "Writing the Body": the example of Grace Nichols', *Journal of Gender Studies*, 3 (1): 55–67.

Featherstone, M. 1991. 'The Body in Consumer Culture', in M. Featherstone, M. Hepworth and B. Turner (eds.) *The Body: Social Process and Cultural Theory*. London: Sage.

Foucault, M. 1988. 'Technologies of the Self', in L.H. Martin, H. Gutman and P.H. Hutton (eds.) *Technologies of the Self: A Seminar with Michel Foucault*. Amherst: The University of Massachusetts Press.

Frank, A. 1991. 'For a Sociology of the Body: an Analytical Review', in M. Featherstone, M. Hepworth and B. Turner (eds.) *The Body: Social Process and Cultural Theory*. London: Sage.

Giddens, A. 1984. *The Constitution of Society*. Berkeley: University of California Press.

Goffman, E. 1959. *The Presentation of Self in Everyday Life*. London: Penguin Books.

Goffman, E. 1963. *Stigma*. London: Penguin Books.

Grosz, E. 1995. *Space, Time and Perception: Essays on the Politics of Bodies*. London: Routledge.

Lowenthal, D. 1996. *The Heritage Crusade and the Spoils of History*. London: Viking.
McCrone, D. et al. 1995. *Scotland the Brand: The Making of the Scottish Tourist Industry*. London: Routledge.
Scott, J. 1991. 'The Evidence of Experience', *Critical Inquiry*, 17: 773–97.
Smith, S. 1993. 'The Bodies of Contemporary Autobiographical Practice', in *Subjectivity, Identity and the Body: Women's Autobiographical Practices in the Twentieth Century*. Bloomington: Indiana University Press.
Turner, B. 1991. 'The Discourse of Diet', in M. Featherstone, M. Hepworth and B. Turner (eds.) *The Body: Social Process and Cultural Theory*. London: Sage.
Urry, J. 1996. 'How Societies Remember the Past', in S. Macdonald and G. Fyfe (eds.) *Theorizing Museums*. Oxford: Blackwell.
Walker, J. 1997. 'The Traumatic Paradox: Documentary Films, Historical Fictions, and Cataclysmic Past Events', *Signs*, 221 (4): 803–26
Walsh, K. 1992. *The Representation of the Past: Museums and Heritage in the Post-modern World*. London: Routledge.
Weigert, A.J. 1981. *Sociology of Everyday Life*. London: Longman.
White, H. 1978. *Tropics of Discourse*. Baltimore: Johns Hopkins University Press.

3

Dissonant Choreographies: Performativity and Method in Socio-cultural Research

Joost van Loon and Hannah Rockwell

Cultural engineering an incorporation – notes from consultancy practice

One of the authors of this chapter (hereafter 'I') was once asked to assist a managerial team of a large organization in the Netherlands. The organization (PULSE), was the product of a recent merger between two competing insurance corporations. Due to increased internal conflicts following the merger, almost the entire management team had been replaced by a new one. A new mission – represented by the slogan 'Human Value in Security' – had been developed to engineer a more effective organizational culture. An instrumental approach to social change may be awkward for those in social and cultural studies whose intellectual heritage is to resist the idea that cultures can be re-created at will and behaviours will fall in line with a new slogan or mission statement. However, organization and business studies have been dealing with issues of organizational culture as engineered since the 1980s – in particular since the publication of Peters' and Waterman's (1982) best-seller *In Search of Excellence*. In the mainstream of management and business scholarship little has been done to counter the unrealistic idea that top-down cultural engineering is desirable and/or possible. Instead, large sums of money have been made by consultants who coin new buzzwords when old ones cease to be fashionable (Feltman 1992).

Most initiatives to provide models for the *cultural* engineering of organizations fail because they are unable to account for the resilient, residual, autonomous and contingent complexity of organizational cultural processes (Koot 1994). In the three years since its creation, PULSE had consumed several organizational consultant teams, including some with prominent reputations. None was able successfully to re-engineer organizational attitudes and practices, and final reports on the failed projects were univocal in their condemnation of this organization, described as 'slow', 'inert', 'rigid' and 'bureaucratic'. Despite costly disappointments, leaders at PULSE kept faith with an idea of professional expertise and continued attempts to change its culture on the basis of a vision inherent in the new mission statement.

On my first visit to company headquarters, I was impressed by the architecture and spatial organization of the reception area. There was a large, empty lobby with a large reception desk and a few couches. The style was a mixture of classic and modern with everything perfectly placed. This spatialization of the 'reception' one gets from PULSE signifies that this is an organization whose style and appearance is highly valued. The office areas, however, give a startlingly different impression. They are mostly the cell-type cubicles of bureaucratic architecture with very few open plan offices (Dutch office architecture had abandoned open plan offices in the 1960s – Veldhoen and Piepers 1995). The contrast with the reception area was striking. Instead of a luxurious breathing space (*Lebensraum*), these offices were small, cramped and ugly. Refurbishment initiatives were being considered, but the lack of resources made the likelihood of a major re-spatialization poor. Another striking feature of the spatial organization was that few people could be observed in corridors or common rooms. Most doors were closed, and where they were not, people were usually working quietly behind computer screens. A cell structure accommodates private and individualized work performances; at the same time, it engenders a cold, indifferent and non-interactive atmosphere. Such an environment was unlikely to support the ideological vision of 'human value and security'.

The team members I met were welcoming, warm and informal. They first began to probe my credentials diplomatically and assess my perspective on 'organizational culture'. It was of my own intent to 'acquire' this account in order to prove to colleagues at the Free University that I was more than a theoretician and could do the 'practical work' of hands-on consultancy. I rationalized my involvement by asserting a belief that it was an interesting way of doing research and gathering data. I justified the experience as action research, in which there is a mutual interest and stake in the work. The voyeurism inherent in ethnography lends itself to situating a researcher in an uneasy place. I assumed I could offer some kind of expertise in return for the information I was about to glean.

I explained to management that if cultural change were to happen at all, it needed to emerge from the bottom up and that this was unlikely to occur since in a climate of economizing and rationing of time and resources, we can expect that most employees had better things to do than reflexively rationalize their own practices in order to adjust them to the new cultural-managerial regime. In spite of my explicit reservations, the team went ahead with its plan to launch a symposium for middle management in an attempt to engage them in a discussion about the way that organizational culture could be re-engineered. I was asked to sit in, make observations and give feedback at a later stage. Later that day I spoke informally with members of middle management. After only a brief meeting, the institutional roles of each cohort became clear. The management team told organizational members what the new mission was supposed to be and what sort of culture should emerge from that. Middle managers withdrew into an oppositional camp, resistant to any idea of change and expressed worries about the material implications and outcomes of the structural incorporation of cultural engineering.

The spatial organization of the day's events reinforced the attitudinal divisions that appeared to be already in place with management 'on stage' and the rest of the organizational members in the 'audience'. Although the meeting place was a neutral conference centre, the event became a simulacrum for the organization as a whole. The aural and visual modes of engagement did not appear to be harmonious. Hostilities became apparent through whispering and frequent eye-contact between members of cliques (some of which were pre-existing, some appeared to have formed on-the-spot). I noticed an atmosphere of general discomfort signalled by expressions of disaffection and indifference to speakers from management, and restless, repetitive body movements. I was not an experienced ethnographer nor consultant, and ultimately could not sustain this dual role. I felt it was necessary to disassociate myself from the performances on stage and the apparent hostilities and actions of audience members.

My strategy of distanciation came in handy because the team had also hired an 'organizational performance therapist' who invited participants of the symposium to dance to a very basic rhythm which was based around the new mission statement. In short, the organizational therapy involved choreographed movements coinciding with a slogan to incorporate a harmonious, collective organizational *espirit de corps*. This experience was apparently designed to evoke the expressive catharsis of pent-up frustration, perhaps aggravated by the cellular architecture of the environment, and to enable a deeper integration of the workers' unconscious identification with PULSE's organization. To speak of an organization's mission is to offer a rhetoric for ideological consideration, but to invite workers to embody (or dance to) the slogan is to engender a physical and sentient involvement in the experience of in-corporation into an artificially constructed rhythm of the organizational body.

Surprisingly, the employee participation rate was initially high; however, after a few minutes, the majority dropped out and began to express themselves in non-sanctioned, improvisational ways, for example by inventing their own movements, often mocking the senior managers who were dancing in front of them and could not see them. It is likely that the visible movement and line of vision of top managers prevented the total disidentification of other employees. I chose to use my role as an outsider to remain marginal to the event and did not participate with the dancers. As a person on the scene, I was not about to be swept up into the dramatic action. Therefore, I improvised as embarrassed observer and aligned my feelings with an apparent disenchantment that some employees seemed to experience having been asked to perform with colleagues.

Spatialization and embodiment as methodological issues

The observations described above reveal the failures of cultural engineering – the (dis)organization of sense and sensibility through central programming. Affective structures shaped by historical rituals and cultural understanding cannot easily be unlearned nor easily manipulated by a slogan and a dance. To assume that such an event will enable employee loyalty or establish the value of membership demonstrates management's lack of understanding about cultural change, human affect and the politics of power inherent in any organizational setting. Change (however positive) generates human fear, an instability in sentient experience and an intensification of regressive resistance to change. To subject employees to a transitional one-day therapeutic dance symposium clearly and sorely misses the dartboard of plausible ways to assure employees of their place and value when an organization is undergoing restructuring.

There is something that always remains ideologically and practically in excess of scripts that have been drafted to establish a rationale for particular forms of organizing. According to the feminist cultural critic Judith Butler, the '*performative* dimension of [social] construction is precisely the forced reiteration of norms' (1993: 94). Social constraints may be thought of as a *condition* of performativity (ibid.: 94–5). While constraints are the outside limits of what employees typically do, say and think in a particular organization, the performance of work rituals is not a single event, but a 'ritual reiterated under and through constraint, under and through the force of prohibition and taboo, with the threat of ostracism and even death controlling and compelling the shape of the production' (ibid.: 95). Put simply, company rules shape the outside boundaries for social practices within an organization, and people express themselves in sustained and repetitive ways within those sets of constraints. The *performative* is the tacit, mundane, embodied repetition of social practices. In addition, Butler's concept of *performativity* includes the leaky excess that is always already destined to escape because of the temporal and spatial nature of social practice (Rockwell 1996). Ironically, the habitual repetitions of daily practices provide an organization with its most resilient limits because of the historicity and momentum of collective understanding in a particular place over time. Concurrently, these practices 'perpetually' re-institute the possibility of their own failure to regulate behaviour. Therefore, the *excessive* power of social practices are produced in the same instances in which they are carried out. Butler suggests that '[t]he question here concerns the tacit cruelties that sustain coherent identity, cruelties that include self-cruelty as well, the abasement through which coherence is fictively reproduced and sustained' (1993: 115). All social practices that take place within an organizational setting have the potential to impinge upon social identity as well as function as a form of socio-political resistance; in order to better understand how this works, it is important to take into consideration all features of performativity, and this is where we depart from Butler to address our concerns.

Performativity in an organization can be understood in terms of two analytically distinct but practically connected processes: spatialization and embodiment. To *spatialize* is to locate oneself in a coordinated way in time and place with others in proximity and to monitor one's extrinsic movements according to an interpretation of apparent social codes. One might think of spatialization as the distinctly social dimension of performativity. *Embodiment* is the active incorporation and reorganization of habituated experiences carried out in speech, movement, thought and feeling, that guides and remembers human activity. Neither spatialization nor embodiment should be thought of as fixed or static experiences; indeed, their analytic value is to consider these concepts in relation to social practice both separately and as coordinates. Taken together, these conceptual distinctions provide a methodological tool for beginning to examine social phenomena while taking into account the role of bodies understood as textured and previously unassumed phenomenon in the practical formation of cultural *incorporation*.

Our understanding of the 'social' as performativity establishes a role for the body in methodological questions. The current rise in attempts to theorize the body in sociology and cultural studies has provided exciting insights into how symbolic representation and practical activity are critical dimensions of social regulation. These attempts, however, have had little to say about the various modalities of embodiment and their implications for research methods and practices. The body is now a relatively well-established domain within socio-cultural theory, and has been subject to numerous empirical studies (Martin 1987; Leder 1990; Featherstone et al. 1991; Lupton 1995). However, it is remarkable that the relatively traditional research methods have not yet been affected by the theoretical force mounted against the methodological objectification of bodies in favour of their constitutive character. In other words, it is ironic that much research on the body has been conducted with a relatively disembodied ethos.[1] Indeed, it seems as if as soon as researchers arrive at the scene to investigate human activity as a subject of analysis, people's bodies (including our own) are quickly taken for granted as self-revelatory and/or as objects of representation. In addition, questions such as 'what is a body?' and/or 'what does it do?' 'how does it function?' are often displaced by an urge to represent it as something else – for example, as a text, an agent, a will-to-power or an institutional product. While the body can function for the researcher in any of those capacities, we find that in examining the productive activities of everyday existence, each of those ways of re-presenting bodies is inadequate for understanding how and what bodies do in the course of performing lived experience. The body's agency is imbued with more than engaging in 'conduct'. This richly lived, active, intelligent organism is our interpreter of all sensibility and shaper of social memory. If we find language to express the richness of cultural life from a point of view in which the self-evident nature of the body is not taken for granted nor understood as a mere instrument of mindful activity, our understanding of human performativity will likewise be enriched.

The concept of method has come under attack in some theoretical zones; however, there are good reasons for maintaining an adherence to methodological rigour. Conventionally, method is a rule-bound, standardized and replicable manner of doing something. Research is a social practice whose ways of 'doing' has its own domain of expertise and counter-expertise. Therefore, to have an identity as a researcher, one must be learned in the symbolic orders that provide the integrating logic for a discipline's content and professional tools. Method represents a particular, rule bound, regulated, standardized and transferable mode (manner) of doing something.

However, methods are also a particular form of disciplinary enrolment. One enters a profession, a discipline, not only by acquiring research skills, but also by allowing its logic to discipline oneself – to become part of it. Method as a form of discipline has implications for the body. To become 'methodical', is to embody a discursive logic and requires a particular kind of posturing. Taking a posture is adopting a docile body by regulating oneself in the service of the performance of a particular task (Foucault 1977). While Foucault laid important groundwork for understanding the relationship between discourse and bodies, he inadequately addressed how every posture-taking has an excessive quality. If the performative is the embodied, tacit and practised repetition of social practices, performativity includes those repetitions plus that which escapes during embodied engagement. Therefore, to take up a researcher's posture is once and at the same time to re-enact learned practices associated with method-proper and to open up a space for alternative performances of method. Posturing opens up an excess-desire, or as Joan Copjec (1989) once called it, inculpation (an endowment with guilt), that it is not really me/you. The posture is always already differentiated from the 'really me/you' and operates as another force, subject to the inducements of disciplinary power and resistances against it. Performativity lives through the methodologist-as-impostor.[2] Hence, the embodiment of method brings something extra – a moment in which the performative turns back to itself and thereby opens a scope for re-interpretation and critical intervention. This doubling of the performative – or what has also been referred to as 'reflexivity' – establishes new limits for methodology by reasserting the necessity of concern for political and aesthetic dimensions of social experience. A total abandonment of 'method' would foreclose critical intervention by disabling any engagement beyond the immediacy of performativity as if that which performs is somehow simultaneously and without distortion, also disclosing itself in full.

Shadows and resonances: cultural research of the non/present

Embodiment, when integrated as a key feature of method, exposes a researcher's posturing stance and foregrounds a radically immediate enpresentation of experience. That is, what we take to be 'present' in the form of a body can only achieve mythical status if it is 'revealed' as a body (van Loon 1996). The body is never itself since it does not stand for the total of the identity of itself. The body is inscribed, marked, shaped, penetrated, infected, shifting, disintegrating and dying. Every body marks the traces of cultural endowment; no body is pure matter/energy but always contaminated with signification. Cultural research needs to recognize a fundamental paradox that accounts for the radical presence of experience not wholly presented in that which is immediately apparent. Two figures might stand as metaphorical actors for this posturing: the shadow and the resonance.

The *shadow* is a classical figure that stands as an originating myth of traditional western metaphysics. It starts in Plato's allegory of the cave, where it plays the role of the impostor (by disguising itself as the 'real object') revealing an untruth. The shadow, from distortion to fallacy, is that which the philosopher must overcome and render obsolete.[3] Plato's search for perfection led him to assume that between the worlds of ideas and things, there is no place for the shady simulacrum – that which is neither original nor copy, but counters the will to know with the fear of knowing (Deleuze 1994). However, as Deleuze argues, the simulacrum may be all we have left once representations have been stripped from the mythical idealism that grants them this divine status as Ideas.

The shadow belongs to zones of liminality, deviance from convention and impurity; it is the figure of the in-between. The shadow emerges when light encounters an obstacle, an object, that thereby spatializes the being-in-the-world; the shadow marks that other side of the object, its less than conscious side. Its darkness hides all secret fears and desires. The shadow marks non-being, the nothing that is no thing, from which all sense emerges.

The resonance, drawing on an aural metaphor, is a figure similar to the shadow, but instead of spatializing, it temporizes. The resonance is sound that comes after, it is a trace that marks the vanishing event, the present that is not sustainable. Resonance is similar to Derrida's (1982) '*différance*', yet its difference defers in time. Resonances can be harmonious as well as dissonant. In harmony, they are attuned to their destiny and amplify the sound-waves. However, in dissonance, the resonance is a remainder that breaks the unity of the whole and marks a minus-that-which-has-been-presented, that element that does not belong, a matter-out-of-time (and out-of-tune).

Sound-traces, or resonances, are of course not purely temporal, as they set into work the specific acoustics, hence space. Likewise, shadows also mark temporality; the earliest forms of time measurement used the length of shadows to indicate the time of day. However, whereas the relationship between the object and its shadow is relatively immediate and mimetic, the relationship between a sound and its resonance is always necessarily delayed. Therefore, we need both figures if we are to make sense out of the body in cultural research and do justice to its im/materiality.

Both shadow and resonance are archetypical forms of spatialization. They highlight that space is always relative and relational to entities which constitute it (Heidegger 1986), be it an object of reflection or an utterance of enunciation. Space is thus articulated in particular, temporal mediations; hence, it is 'indexical'. Indexicality is a term used by Garfinkel (1967), who appropriated it within a phenomenological perspective to describe the necessity of the particular, context-specific and relational character of understanding any enunciation. Shadows and resonances are indexical forms of spatialization because they make sense only in relation to the specific situations in which they emerged into being. Shadows are always 'of' some entity, just as resonances always belong to some utterance of sound. They only become figures of obscurity if they lose their indexicality.

However, indexicality can be used in a second way that relates not to a phenomenological, but to a more hermeneutic tradition; in particular that of the pragmatic language philosopher Charles Sanders Peirce (1940). Peirce used the term 'index' as a category in between 'icon' (a form of signification that works through resemblance) and 'symbol' (a form of signification that works through a complex system of rules). For Peirce, the index is a form of signification that operates on the basis of a natural referential relationship, such as smoke in relation to fire. However Eco (1977) refined this and criticized its rather naive naturalist assumption. According to Eco, the index must be seen as a relational signifier that operates on the basis of material tracing, but without exclusively those of cause-and-effect. That is, an index is like a trace of something else, indicating that this 'other entity' was once, but no longer, 'present' (also see Derrida 1978). Here, the shadow and the resonance are indices of particular entities and utterances, whose presence is deferred by the difference that has set these figures 'into work'. Combining both notions of indexicality, we can see how it relates to spatialization. Spatialization takes place through indexicality. In this sense, space is always particular and relational. As such, it constitutes the primary form of cultural research, which always requires a specific attunement to particular modes of sense-making that are relational.

Choreography, dissonance and creativity

In previous sections, we have outlined that we understand the social in terms of performativity, and method as an effective way of mapping the complexity of traces, operationalized as shadows and resonances. We now deepen our concern with their implications for understanding 'the body'. The concept of embodiment is linked to experiences of spatialization and only exists socially in the moment of performativity shaped by history and convention. Productions of individual and collective bodies relate to each other – empathetically, sympathetically, antipathetically or simply pathetically.[4] In other words, performing bodies are inflected with a totality of experience that is shaped by context – time and space. This enacted-relational understanding of embodiment is necessary to resist the tendency to project a concept of the body as a self-enclosed entity, identical with itself, as the physical anchor of subjectivity versus a time-space experience through which (always partial) subjective experience may be traced.

Indeed, if we view bodies as instigators of and memory sites for social experience, never equalling themselves-as-matter, the social is not simply the space that lies in-between and beyond bodies. Instead, the social is that which is inaugurated by forms of embodiment that engender 'affect' and the accent and tone of any experience. These bodies take on particular postures – constituting their performativity – and are attuned to each other in the form of shadows and resonances, that is, in particular and temporary forms of mediation. It is this attunement that constitutes particular modalities of sociation. Attunement is a form of indexicality, a pointing towards the tracing of the present, which is always differing and deferred. Attunement is a form of spatialization, a pointing towards that brings forth an in-between/beyond through which embodiment literally 'takes place'.

The social is not a random collection of embodied entities, but is complexly structured through an infinite residue of traces of discourse and experience. Social spatialization is not a haphazard gathering of indices, but a highly organized and managed performance of relationships and references. For more than a century now, sociologists have tried to account for the nature of social order and tried to explain how it comes about. Most explanations have focused on the rule-bound nature of social structure, and suggested that it should be analysed as something external to, and imposed upon, members of society. Durkheim's (1984) '*conscience colléctif*' is an example of such an explanation that tries to locate the sense of social order as residing beyond the scope of individual embodiments.

A figure we may draw upon is the concept of choreography. As in a dance, the social consists of coordinated movements of bodies that individually may be following their own patterns, and in total perform a balanced 'act' whose entirety is more than the sum of the parts. Durkheim's 'organic solidarity', points us in a useful direction. This concept integrates mutual interdependence and functional specialization into a totality whose structure is written as a moral code that one is obliged to follow. However, this view conceives of social experience principally as static text. Choreography, however, exists only in its performativity – in the embodied actualization of coordinated movement. The script allows us to interpret and rationalize the performative, and subject it to discursive manipulation. Durkheim acknowledged that the social is in actuality quite different from an ideal of complete harmony. There were always deviations from the moral code that had the potential to disrupt organic solidarity and bring society to the brink of chaos. The indexicalities of an ensemble of embodiments are not always attuned to each other; there are liminal zones, which could be spatial (e.g. ghettos), temporal (e.g. war, revolution, riot), or both (e.g. urban guerrilla warfare).

However, if we look at the nature of the social in actuality, disorder seems far less exceptional; indeed order is far less common and seems to exist only as an ideal. Attunement, therefore, cannot simply or even predominantly be seen as an attempt to harmonize according to an already existing script (e.g. the old sociological model of 'norms and values'). It is an enactment in which a mode of engagement is established that takes its engagement with others as primary. This does not necessarily foreclose any evil intent to violate the other. Violation may be seen as a form of engagement. Enactment, not intentionality, is our point of departure for the inauguration of the social.

The decline of structural-functionalist and Marxist paradigms in sociology in the 1960s and 1970s followed a trajectory that was similar to that left behind by the then up-and-coming paradigm in the natural sciences. Anti-positivism, which was already dominating the epistemological debates in philosophy of science, became an accepted position within sociology too, and in the wake of the new mood came new forms of theorizing the social. A new de-emphasis on externally existing rules was elaborated by ethnomethodologists, phenomenologists and poststructuralists as they stressed the emergent nature of social order while admitting that it is something that is inherently unstable and prone to particularities that make a generalization of rules into moral codes problematic. In these views, rule-boundness is far less an effect of an external logic, but inherent in the very regularity of its performance and temporal repetition. Whereas there may seem to be a logic to the social, it is only a temporary sedimentation, externalized rather than externally imposed. It would therefore be wrong to state that such theoretical perspectives have no sense of structure (also see Giddens 1984).

However, it is still possible to discuss the social in terms of choreography, as long as we acknowledge that (a) it involves dissonant as well as consonant elements; and (b) the choreography is not a fixed script, but an enactment, indeed, an inscription. The script that social and cultural researchers encounter (render an account of) in their interrogation of practices is thus a reconstruction of performativity, a sedimentation of the enactment of pathology. Choreography and the performative are mutually engaged in the production of affect. Hence, choreography necessarily entails traces of creativity and improvisation which refer to those embodied movements and indexicalities that have a self-generating life-force (*puissance*) 'of their own', and are the setting-into-work of irregularities that engender transgressions of rules. Indeed, all practices entail some form of creativity and all practices are to some degree transgressive of the settings in which they are enacted. This resonates with some of the more established neo-functionalist arguments that full systemic enclosure around norms and values is never realised because actors always bring in something 'extra', be it deviance or simply strategic action (e.g. Merton 1968; Alexander 1988).[5] However, we differ from such neo-functionalist accommodations of deviance and transformation on the issue of the status of the normative order itself. In dissonant choreographies, there is no 'order', there are only 'ordering' practices. Hence, what is being transgressed is not a system of rules, regulations, norms and values, but particular forms of inscription that regulate the setting of embodied enactments and emerges from the attunement of our being-in-the-world. Settings can be differentiated in degrees and modalities of 'ordering'. These degrees of ordering are contingent upon the degrees of regularity (frequency + tempo + rhythm) and repetition. Every repetition, however, entails a deviation from that which is repeated (Deleuze 1994). Scripts, which are the product of social and cultural research and writing, are the accounts that have been rendered of these settings. The confusion between settings and scripts has led to 'structural functionalism'.

In highly schematic terms, we argue that ordering and disordering take place in at least two ways which are analytically distinct but practically often indistinguishable:

1. *Dissonant choreographies,* which are more or less intentional deviations of attunement and engagement of bodies and indexicalities during performative moments of social spatialization (overdetermination).
2. *Improvization,* which is in its core a form of spontaneous deviation because it is engendered in the puissance of embodiment and indexicality; that remainder that is not tamed by the regularities of repetition and rehearsal but lies beyond identity, as the *minus-in-the-origin* (Bhabha 1994) without which (double negative) total unification would have been possible (underdetermination).

To sum up, the social is to some degree ordered and there is some pleasurable experience in this order as bodies find in their movements spontaneous and intentional attunements to each other's indexicalities. Social spatialization involves complex choreographies of such attunements which, however, are not always in tune and harmonious. Some embodiments remain obscure in liminal forms, some resonances do not find consonance with leading tunes.

Methodology revisited: the case of (auto)biography

The themes of dissonant choreography and creative indexicality, which we distilled from the figures of the shadow and the resonance, highlight that the fundamental problem of any empirical methodology is always the elusiveness of the present. Method, we argued, always entails forms of (im)posturing; this is because it is an embodied form of social spatialization. For every question leaves a trace; every observation denotes a trajectory. What sort of presence comes to our senses in empirical form? They are always shadows, resonances, traces of something in passing. The methodologist has to perform Plato's trick (dismissing the shadows) to impose a sense immutability onto these traces to turn them into 'data' that take the form of 'facts'. At the same time, the researcher has to conceal the actual performativity of researching so as not to disturb the unfolding of reality that shows up before her/him.

Of course, the vast majority of social scientists who are concerned about methodology already know this and hence acknowledge the false pretences of 'pure' empirical observations. Every observation entails a translation, which is inherent in the passing of the event, and its inscription into textual form. However, many in the social sciences and cultural studies concluded from this that this means the end of 'method'. This response is premature, logically incorrect and impractical. To state that because no method gives us pure access to the present, we therefore can dispense with any organized way of accumulating traces with which to make sense, resides on the same false assumption that there really are such things as a 'pure present' and 'pure writing'. Even if an unbridgeable gap exists between these two temporarily arrested forms of reality, we may still continue to work on the asymptotic relationship that may be projected onto that gap. Second, a dismissal of method on the basis of its inability to access 'pure' empirical reality still suggests that that is what research 'should' be; hence reiterating similar assumptions about the role of science as those advocated by modern thought. Third, a denial of method leaves social sciences and humanities to be just other genres of 'running commentaries' on interpretations of the world. However, compared to philosophy, the social sciences are ill-equipped to engender conceptual innovations; and compared to the arts, they are far too unimaginative to spurn any radical creative energy. It is method which sets the (social) sciences apart from philosophy and the arts (cf. Deleuze and Guattari 1994). Without method, there is no element of surprise, as all has already been anticipated. Method allows a doubling of the inscription as it acknowledges that the inscribing is a process rather than a timeless-spontaneous happening. Method engages with the mapping of traces and the tracing of maps; it thus allows the social and cultural researcher to engage – ethically, politically and aesthetically – with her/his being-in-the-world.

Not just any method will do. In order to work within a non-positivist and non-representational epistemology, i.e. to be engaged in tracing shadows and resonances, our method should depart first, from an acknowledgement of (im)posturing. Methodology itself should be embodied and indexical. Embodied indexicality brings together two different traditions of thinking: one involves the immediate responsiveness of the body in terms of matter/energy, the other a form of temporization/spatialization resembling *différance* – a differing/deferring movement away from the immediacy of the present. Both could actually be combined into one word: reflexivity; this combination invokes both the German and English usage of the word. The German usage of *Reflex* refers to an immediate-embodied, non-cognitive response to a stimulus; whereas in English, being reflexive refers to maintaining a distance in order to contemplate. Of course, the uses are complementary by providing the conceptual framework for experiencing the doubled movement of a methodological loop. In order to diminish a metaphysics of static presence, it is important to emphasize that such a repetition is not of an identicality. Whatever it is that reflexivity induces, it is not an identical same (e.g. vulgar mimesis) but a deviation. The index is not the same as its object. No body is ever fully present to itself, even at its highest possible state of reflexivity.

In its repetition, reflexivity undermines the conditions under which it was set into operation. It transforms the reality it works with. However a method that requires reflexivity and a richer understanding of embodiment and indexicality is more likely to disrupt than to affirm the harmony of coordinated bodies. Of course, as every form of life involves a complex ensemble of ordering principles (which may not always work according to plan), the choreographies that reflexivity creates are likely to be dissonant. Hence, sense-making practices that are without dissonance should be taken with a great degree of suspicion. It is those elements that do not add up which point towards the residual, inert matter/energy that reflexive-embodied-indexicality sensitizes. In their turn, they allow cultural theorists to further cultivate their sensibilities towards embodiment and social spatialization and really start to move beyond the debilitating dualisms of general/particular structure/agency and reality/representation.

Conclusion

A week after the mishappening at PULSE, I was asked to give an account of the day and to suggest ways of improving on it. I explained I was unable to continue with my consultancy on the basis that more research was needed to examine what was going on in the offices of regular employees. The management team wanted a quick technological fix. It was not in their interests to have a researcher looking for lost traces and bringing back resonances from a past. In one sense, the observations I have presented suggest a 'failed project' because it was an action intervention that did not deliver any substantial 'product'. However, it is also arguable that it was a highly successful experience. The observations show the resilience of embodiment against processes of incorporation that are directed by cultural engineering. The bodies of the middle managers refused to be attuned to the new rhythm of the PULSE mission. What these bodies inhabited were the sedimentations of years of machinic-bureaucratic practices, welded together by frustration and resentment. Hence, second, the observations revealed that the socio-cultural incorporation of PULSE took place in a rather antagonistic spatialisation. There was a lot of dissonance. The dissonance, however, was not part of the choreography of senior management and their team of energetic cultural engineers. Their imagined choreography of harmony and flexibility failed to effect significant changes in the already established patterns of embodiment and spatialisation.

Third, when the role of the researcher, and more specifically the embodiment of the researcher, is drawn into the rendering of an account of this event, something strange happens. Suddenly, the event opens up into a new dimension. An element of surprise is introduced that would have been absent from a disembodied 'point of view'. This doubling of writing – of the person and the persona – is a repetition of the social event. Repetition does not mean identicality, however. Hence, no reflexive account will ever be the same as the life-events that have produced it.

The main insight of poststructuralism may be that every rendering of an account, every historiography of an event, is a fabrication (de Certeau 1984). However, what constitutes this fabrication is always in excess of the scripts that can be written about them, these are the traces of affect, of pathos. These traces are themselves not fabricated as scripts, but are resonances, shadows, simulacra, indeed, excesses of other fabrications. The traces are never fully present in any account. However, what matters is their enactment, their actualisation, which can be 'mapped'. Every mapping is thus a pathology, a liability to affect. As far as liability goes, mapping the traces is a deeply ethical engagement. Poststructuralism sensitizes us to the fabrication, the tracing and the mapping of accounts of embodiment and spatialization. These are the enactments of writing, which is the performativity of social and cultural research. Writing is enacted by embodiment and spatialization. It is through writing that we may be able to cultivate a sensibility of our own being in the world.

In other words, methods in social and cultural research are always performative, hence engage in processes of embodiment and spatizalization. The researcher is always part of the research process in three modalities: (a) as constitutive of the traces of setting; (b) as an embodied impostor; and (c) as the transcriber (script writer) of the fabrication of the event. Hence it is not simply the complexity of the world that prevents any form of complete understanding, it is the spatio-temporal specificity of any 'being in the world' that such an understanding enacts, which prevents a complete scripting of being. Issues of validity and generalization, therefore, cannot be answered simply by optimizing the methodological performativity of the actualization of 'research'. What makes a good research method is contingent upon the pathology it actualizes. This pathological concern thus reveals that before questions of validity and truth, there are always already questions of ethics and aesthetics, and most importantly, questions of faith, belief and trust.

Notes

1. Significant exceptions are the works of Arthur Frank (1991, 1995) and Jackie Stacey (1998) whose autobiographical approach focuses on embodiment in terms of suffering and personal experience of illness.
2. The term 'impostor' does not refer to a person 'faking it', but to the inevitability that every 'posture' implies an inauthentic identification with a wider set of abstractions, discursive as well as institutional. Whilst relatively intentional and strategic, the methodological deception is still genuine and not necessarily malicious. Hence we are not proposing a cynical view of research methods here but simply emphasize that methods are never inconsequential and performed innocently.
3. It is of little surprise that feminist theorists, in particular, Luce Irigaray, have taken the myth of Plato's Cave to task by subjecting it to epistemological questions about the relationship between language and bodies.
4. The Greek word *pathos* is a quality in speech of exciting pity or sadness and is related to *pathetikos* (sensitive) and *pathetos* (liable to suffer) (*Oxford English Dictionary of Etymology*, 1986) As such 'the pathetic and the pathological are fundamental modalities of sociation – the ability to be affected'.
5. We are extremely grateful to one anonymous referee who commented on this in an earlier draft.

References

Alexander, J. 1988. *Action and its Environments*. New York: Columbia University Press.

Bhabha, H. 1994. *The Location of Culture*. London: Routledge.

Butler, J. 1993. *Bodies that Matter. On the Discursive Limits of 'Sex'*. London: Routledge.

Copjec, J. 1989. 'The Orthopsychic Subject. Film Theory and the Reception of Lacan', *October*, 49 (Summer): 53–71.

de Certeau, M. 1984. *The Practice of Everyday Life*. Berkeley: University of California Press.

Deleuze, G. [1968] 1994. *Difference and Repetition*. London: The Athlone Press.

Deleuze, G. and Guattari, F. 1994. *What is Philosophy?* London: Verso.

Derrida, J. 1978. *Writing and Difference*. Chicago: University of Chicago Press.

Derrida, J. [1972] 1982. *Margins of Philosophy*. Hemel Hempsted: Harvester Wheatsheaf.

Durkheim, E. 1984. *The Division of Labour*. London: Macmillan.

Eco, U. 1977. *A Theory of Semiotics*. London: Macmillan.
Featherstone, M. Hepworth, M. and Turner, B.S. (eds) 1991. *The Body: Social Process and Cultural Theory*. London: Sage.
Feltman, E. 1992. 'Adviseren na het postmodernisme: Naar een buitengewone interventiekunde?' *M&O*, 46 (1): 133–60.
Foucault, M. 1977. *Discipline and Punish. The Birth of the Prison*. New York: Vintage.
Frank, A. 1991. *At the Will of the Body: Reflections on Illness*. Boston: Houghton Mifflin.
Frank, A. 1995. *The Wounded Storyteller: Body, Illness, and Ethics*. Chicago: University of Chicago Press.
Garfinkel, H. 1967. *Studies in Ethnomethodology*. Englewood Cliffs: Prentice-Hall.
Giddens, A. 1984. *The Constitution of Society: Outline of the Theory of Structuration*. Berkeley: University of California Press.
Heidegger, M. [1927] 1986. *Sein und Zeit* (16th edition). Tübingen: Max Niemeyer Verlag.
Koot, W. 1994. *De Complexiteit van het Alledaagse*. Bussum: Couthino.
Leder, D. 1990. *The Absent Body*. Chicago: University of Chicago Press.
van Loon, J. 1996. 'A Cultural Exploration of Time. Some Implications of Temporality and Mediation', *Time & Society*, 5 (1): 61–84.
Lupton, D. 1995. *The Imperative of Health: Public Health and the Regulated Body*. London: Sage.
Martin, E. 1987. *The Woman in the Body*. Open University Press.
Merton, R. 1968. *Social Theory and Social Structure*. New York: Free Press.
Peirce, C.S. 1940. *The Philosophy of Peirce. Selected Writings*, ed. J. Buchler. London: Kegan Paul, French, Trubner and Co.
Peters, T. and Waterman, R. 1982. *In Search of Excellence: Lessons from America's best run companies*. New York: Harper & Row.
Rockwell, H. 1996. 'An Other Burlesque: Feminine Bodies and Irigaray's Performing Textuality', *Body & Society*, 2 (1): 65–89.
Stacey, J. 1998. 'Teratorologies', *A Cultural Study of Cancer*. London: Routledge.
Veldhoen, E. and Piepers, B. 1995. *The Demise of the Office. The Digital Workplace in a Thriving Organization*. Rotterdam: 010 Publishers.

4

Refusing to Fight: A Playful Approach to Chronic Disease

Gerald Pillsbury

> I do not want to end up in isolation, even in the midst of things; I never want to become accustomed to a dry, little life. And I realize fully that to live otherwise is up to me.
>
> Maxine Greene, 1995

Rarely have I found any experience to be wholly beneficial or wholly harmful, yet the literature and our common ways of speaking depict the experience of chronic disease as uncompromisingly negative. We conceive of it as always intrusive, restricting, dreaded. Such thinking leads us, when discussing the social consequences of the experience, to focus almost exclusively on the troublesome, limiting, separating effects. We talk about loss of functioning, the dissolution or hardening of relationships, and the diminishment of self. You may object that, in fact, we do regularly acknowledge a positive effect of disease on people's lives. Those living through such experiences frequently report that they reprioritize their lives, curtailing unrewarding, unimportant activities. Cancer survivors often adopt healthier patterns of eating, begin regular exercise schedules and stop smoking. Migraine sufferers may more consistently monitor levels of stress or take up yoga. Multiple sclerosis (MS), lupus, tubercular and Parkinson's patients, among many others, may spend greater amounts of their limited energies on enriching productive relationships with loved ones. But these advantages, however, come from the patient's reactions to the disease which he or she likely continues to experience as an unwelcome intrusion necessary only to force oneself to break through bad habits, animate deadened sensibilities, or awaken a hardened heart. One learns, perhaps creatively, heroically, honorably, to make the best of an unfortunate situation. If, prior to the disease, the patient had been sufficiently reflective, the unpleasant experience would be wholly unnecessary, at best merely unenlightening and at worst profoundly pernicious.

Surely, from our customary perspective it seems only natural to think negatively of disease itself and so perhaps, you will find what I will attempt in this chapter quite perverse, for I intend to search for the positive effects of chronic disease – the benefits such a disease may offer. I seek to extend Oliver Sacks' foray into those 'strange waters where... illness may be wellness' (1990: 107). In this nebulous realm, illness and health mix, with illness sometimes constituting a greater good than normality. Here, rather than debilitating, we come to see disease as 'enabling'. Thus, this chapter carries out a thought experiment. If we imagine a subject who is already reflective and self-reflective, what advantages could he or she gain by having a chronic disease? I look for advantages that make the experience of the disease as a whole a true advantage over not having it, benefits that might even make it an experience worth choosing. Such an experiment attempts to change the metaphors, in Lakoff and Johnson's (1980) broad sense of the term, that structure the experience of disease. Would it be possible to experience a chronic disease, even a progressively debilitating and generally feared one, as, if not a welcome experience, at least one that offers advantages as well as limitations? What would such a transformation in our thinking take?

For me, such an experiment is not simply a thought experiment, nor an academic exercise. For the past twelve years[1] I have lived with a slowly progressive form of multiple sclerosis. I am brought to wonder about altering the perspective because the idea that for the next 20, 30 or 40 years I must engage in a fight to the death against the disease feels exhausting. Moreover, the combative metaphor greatly restricts the meanings I can make of my life. Nor, I suggest, should the answer seem irrelevant to the reader even if you are currently not living with a chronic illness. After some point in our lives, chronic rather than occasional illness will be the rule rather than the exception for the majority of us. To this point, Hoffman and Rice (1996) estimate that 100 million Americans, more than one in three, currently live with some kind of chronic disease.

What we will find through this investigation is that it is possible, albeit perhaps only temporarily and with great difficulty, to alter purposefully our experience of chronic disease. Admittedly, I have enjoyed only temporary success at doing so. At times, anxiety and depression still take over returning me to the metaphors of loss and limitations from which I seek to escape. At other times, what obstructs me, often before I am aware that I am using them, are our common ways of talking about and perceiving the disease. But so far at least, I have been able at times to work through these limiting emotional and experiential states and into a much more rewarding perspective on life with the disease. This perspective consists of framing the disease as a form of play. My body, much as an intimate friend might, is asking me to play, in particular play with how we create and maintain reality. The type of play I seek to engage in is a serious one and thus not for everyone. Success comes from accepting the offer unconditionally, enjoying the game and responding imaginatively.

Since this chapter focuses on social knowledge, I will specify the investigation's driving question even further to 'What can chronic disease reveal about the social dimension of self? That is, how people connect with one another?' Merleau-Ponty (1962) argues that the intersubjectivity that connects us to each other and allows us to understand one another depends upon our being able to take our bodily experience as essentially similar to each other. Our being able to construct common projects to engage in requires this assumption of commonality of bodies. If that assumption is threatened, my ability to sustain the life-world (Schutz and Luckmann 1973) we have built and shared is compromised. To continue to live together, living together in the sense of meaningfully enriching each other, we will have to find ways to construct a new world out of recognizing just the opposite of intersubjectivity; we must begin by acknowledging that our fundamental bodily experiences may radically differ.

My task in this chapter, then, is to elaborate in what sense one can see the experience of disease as play, what it takes to adopt such a perspective, and the relationships with others that such a perspective generates. The plan of this chapter is first to present the assumptions that will direct this investigation, second to use a phenomenological approach to articulate the linguistic constraints that limit the relationships I have and then explicate a playful perspective toward my experience. Finally, we consider the social possibilities of this form of play including the moral dimensions of such relations.

Three assumptions

A first assumption guiding this inquiry is that all knowledge is embodied (Polanyi 1958; Merleau-Ponty 1962; Johnson 1987; Shotter 1993). What we know and how we know it greatly depend upon our bodily experience. Our bodies 'know' things we cannot always express. For example, our bodies recognize situations and probable outcomes for good or bad (Dewey 1934). They habitualize knowledge that would be too cumbersome to keep conscious (Camic 1986). They determine the 'aptness' of metaphors fundamental to further thinking processes (Johnson 1987). They allow us to recognize the identities of people and things (Polanyi 1974). Indeed culture itself is grounded in the body (Csordas 1994). In short, a great deal of recent scholarship returns us with ample support to Mauss's observation a half-century ago that 'the body is at the same time the original instrument through which humans shape their world, and the original substance out of which the human world is shaped' (1950, paraphrased in Csordas 1994: 6). Should our bodily experience change in fundamental and lasting ways, as it may do with chronic disease, it seems inevitable that one's knowledge – the practical and eventually, if attended to, the contemplative/theoretical as well – would undergo a fundamental transformation.

A second assumption concerns the nature of this world we live within. It has two orders (Berger 1987; Kirmayer 1992): one of the body and the other of the text and the two are inextricably intertwined. Thus, the sick body and how we talk about illness and the body are intimately connected. Both orders are worlds of meaning. Meaning infuses itself throughout everything we experience and how we experience it. For further elaboration of the idea of meaning, I turn to the radically social constructionist view of Gergen (1994) and Shotter (1993). Our lives consist of hopes, purposes, plans, histories, memories, emotions, and play – all constructed through language. Language and the meanings of our words come prior to and after any form of individual perception, contact, awareness or behaviour. Meaning is not individually or personally created or arrived at, a view that contrasts sharply with many others called constructionist; rather, it is always negotiated within each context and between conversants (Garfinkel 1967; Gergen 1994). Social constructivists do not view meanings as housed within individuals because they do not arise out of individual accommodations to the outside world as Piaget argued. Rather they are continuously constructed and reconstructed through dialogue and interactions with others and, as a result, can be located only in the social world, that common realm between individuals.

The most salient feature of the meaning of words for these social constructivists is not the referential function of words. In fact, they argue that we have been profoundly mistaken in our psychology, sociology, anthropology, political science and the other social sciences because we have been captivated, indeed hypnotized, by the referential conception of language. Language primarily serves rhetorical, that is persuasive, argumentative, and performative, ends. Even the referential functions of language are often preformative. They are of the variety, 'If you attend to X, you will see things in this way and want to do Y' (Shotter 1993: 34). For example, if during a conversation I say, 'I have little feeling in my legs', I have created a situation that directs our attention and behaviour including at least the next few comments. To be intelligible and polite we must connect what we say next to that statement. With my next words, I am now obliged to show you how to take the comment, either as a fleeting observation not worthy of further attention, as a grave concern that requires empathy, attention and caring words and actions, or as some other familiar linguistic tool of social action. Once I commit us to one understanding, I have ruled out a great many other possibilities, at least temporarily. I have limited the replies you can make. You must attend to the aspect of our environment I have pointed to and respond, either in support, indifference or disbelief. Whether you want it to or not, how you respond expresses your moral character. You can then continue our attention on my experience or refocus it elsewhere, but if you do not do either in a socially acceptable fashion, you have made yourself nonsensical.

My third assumption concerns the nature of the self. I turn to Mead (1934), and more recently Crapanzano (1982), to adopt a highly linguistic and a highly dynamic view of selves. How, where and with whom I locate myself fluctuates continuously and may be only tangentially related to where my body is or what it does but is nonetheless never wholly unrelated to my body. At times I expand and enter into a commonality with others, such as when I use my body and the pronoun 'we' to create solidarity (Pillsbury 1996). At others I impose distance or withdraw, constricting myself into an 'I' (Pillsbury 1998). Together these three assumptions lead us to take language very seriously as the primary tool in the construction of our experience and remember that play is a perspective created through words.

Restrictive roles

Chronic disease narrows appreciably the range of social roles available to a person. The person lives considerably restricted even though many times, perhaps most times, he or she may have little awareness of these constraints. Let me spend a little time articulating the box I have found myself in before exploring how I might get out. I regularly find myself acting sick. By acting I do not mean pretending or any kind of theatrics or histrionics. Rather I watch myself engage in behaviours that fit a role. Often it is not clear even to me whether I am doing it intentionally or not. Do I limp more when I park in a handicapped spot or is the stiffness simply a result of sitting too long? Or perhaps it is a result of the subtle reminder of my condition evoked by the symbol on the parking sticker. Aspects of this role include accepting help for many physical tasks more readily than before I was diagnosed, engaging much more often in talk about the state and capabilities of my body, responding regularly to people's reactions to the state of my health. These responses vary widely and often include explanation, flippancy, accepting sympathy or sometimes expressions of anger. I avoid even moderate walks, warm environments and exposure to the sun. I rest often by sitting or lying on a couch and severely limit the plans I make for the future whether those plans are for future years or simply a list of the day's tasks.

But what I mean by the sick role goes much further than those rather obvious limitations. It involves a certain quality of passivity in my relations with others. I find myself restricting gestures while I speak so as not to wear myself out but also, when conversing, I measure the energy it would take to dispute a point or engage in thoughtful discussion. Because we can never anticipate all the ways in which our words can be taken, I can never be quite sure when my usual speech is going to reveal myself. Common phrases, such as 'I need to run an errand', now regularly take on an ironic quality in my mouth. The sick role involves concern and sensitivity that the exchanges that constitute friendship may have become unbalanced. I worry that others may be doing more for me than I am for them.

As Goffman (1959) showed us, in our presentations of self to others, we constantly construct and reconstruct ourselves. Much of my self-work involves dances[2] to stay between the two extremes of (1) self-indulgent hypochondriac and (2) disinterested in myself, disconnected from my body, unrealistic about my future. I frequently question how descriptions of my current state depict, and construct, me. As continuing the same discouraging tale? Can I express myself, that is portray myself, as depressed, or will that move lead to living out what is not yet fully real? Or do I depict myself as accepting, not dwelling on the losses and limitations, perhaps even unrealistically happy? As refusing to accept my future? As distressingly reversed when I do attend to symptoms? Recall the social constructionist assumption guiding this investigation. I do not see either description, or any other, as portraying a 'real me'. Rather, my language constructs me as I continuously shift among several linguistic alternatives.

While constructing myself I am constantly alert to the effects of each construction on my relationships with others. A negative depiction risks making interactions with me more difficult and less rewarding for others, which may encourage them to be more reserved, take fewer risks, and seek specific kinds of conversational or interactive rewards before continuing. More positive self-portrayals may put the other into a supportive but wary role. If the other sees me as needing to deflect attention away from the disease, he or she may steer the conversation away from the disease and yet at the same time remain watchful in case we move into unhealthy delusion. He or she may hesitate to direct attention to the negative aspects of the disease. Other descriptions of my experiential state similarly restrict the roles through which others can respond to me. In every case, people are likely to monitor their interactions with me a bit more closely than with 'healthy' others, for our culture sees interactions with diseased persons as particularly revealing one's moral qualities, particularly the depth of caring, the extent of generosity (of time and concern) and a host of related virtues. Friends, and those who offer interest and support, similarly find their roles stilted, unfamiliar, even uncomfortable. They are likely to monitor more self-consciously than usual the effects of words and actions on me. Recently the irony of a friend's comment drew across her face when she hoped aloud that she had not 'run me ragged'. People interacting with me may find themselves devoting unusual amounts of energy to monitoring my condition and attending to even small signs of change in my condition. Or, in the opposite direction, they may find themselves somewhat anxious and uncomfortable around me, chafing at the limitations that come from sticking with me for a while.

When I report improvements, determining an appropriate response is rarely easy. I can imagine a number of dilemmas such people may find themselves facing if they reflect before speaking. How can one show oneself to be caring and yet at the same time realistic and respectful? How does one express compassion without treating me as less than a fully responsible and capable adult? How does one show caring and support for chronic illness without insinuating an unrealistic expectation of recovery? How does one signal supportive empathy by expressing sadness, alarm or disappointment without initiating or heightening such feelings in me? While common to many relationships, as noted above, in relationships with diseased people such reflections regularly carry a heightened moral poignancy. There is always the moral expectation to care but considerable ambiguity about how best to exercise this obligation. As a result, these worries and reflections constrain the flexibility of established relationships and the creative generation of new ones.

Disrupting the linguistic basis of social reality

To live in the human world means to live with others, to coordinate[3] my actions with theirs, and vice versa (Shotter 1993). The most pervasive system for organizing such coordination is language. Notice that by language constructing and sustaining the world we live in, our world and our lives are socially, not personally, constructed. But for me, MS has thrown into doubt language's ability to sustain this world; it has limited the range and diminished the quality of the relationships available. Consider the various ways the experience may be expressed. Can I adequately share my experience with you through descriptions? Have I any practical alternatives? 'Adequate' and 'practical' in my two questions must be judged by the quality of the relationship the words create between us. I am following the lead of the social constructionists previously mentioned and Billig (1987) and Crapanzano (1982). What concerns me here is not sharing, conceived of as reporting an essentialistic slice of reality originating from an individual source; rather sharing as a form of joint action. It is a type of participation in our mutually constructed social life and one in which mutuality is explicitly highlighted. My shift from the verb 'report' to 'participate' is deliberate. Again, I want to highlight that contrary to common assumptions, the slices of illness experience that concern this investigation do not emanate from a private reality identified through feeling or introspection and reported in speech. Rather, we create them through our engagement with and in one another, through our joint participation in mutual activities which includes dialogue. 'Adequate' and 'practical' in the questions above ask us to consider whether a particular form and instance of sharing enables us to engage in meaningful joint activities, whether it enables us to go on together.

To exemplify the difficulties MS creates, consider the limited relations established when I try to describe the sensation in my feet. I might start by saying that my feeling there has changed considerably from what I remember it being 10 or 15 years ago and go on that I experience tingling, sometimes burning, sometimes a deadening, heavy sensation. I might point to a specific spot almost anywhere on my feet and lower legs and tell you that if you poke there with a pin, it feels sharper than if you poke my arm.[4] At another spot even close by, the poke would feel duller or I might not be able to feel it at all. To paint a more accurate picture, I would need further to explain the temporality of such sensations. The various sensations change constantly, though seemingly without pattern. Where I today feel acute sharpness from a poke, tomorrow I may register nothing at all.

I am tempted to say I lose the feeling in my legs, arms, hands and parts of my torso and often do say just that. But that description is shorthand; it does not hold up to thoughtful reflection for loss is an oversimplification. Most often I do still feel in these affected parts. In fact, in one sense I feel more constantly, urgently in that part of my body. The sensation is somewhat like when a limb falls asleep but different enough that I cannot comfortably use that image. These body parts 'buzz', clouded by diffuse sensations that insistently draw my attention back. Usual sensations, what I can take without attention, feel covered over, cloaked by another layer of sensations. The 'noise' or buzzing felt there occupies a great deal of my attention, but my body/my self – the interpreter that I call 'I' – cannot make sense of these foreign sensations. Perhaps it is lack of practice. Certainly, over time I have been able to put the new sensations in my feet and legs aside even as they continue, just as I had with usual 'normal' sensations there before I had MS. The buzzing is not the only change in these body parts. The coordination has changed. From inside, the skin feels stiff and swollen. Grasping items and bringing them in front of my face for inspection while not yet difficult has become much more of a thoughtful, intentional process. Nevertheless the central occupation of my attention is this noise.

Attempts at literal description do not, though, establish particularly satisfactory relationships; they do not invite you into my experience. Literal language sets up a reserved relationship, the kind of relationship typical to patient and doctor – a relationship, it is often pointed out, which focuses on managing the disease as a biological problem rather than understanding the phenomenal experience of the human being (Toombs 1990). What Buber (1965) calls 'I–it' relationships are those in which one person 'manages' another, treating him or her as a problem to be solved, which means treating the person as less than fully human. Literal, straightforward descriptions of disease experience regularly establish such I–it relationships and so seem artificially limited. The linguistic device we use most frequently to relate complex or idiosyncratic experience, and thus relate to the other as a full human being, Buber's 'I–thou' relation, is metaphor.

I suspect all MS patients search for metaphors whenever we seek a close relationship with another person, the kind of relationship that invites another to enter into our experience. These relationships require language that moves the other out of him- or herself. Such movement requires metaphor even when we are not aware of using such tropes. In fact, the more we ask 'literal' descriptions to do such work, the more they become metaphoric. Certainly many of the descriptors I used above – 'buzzing', 'tingling', 'burning', 'deadening', 'heavy', even 'sharpness' – are metaphoric. Only when understood as metaphors, can we begin adequately to understand each other.

Though better than those established by literal description, relationships created through metaphor have critical limitations and obfuscations that prevent solidarity, holistic understanding, immersion in a common MS experience, and complete sharing of each other. While it is undoubtedly the case that all metaphors, indeed all language, cannot establish the relations with others desired, and so we feel that our understanding is not adequate, in the case of chronic disease, language's failure is accentuated and thus more disturbing. To illustrate how metaphors tend to limit relations, consider two metaphors I use in the hope of capturing and sharing some of my physical sensations.

Two illustrative metaphors

The metaphor that perhaps most satisfactorily captures one of my symptoms is that of feeling sunburned. The sensation occurs regularly now towards the end of the day. Even though I have not been outside, my feet and lower legs feel sunburned. The skin stings and stiffens, the sensations of the skin's pliability and resilience diminish. The metaphor feels appropriate in that my legs feel much the same as I remember feeling when sunburned. Admittedly the last time my legs were actually sunburned was some time ago, perhaps 10–15 years. If I were to have the two experiences closer together, I might well notice differences more clearly, but for now my sense is that they are rather similar.

The metaphor fits, though, only for the aspects of the sensation I habitually concentrate on. I can, with a little effort, call up to awareness other aspects of that experience that do not fit the metaphor and make it feel less apt. The skin is not red, nor does it feel hot, nor does it radiate heat. Touch and pressure do not increase the discomfort as they do with a real sunburn. Nor do I associate with it memories of activities such as playing at the beach or working in the garden. Sunburn does not usually go away by morning, but these sensations largely do. The burning sensation is often accompanied by great fatigue, more pronounced in the legs than the rest of my body. The fit of the metaphor gets further complicated if I focus on the difficulty I have in relaxing the muscles in the legs, the seeming opposite of what one experiences after an exhausting day at the beach. Even when I have let go of my legs attempting to rest them on the couch like sacks of flour, I find muscles in them – found through visual inspection and physical manipulation, not by intuitive perception – that continue to tense and exhaust themselves. To the extent that the sunburn metaphor directs me to overlook these aspects of my physical state, it fails to capture my whole experience. To the extent that it makes it more difficult for my conversant to grasp any of these characteristics, the metaphor fails to share the experience.

Another everyday experience seems even less satisfactorily conveyed by the best metaphor I have found so far. An exacerbation seven years ago left me without much feeling in my legs for a period of several weeks. What my partial recovery returned is a feeling which I can best describe as that of continually wearing heavy wet socks. While the best I have found, the metaphor feels even more incomplete than the sunburned metaphor. It misses the buzzing feeling reverberating in the legs and overlooks the replacement of a unified sense of agility, strength and readiness with (disjointed?) sensations of stiffness, fatigue and weakness. And of course, each of the descriptors I just used 'buzzing', 'stiffness', 'fatigue' and 'weakness' are likewise metaphoric and so incomplete and inaccurate, even potentially misleading, expressions for the experience.

What comparison of the two experiences highlights is that metaphor and language generally are ways of directing attention: what to emphasize, what to overlook or ignore, what to remember and how to remember it. While every metaphor has aspects that do not fit, good metaphors direct attention away from these aspects to those that do. My metaphors may be most effective at directing my own attention and I use them in an attempt to do the same to my conversant. Good metaphors help one overlook what does not fit the description.

The desire to 'get it right', that is, to find a metaphor that embraces every aspect of the experience, reveals the limitations of metaphor for establishing relationships. As indicated earlier, my goal in sharing experience, though often not acknowledged, is ultimately not a matter of giving information. Rather it is a matter of establishing and continuing relationships that enrich and educate both parties. Worries about 'getting it right' mislead us, deflecting attention away from relationships and towards the empty pursuit of essential experiential realities. I seek rewarding, enriching, malleable relationships which means necessarily, fully embodied, relationships. These are relationships which enable us to carry on with our lives and our interests; they do not restrict us or encourage us to stop or hesitate.

Artistic play

Such meditations on the limits of language have allowed a new perspective towards my interactions with the disease to emerge for me now, one that does not attempt to disregard or make light of it, but one resolved not to accept settled, 'appropriate', singular approaches to the experience. To explain this transformation, I appeal to Kenneth Gergen's concept of serious play and James Carse's of infinite games. We often think of play as meaning very little or having no real consequence. We contrast it to the serious and important. Thus, playing with disease seems, at least at first, disrespectful of myself and openly disrespectful of others' experiences, particularly those with more severe cases. But Gergen (1991) reminds us that play need not be taken lightly, as mere amusement. It can be the site of earnest endeavours, intense concentration, a tremendously influential context for the expression and development of self. Examples of serious play that first come to mind are athletic contests and then dramas in all genres. In fact, some of our most serious endeavours – including politics, marriage, religion and intellectual life – are regularly conceived as games often without intending any disparagement. Gergen pushes us to consider a broad conception of play, one that is both serious and nonserious at the same time. Such a conception challenges rigid or narrow constructions of disease experience, opening the patient to the possibilities of renegotiating the forms and meanings of this experience. When such opportunities are held in mind, play expresses a higher regard for the person than the disease. Play represents a higher form of respect than seriousness.

The notion of serious play turns us to Carse (1989), who distinguishes two kinds of games – finite and infinite. Finite games have clear, mutually accepted rules and outcomes. Examples include, of course, children's board games, athletic contests, lotteries, graduation rankings and political contests. Infinite games, in contrast, invite players to renegotiate boundaries, meanings and purposes. The purpose in infinite games is not to win but to continue and extend the game.

Examples of these games include a variety of cultural forms, including art. Art genres play with the forms of expression, continually renegotiating how art itself is constructed and what counts as art. Genres tend to work out modes of expression until imagination begins to run dry. Subsequent genres react against previous ones extending the play of art. Art often tries to rub up against the limits of what we can say. It often seeks to say what cannot be said in words. It seeks to create understanding we cannot otherwise reach through didactic means. And perhaps most pertinent to the kind of play I seek, art often seeks to disturb, awaken and thereby enrich everyday experience (Dewey 1934; Jackson 1998). Rush (1996) argues that art is a fundamental means of solving problems of understanding and expression. Through art, we pay special attention to the relationships between parts and wholes, reconfiguring, highlighting, disturbing experience as necessary to expand and enrich the understandings which structure our social lives.

What I am suggesting is that it is possible to see multiple sclerosis as presenting us with an infinite game of artistic experience. When my symptoms intensify, whether as a part of a new exacerbation or the continuation of prior appearances, I first feel a sense of panic. But once controlled, though, a much more positive sensation emerges. I begin to watch myself, fascinated with the change, for the difference from expectation is entrancing. When changing, my life-world has an unusual characteristic: I live at a greater distance from my own experience than usual. I watch as I try to touch the tip of the index finger on one hand to that of the other (one of my neurologist's tests). I watch my right leg bounce up and down uncontrollably when positioned at a certain angle. When I reach out for a glass of water, I gaze at my arm, as if not fully my own, suspicious that this may be the time I cannot pick it up, cannot close my fingers around it, will drop the glass, or may not even feel a solid object.

The disease plays on and in my body and I can choose to play with it. The game the disease invites me to play concerns how we create reality. Reality at a fundamental level can change; what it becomes is largely up to us. Consider one experience. One morning shortly after the feeling in my hands changed, when I tried to shave, I cupped my hands under the warm water to splash on my face. But once I did, the water scalded. Was the water hot or was my face highly sensitive, such as my feet often are? Our world is made up of temperatures and the body's understanding of them. What if temperatures were unstable or the body's responses to heat and cold unreliable? The game is to construct and live within a world where temperature was always unknown but dangerous. Could this be a real, and not simply imaginary construction? But for our bodies, this is the world we live in now. The meaning of temperatures 'objectively' measured by thermometers still depends upon the body's reaction. That is the meaning of wind chill and the heat index. Temperature remains constant only when, and only because, our bodies react in predictable and consistent ways. MS makes us wonder what if... What would the world be like if our bodies changed? The MS game goes on. It changes a great variety of the forms and boundaries of experience, one time centring on what my legs feel, the next changing the hearing in my left ear, and recently playing inside my right hand. Each move offers a new game for the taking.

I can alternatively experience the disease as sculpting, or painting or playing music on my body. It sculpts the fingers into stiff appendages – how might I think of them? Cocktail sausages, or small beef sticks might work. I do not, of course, eat my fingers, though I do sometimes somewhat absentmindedly nibble on them and have also allowed my infant daughters to do the same. In a sense, then, I do know my fingers as food. This reflection leads me to contemplate the difference between experiencing from within versus from without. One might then pursue the relative weight of both kinds of knowledge. When do we devalue inner knowledge? Phenomenologists have contended that our culture regularly holds outer knowledge in higher esteem. We tend to find, they assert, outer knowledge more scientific and thus, more trustworthy. Certainly this is the medical perspective. But I am not interested in 'getting well' in this case. Rather, I want to play; I want to enjoy the experience. Can I not see my fingers legitimately as small beef sausages and enjoy the experience? Where can I go next if I start here?

Or I can start over. How else can I think of my symptoms, a more appetizing or less culinary image perhaps? The disease paints the skin on my shins and feet with an antiseptic wash, but the painting simultaneously 'morphs' into a cacophony of noise. I try to develop the right perspective for hearing (with the torso, not the ear) this musical tone. How does painting change into music? Perhaps that is a misleading question. Are these really two different 'things'? Perhaps it is this 'I', myself, that creates the distinction. The bodily element that underlies all forms of our understanding seems particularly pronounced in artistic expressions. Perhaps with practice, our bodies can understand all painting as a form of music or all music as a form of painting and seeing the connections is a matter of becoming more finely tuned to the understandings of our bodies. What I am attempting here, of course, is not to articulate settled conclusions about the nature of music or painting or the disease but to outline suggestive positions from which we might proceed.

The games I am proposing are certainly quite academic kinds of games and thus not for everyone. I have presented above merely initial fumblings towards creating games, perhaps somewhat akin to the cavemen's initial stirrings towards art on cave walls. I expect these games will be thoroughly transformed and usefully elaborated or scrapped and replaced as others play with me. Whatever games we come up with will require playing with words. Such play will undoubtedly feel as though we are putting experience into words but it will be just as much creating experience and expressing it. We will phrase and rephrase sensations, uncover the new realities each phrasing creates, live through the relationships established by these realities, and test the boundaries created.

To play these games, we must be willing to examine the ways we have constructed our experience and our bodies' roles in these constructions, and bracket these constructions, setting them aside, out of their usual role in our experience. We must be willing to put every understanding of our world in play, ready to be examined as social constructions and transformed. We must ask how our constructions might be different and how we might live together within these new worlds. In many ways such games are localized versions of the academic games that social constructionists are currently engaged in (Gergen 1994).

I am not trying to win the game, only continue it. My moves in this chapter, and in my life, are not conclusive or settled, only next moves from where I am now, moves from which I might proceed. The perspective I am advocating refuses to stick with what is, but continually launches into what might be, what could be and what I can only imagine. MS offers the chance for me to play with how we create reality, the critical role our body plays in the creation of our everyday experience, and how it could be otherwise. Indeed, 'offering' is too gentle a verb, for the disease throws me into the game without warning and without choice.

Now I am a sclerotic. I have lived a significant portion of my life to date with MS, my ever-present partner. Indeed, at this point over a quarter of my life. I have made decisions, concessions and accommodations occasionally with the disease pressing on my mind, more often with it gently lingering at the side, but with it always present. The disease has been a constant force on this self I have come to construct. The self I know is sclerotic. I know no other. I would not be who I am now without the disease. If tomorrow the disease is cured, who would I be? I am not sure I would know what to do. I am not sure I could recognize myself and without that fundamental assurance, how could I project myself forward into the future? Such reflections about identity are reinforced by what medical knowledge tells us about the disease. Current medical knowledge about MS is in doubt that an invading virus causes the disease. Indeed, what we know is that the immune system behaves erratically, mistakenly killing healthy myelin cells. The symptoms I experience come from my body attacking itself. The disease is no other. My body is both the healthy patient and the illness. I am both disease and self. There is no division between the two. In fact, there are not even two entities here, only one: me. All that may sound flippant but I mean to play it seriously. This perspective may become more difficult or even impossible to maintain as my disease progresses. Will I continue to play with the disease if I become blind, when I am in a wheelchair, or if I cannot use my arms? I do not know, but I hope so.

The social dimension of this play

But I have given this discussion too individual of a flavour. A second key feature of artistic experience is that it is always social. It does not count as art until the receiver sees it as art (Goodman 1978). In order to construct his or her work, the artist must adopt a social reference point. An artist's concern while constructing a work must be how the observer will see, hear or otherwise experience the piece. According to Dewey (1934), a central function of art is to reconfigure the way we experience not only ourselves, but also others and our world. The very notion of play invites sociality. I do not want to engage in this game alone. Games are often social and this one should be no exception. We can play this game together not merely by your listening to me, nor even by your suggesting images, perspectives and metaphors that I try on, retaining the final say about their accuracy. I need you to be an active player. We shall use the disease to create a mutual space where we both try out and expand understandings. Each of us must retain judgement over the appropriateness of conceptions in capturing not our individual but our mutual experience and productivity for proceeding.

The kind of play I am seeking will certainly require us to find and push up against the boundaries of our worlds but what is essential is that the game provide points from which we can continue to make moves together rather than seek a final, and almost surely individual, determination of a fixed reality. Because we have used our bodies to make the worlds we live within, I inhabit phenomenal worlds that differ significantly from the ones we used to share. A prime task now is to entice others to join me in the construction of a new joint world, a playful world where we keep boundaries and limits fluid and we remain quite conscious of our constructive abilities. Together we can create common realms for joint exploration and re-creation using elements of our divergent worlds. To create these realms, we must through coordinated actions feel, assume and enter into common images and mutual perspectives. We produce ideas as in a fencing match: parry, counter-parry, anticipation, expectation, denial, surprise. Each move adapts, enriches, extends or challenges the previous one, thereby improving our own fit to one another and within this created world. If we accept the invitation chronic disease presents we not only change the way we experience the everyday world, we transform ourselves and broaden the range of relationships with others open to us.

Let me say a word about the relationship with my wife, a topic certainly not common fare in academic studies but certainly of relevance here. Together we are learning to play. Perhaps the development of play around disease goes through a series of stages. If an initial stage consists of joking, we have very comfortably reached this stage. With her, I can frequently call myself a 'spaz' when I trip or say 'Yeah, in your dreams' when a pathway leads to a steep flight of stairs. We laughed together after a telephone solicitor informed us that we had won a prize especially selected for us: dance lessons. When she pushes me in my wheelchair and someone asks her 'Can he walk?', she sometimes replies 'No, but he can talk.' We seek, however, to go further. As I have tried to indicate, play can embrace the serious as well as the light-hearted. The imperative to care, which I know constantly informs my wife's perspective may, as I have indicated earlier, complicate our ability to go further together into this play perspective. Perhaps our selves have become so intertwined – I in her and she in me – that the meaning of certain possibilities cannot be fully explored. They simply feel too dangerous. In certain respects the play perspective may be easier to attain with someone who offers more distance to myself. Yet, I may be wrong, for the possibilities and rewards that have come through our marriage continue to surprise me.

I was mistaken in first taking the challenge MS offers as one of finding the 'right' metaphor to depict the experience. That is a hopeless task that pushes one further and further into isolation. The challenge is not to identify a single true reality. Rather, the challenge is to find artistic modes of expression that create new realities which in turn extend and enrich relationships. Changes in bodily experiences would present game-like challenges to each understanding and require new moves on our part. The game offers new selves for me to be, new selves for you to become and new ways for us to relate to one another.

The diseased self

The perspective of artistic play towards chronic disease transforms the self who is diseased. Indeed the influence is akin to the influence Dewey saw of art on the self. Dewey wrote, 'For the uniquely distinguishing feature of esthetic experience is exactly the fact that no such distinction of self and object exists in it, since it is esthetic in the degree in which organism and environment cooperate to institute an experience in which the two are so fully integrated that each disappears' (1934: 249). When I was first diagnosed, the disease was other than me. It was an invader who had come into my life uninvited and unwelcome. I remember clearly the first time a doctor referred to it as my disease. I resisted vigorously. It was not my disease. It was another that I wanted to have nothing do with. To some extent, it was his disease I was experiencing. Certainly he knew it better than I did.

Earlier I described what I experience in the first stages of an exacerbation: panic followed by fascination. In that discussion, I said I live at a greater distance to my own experience than usual. While I do not experience the undergoings that lead to such fascination as happening to or caused by someone else, yet they are not happening to me quite as personally or as vigorously as they used to. Such distance gives birth to not just a different self, but an entirely different kind of self: a playful one. One able to forget itself in a way not possible when playing a finite game. The self that can forget itself experiences freedom to create and experiment, for the consequences are never settled, never permanent, never disclosing of a solemn essence. Reality at a most basic level is being created and reformed 'in front of my eyes', so to speak, and I am a fundamental participant in this creation. The fun, however, is stunted unless I can find people with whom to share it and a means of doing so. Imposing this distance, however, does not make the disease an other that I remove from myself. There is no 'other' here, only myself. I am both self and disease, though I can nevertheless stand apart from myself. The critical move involves 'intersticing' a distance between my own experience and myself. This move opens the possibility of renewed, flexible and enriching relationships with the disease and others I have been seeking.

Moral considerations and the respect for life

Emphasizing this game as a social rather than individual affair, however, presents special difficulties, particularly for the others that I hope will join me. Generally, others may feel that by virtue of a special moral sanction, I and other chronically ill individuals can do what they cannot. For us to adopt this perspective is less repugnant than for them to do so. By accepting this perspective, they would, they often feel, be participating in practices that do not take our lives seriously. They may be encouraging us in practices that may lead to earlier and more complete disability than if we had resisted. Can they accept themselves if they do? Even if we give them permission to play with us and invite them to do so, the moral restraints will continue to weigh heavily upon them.

But such a view confuses quality of life with extension. Some of the moral qualms generated by this perspective come from the apparent trade-off of length of life for quality of life. Will I live as long by not fighting the disease as I would if I did fight it? Included in what we mean by fighting a disease is to follow medical practitioners' directions and take medicine regularly. I do take these actions and precautions so that possibility cannot form the basis of this question. Have I given in or given up? The question inquires into the effects of psychological disengagement. I learned through a long athletic career that, even when performing all the desired actions, diminishing the desire to win, refusing actively to resist, opening the possibility for defeat, or turning attention to other phenomena besides the competition itself can be enough to throw the contest to the other side. As coaches would say, such actions take the edge off a competitor. Will turning my attention away from actively resisting the disease shorten my life? I do not know. Perhaps.

Such a possibility, however, does not compel my attention. Other qualities of life besides duration concern me, and this choice provides the sticky moral ground of the perspective I have been developing for myself, and the reason why I cannot advocate it as a path for anyone else. We often praise individuals for their heroic struggles against disease. We have come to see struggling for extended length of life as a moral virtue but does this mean that we see a refusal to struggle as less than virtuous, or worse? As giving up? The alternative perspective sees quality of life, defined in terms of enriching relationships of value, growth of understanding and extension of self into others as preferable to simply extending life in any form. This perspective does not come from a refusal to take the measures necessary to keep my life going; rather it evolves from not giving those measures highest priority, resisting the mandate to see my life as one of struggle, choosing to spend the attentional energies required for active resistance elsewhere, and recoiling from taking life as a solemn and holy affair.

Concluding remarks

I began this investigation with three questions: 'Is it possible to experience a chronic disease as one that offers advantages as well as limitations, what would such a transformation in our thinking take, and what can such experience tell us about our relationships with each other?' Let me summarize what we found to answer each of these questions in the order above.

The answer to the first question is a qualified yes. With a change in perspective, it is possible to see the disease as offering advantages that might enrich our understanding of experience and ourselves. Perhaps these 'advantages' are better identified as a series of challenges. So far, at least at times, I am able to take my disease as inviting me to play with how we recognize and understand reality. Without the disease, it is unlikely I would be as ready to play or be as insightful in contesting the boundaries of our reality.

The answer to the second question qualifies the answer to the first question for among the conditions for realizing the advantages of the disease are the social conditions of such recognition. I cannot play for long alone. By myself, the play is stilted and does not get very far. Realizing the possibilities offered by disease requires, as I mentioned, a change in vision. But such a change can only be effected through social, not individual, efforts and these efforts require mutual rethinking and reinscribing[5] our moral understandings. The moral understandings that prohibit playing are extremely difficult to get beyond. They can paralyse us. Somehow others and I must find ways around the limits of our engagement to make such play a truly joint activity that is both insightful and generative for both of us.

And in the answer above lies a beginning answer to our third question, what we can learn about our relationships with one another. We are reminded once again that fundamentally, we are social animals. We live through social processes and experiences, never through individual or isolated efforts even when we think we are doing so. The play outlook establishes relationships unlike, of course, serious realistic ones, but also unlike steadfastly caring ones. And yet, at the same time, a true play perspective embraces both of those and numerous others. My response to this question can only be an initial foray. Until we find ways of playing together we will not be able to extend the lessons chronic disease offers us concerning our social natures.

Until we can develop joint forms of the kind of play outlined here, my success at holding on to the playful perspective I have outlined here will never be more than partial. During those times when the disease is progressing, the reactions of alarm, depression and worry may continue to prevail. At such times, I become concerned with myself, withdrawing from others. I expect caring from others to come in the form of empathy and concern. I am not able to play. I certainly am not admonishing others for having these reactions as well.

I am learning to expect those reactions and wait with a certain element of patience for the opportunity to play again. Once again caring can be expressed in the form of play. Others have written about living with MS for 20 years or more. As of 1998, I have lived with it for at least twelve years. How will I see the disease in years to come? I do not know. Will the disease take away my sight, my ability to walk, my ability to talk? Perhaps. Could I continue to play with the disease then? I hope so. Will I be able to bring others into this play? I am certainly committed to trying.

Like Maxine Greene, whose epigraph opened this article, I do not want to grow accustomed to a dry, little life and indeed even with a chronic disease, the difference is up to me. No, it is up to us.

Acknowledgements

I would like to extend my sincere appreciation to the British Sociological Association for allowing me to present a first draft of this chapter, Cheri Beuhl for helping to type this manuscript, Darlene Beuhl for her essential assistance, and my wife, Clar Pillsbury, for carefully reading and commenting on it. Their efforts have helped me more than they know.

Notes

1. Or is it seventeen years? Five years before I was diagnosed, I lost virtually all the feeling in my right index finger. That symptom, my only symptom, was tentatively diagnosed as a pinched nerve. One of the hallmarks of MS is never being sure when one first 'acquires' the disease.

2. A sign of the constriction of language I am attempting to expand, instead of 'dances', I first wrote 'struggles' here.
3. Shotter's phrase uses a very wide conception of actions that encompasses mentalistic states, such as intents, values, hopes and fears as well as physical behaviours.
4. The image was not picked capriciously. In their examinations, neurologists have often poked me in various locations with a safety pin.
5. Bourdieu's (1980: 53) term which points to the bodily nature of moral understandings.

References

Berger, H. 1987. Bodies and Texts. *Representations*, 17: 144–66.

Berger, P. and Luckmann, T. 1966. *The Social Construction of Reality*. New York: Doubleday/Anchor.

Billig, M. 1989. *Arguing and Thinking: A Rhetorical Approach to Social Psychology*. Cambridge: Cambridge University Press.

Bourdieu, P. 1980. *The Logic of Practice*, trans. Richard Nice. Stanford: Stanford University Press.

Buber, M. 1965. *Between Man and Man*. New York: Macmillan.

Camic, C. 1986. 'The Matter of Habit', *American Journal of Sociology*, 91: 1039–87.

Carse, J.P. 1987. *Finite and Infinite Games*. Harmondsworth: Penguin.

Crapanzano, V. 1982. 'The Self, the Third, and Desire', in B. Lee (ed.) *Psychosocial Theories of the Self*. New York: Plenum Press.

Csordas, T.J. (ed.) 1994. *Embodiment and Experience: The Existential Ground of Culture and Self*. Cambridge: Cambridge University Press.

Dewey, J. 1934. *Art as Experience*. New York: Minton, Balch & Company.

Garfinkel, H. 1967. *Studies in Ethnomethodology*. New York: Prentice-Hall.

Gergen, K. 1991. *The Saturated Self: Dilemmas of Identity in Contemporary Life*. New York: Basic Books.

Gergen, K. 1994. *Realities and Relationships: Soundings in Social Construction*. Cambridge, MA: Harvard University Press.

Goffman, E. 1959. *The Presentation of Self in Everyday Life*. New York: Anchor Books.

Goodman, N. 1978. *Ways of Worldmaking*. Indianapolis: Hackett.

Hoffman, C. and Rice, D. 1996. 'Persons with Chronic Conditions: Their Prevalence and Costs', *The Journal of the American Medical Association*, 276(18): 1473–9.

Jackson, P.W. 1998. *John Dewey and the Lessons of Art*. New Haven, CT: Yale University Press.

Johnson, M. 1987. *The Body in the Mind*. Chicago: University of Chicago.

Kirmayer, L. 1992. 'The Body's Insistence on Meaning: Metaphor as Presentation and Representation in Illness Experience', *Medical Anthropology Quarterly*, 6: 323–46.

Lakoff, G. and Johnson, M. 1980. *Metaphors We Live By*. Chicago: University of Chicago.

Mauss, M. 1950. Les Techniques du Corps. *Sociologie et Anthropologie*. Paris: Presses Universitaires de France.

Mead, G.H. 1934. *Mind, Self and Society from the Standpoint of a Social Behaviorist*, ed. C. Morris. Chicago: University of Chicago Press.

Merleau-Ponty, M. 1962. *Phenomenology of Perception*, trans. Collin Smith. New York: Humanities Press.

Pillsbury, G. 1996. 'Creating the Plural Self: Athletic Teams' Use of Members' Bodies', *International Journal of Qualitative Studies in Education*, 9: 35–48.

Pillsbury, G. 1998. 'First-Person Singular and Plural: Strategies for Managing Ego- and Sociocentrism in Four Basketball Teams', *Contemporary Ethnography*, 26: 450–78.

Polanyi, M. 1958. *Personal Knowledge: Towards a Post-Critical Philosophy*. Chicago: University of Chicago.

Rush, J.C. 1996. 'Conceptual Consistency and Problem Solving: Tools to Evaluate Learning in Studio Art', in *Evaluating and Assessing the Visual Arts in Education*. New York: Teachers College Press.

Sacks, O. 1990. *The Man Who Took His Wife For a Hat and Other Clinical Tales*. New York: Simon & Schuster.

Schutz, A. and Luckmann, T. 1973. *The Structures of the Life-World*, trans. Richard Zaner and H. Tristram Engelhardt, Jr. Evanston: Northwestern University Press.

Shotter, J. 1993. *Conversational Realities: Constructing Life through Language*. London: Sage.

Toombs, S.K. 1990. The Temporality of Illness: four levels of experience. *Theoretical Medicine*, 11: 227–41.

Part II

Neglected Bodies and Everyday Life

5

Disability Studies and Phenomenology: Finding a Space for both the Carnal and the Political

Kevin Paterson

Introduction

Disabled people are engaged in a collective struggle to transform a socio-spatial environment which denies them full citizenship (Campbell and Oliver 1996). The disability movement has successfully highlighted the ways in which dominant ablist norms and practices work, on the one hand, to exclude people with impairments from public space, while, on the other, intern them in 'special' enclaves. This politicization of the spatial environment is rooted in the writings of UPIAS (1976), Finkelstein (1980) and Oliver (1983). Their work has inaugurated a 'theory' (the social model of disability), which posits a clear separation between the impaired body and the socially imposed disability, and it is this Cartesian heritage which informs disability studies.

This chapter questions the value of disability studies' reliance on traditional Cartesian modes of thinking about impairment and disability, body and culture. It considers a possible response to the assertion that it is both mistaken and politically naive to speak of 'incorporating' impairment into the social model of disability. New social movements have realized that to be a force in what Bryan Turner (1992) has termed 'somatic society', they must reject the modernist separation of the body from politics. The body, or embodied subject, has become the primary site for social, political and cultural debate and activity within late capitalism (Turner 1994). While it undoubtedly made good political and theoretical sense for the advocates of the social model to make an explicit distinction between impairment and disability, the 'Cartesianized' subject it produces closes off any likelihood of an emancipatory politics of identity. Thus, it is time for disability studies to shed its traditional reluctance to posit the impaired body as anything other than a passive pre-cultural object. This chapter explores the theoretical contribution that phenomenology might make to remedy this, namely, the necessary development of a sociology of impairment.

In this chapter, it is my intention to demonstrate that a phenomenological approach to impairment is not an apolitical discourse. Phenomenology provides the conceptual tools to trace the ways in which oppression and discrimination become embodied and 'lived' through everyday reality (Hughes and Paterson 1997). I will also argue that disability studies' structuralist account of disability is limited by the politics it allows. Its weakness is its failure to interrogate the *Lebenswelt* (everyday world). Within the *Lebenswelt*, oppression is not simply produced by the spatial environment, it is a question of intercorporeal norms and conventions, it is about the extent to which 'social competence' is negotiated in everyday life and how this negotiation hinges on carnal factors. The social model does not provide a basis for a 'carnal politics of everyday life' (Paterson and Hughes 1999).

Formal and informal policing of bodily comportment

The denial of 'social competence' from disabled people is manifest in the view that they are dependent on others to arrange their life. Disability studies offers a structuralist argument that dependence is not an intrinsic feature of impairment but that welfare policies have propagated such an assumption. I want also to argue that such paternalistic policies and procedures reflect a colonialization of disabled people's lifeworlds (Habermas 1975; Imrie 1996) which is carnally formed and informed by non-impaired bodies. Conceptions of competence/independence are therefore predisposed to the exclusion of disabled people. Exclusion is not simply a 'product' of structural disadvantage and oppression: it is bound into the everyday network of intercorporeal association, into what Young (1990) refers to as the 'meshes of microauthority'.

The parameters of micro-authority need to be understood in the context of the rise of the philosophy of integration and the view that 'the community', rather than segregation, is the best 'cure' for disabled people. Integration effectively sought to establish ablist rules and conduct through the extension of bureaucratic control (Imrie 1996). The policy of 'community care' extends surveillance and regulation into the *Lebenswelt* and epitomizes the omnipresence of micro-authority (Donzelot 1979). Integrationism is policing, either formally (a visit from the benefits officer) or informally (an everyday encounter) and it is often policing by xenophobia (Imrie 1996). Contrary to received wisdom, the reversal of segregation can mean the exacerbation of xenophobia and prejudice. Intercorporeal encounters become 'demands' for disabled people to normalize themselves, to express themselves carnally in a manner conditioned by ablist norms of bodily comportment. The price of integration is 'normalization'. Disabled people are expected to reject their own bodies, adjust to carnal norms: they are expected to, as Young (1990) put it, 'scale their bodies'.

Disability studies and sociology of the body: a mutual disengagement

Sociology of the body and disability

Works that utilize phenomenology as a theoretical tool can be found in the emerging sociology of the body. However, sociologists of the body have not only neglected the experience of being disabled, but have also overlooked the conceptual developments arising out of disability studies or sought to locate such work at the margins of sociological theory (see Shilling 1993; Turner 1984, 1996). This is, of course, nothing new. The discipline of sociology has consistently failed to view disability as a subject deserving any serious examination. Even medical sociology appears unwilling to challenge dominant understandings of disability (Barnes and Mercer 1996; Shakespeare and Watson 1997).

Sociologists of the body have failed to satisfy the expectation that they would provide a more adequate account of disability than that offered by medical sociology (Shakespeare and Watson 1995a and b; Abberley 1997). For example, Turner (1992) argues that a phenomenology of the body or embodiment has particular importance as it provides sociologists with a sensitive and sophisticated perspective on issues such as pain, disability and death. It could be easily assumed from this argument that the 'disabled body' (or rather, the impaired body) would feature large in any theoretical and conceptual innovations (Oliver 1996b). Unfortunately, Turner's analysis holds faithfully to a medicalized and individualized understanding of disability. It is understandable why disability studies has not engaged with the sociology of the body. Nevertheless, it is possible to manoeuvre a path which checks the disablism of the sociology of the body on the one hand, while utilising phenomenology to overcome the social model's disembodied view of disability on the other. Furthermore, an embodied view of disability also offers a basis for a sociology of impairment (Paterson and Hughes 1999).

Disability studies and the impaired body

Historically, radical perspectives which present disability as a form of social oppression have included impairment in their discussions. Finkelstein's (1980) central point is that disability is the relationship between impairment and social context/structure, and Abberley (1987) argues that a social theory of disability must stress the social origin of impairment. This standpoint, however, is premised on the typical Enlightenment view of the social and the biological as binary opposites. The problem with this Cartesian move is that it compels the social model to adopt a disembodied view of disability and an asocial view of impairment. Abberley's position on impairment is echoed by Oliver (1990). He acknowledges the social property of impairment through a structural analysis and then shelves it as non-problematic. When faced with the charge that disability studies presents a disembodied view of disability, Oliver has been keen to voice Abberley's assertion that a social theory of disability must take impairment into account. However, while Oliver (1996a) concedes there may be a need for a 'social model of impairment', he is clearly sceptical about – and would prefer to distance himself from – such a task.

Finkelstein has recently expressed severe irritation at the moves to re-conceptualize the role of impairment within disability studies (see Finkelstein 1996). He sees marked differences between the contemporary politics of disability and the pioneering stance of the 1980s. Originally, in an effort to claim ownership of how disability was understood, disabled people concentrated on challenging the disabling 'world outside', rather than exploring the attitudes and emotions that came from those experiencing discrimination. The focus of attention was 'outside in' rather than 'inside out'. Since then, according to Finkelstein, disabled academics have 'hijacked' the movement's agenda to serve their own priorities, replacing the active vision with a passive abstraction. He believes that the elevation of the importance of personal experience is a discredited and sterile approach to understanding and changing the world, and that there is now a definite division in the disability movement between two social models of disability – an active one (outside in) and a passive one (inside out).

Where Finkelstein sees a creeping revision of the radical definition of disability one might just as easily see realignment. This reliance on Cartesian modes of thinking about impairment and disability ignores the fact that in somatic society the body is not a passive component in politics: it actively contributes to the shaping of the social world. In this context dualistic outside/in or inside/out models of emancipation are negated. Contemporary 'pride movements' – Black; gay; disability – are all forms of a politics of proprioception; a contemporary politics of bodies, in which aesthetic, as well as political and economic tyrannies, are deconstructed by excluded groups (Hughes and Paterson 1997). They 'target' simultaneously the inside and the outside. Their project is transformation of self and society, a declaration of self-respect which is, at one and the same time, a challenge to prejudice and oppression: a challenge to the cultural and socially sedimented practices and discourses that propagate the 'gold standard' norms that produce otherness and exclusion. The politics of 'outside in', the standard politics of the disability movement, have tended to stay 'outside' and never get 'in'. A sociology of impairment becomes necessary for disability studies to break from traditional dualistic modes of thinking, and in so doing, be a force in body politics (Paterson and Hughes 1999).

The impaired body in disability studies

Disabled people have always discussed and written about their bodies within the major sphere of disability studies (see Campling 1981; Oliver et al. 1988; Morris 1989; Hales 1996). However, the term 'body' has tended to be used without much sense of bodiliness, as if the body were little more than flesh and bones. This tendency risks the body being treated as an object, lacking intentionality and intersubjectivity (Paterson and Hughes 1999).

Interactionist perspectives predominate within much of the work which features disabled people talking about their bodies. Such approaches have been criticized for offering mere descriptions of the discrimination faced by disabled people rather than examining the conditions which produce their experience of oppression (Finkelstein 1980; Abberley 1987, 1993). However, just as interactionist perspectives can be criticized for their micro-analysis of disability at the expense of any macro-analysis, the converse can be said of disability studies. It suggests that research should be concerned with spotlighting the ways in which society disables people with impairments rather than the effects on individuals (Oliver 1992; Zarb 1992). Here, the everyday reality of lived experience is neglected in favour of a purely structural analysis of disability (Shakespeare, in Shakespeare and Watson 1995b). Indeed, the critique of interactionism from the perspective of the social model of disability (Oliver 1990) is restricted by its structuralist slant. Whilst a structuralist critique of 'stigma' is valid, it is possible to provide an embodied critique of the category. Stigma reproduces disability and impairment as otherness (Wendell 1996). The concept of stigma is discursively mired in disablism, not simply because (as the social model would have it) it is pre-structuralist, but also because it is overdetermined by its existential origins. In summary, one can argue that the concept of stigma is carnally ill-informed.

The body is both active and acted upon

This neglect of embodied experience mirrors the development of second-wave feminism, where difference among women was initially denied in the formation of a structural and generic analysis of sexism. Feminism steered away from admitting difference because it runs the risk of strengthening reactionary arguments. This illustrates that political needs can inhibit a sociological understanding of the body. This has been the case within disability studies (Shakespeare 1994; Shakespeare and Watson 1995a and b).

Disability studies' understanding of disability does not deny that the impaired body is a subject of (and subject to) social power, Abberley (1987: 14) asserts that 'For disabled people the body is the site of oppression, both in form, and in what is done with it.' However, the experience of being disabled is not just inscribed on the body as disability studies implies. A person's everyday relation to the (disabling) social world comes from their lived experience of embodiment. New social movements are moving away from theoretical perspectives which regard the body as a recipient of social forces in which it has no formative role (Lyon and Barbalet 1994). Disability studies must also address the fundamental issue of bodily agency. As Imrie (1996: 145) points out, disabled people are 'not merely passive recipients of the built environment, but actively seek to challenge and change it'.

The phenomenological body

To be a body and to have a body

Phenomenologists have sought to reconcile the traditional Cartesian dualisms through which scientific medicine – and likewise disability studies – refer only to the body as a passive pre-cultural object. Thus, the phenomenological body is constructed as subject/object. This serves to highlight the tension between having and being a body (Lyon and Barbalet 1994). In his book 'The Phenomenology of Perception', Merleau-Ponty (1962) developed a conception of human embodiment which attempted to transcend the mind/body dualism. He grounded perception in the experienced and experiencing body. The world as perceived through the body was, for Merleau-Ponty, the ground level of all knowledge, for it is through the body that people gain access to the world (Lyon and Barbalet 1994). Our perception of everyday reality depends upon a 'lived body' (Bendelow and Williams 1995), that is a body which simultaneously experiences the world but also produces it.

Thus from this perspective, human beings can be seen to have a double nature; a situation illuminated by the German terms '*Lieb*' and '*Korper*'. The former refers to the animated, experiential, living body (i.e. the body-for-itself) and the latter refers to the objective, exterior, instrumental body (i.e. the body-in-itself). Bendelow and Williams (1995: 147) assert that this approach 'expresses the essential ambiguity of human embodiment as both personal and impersonal, objective and subjective, social and natural. Moreover, it serves to highlight the weakness of the Cartesian legacy for sociology which has resulted in an almost exclusive representation of the body as Korper rather than simultaneously as Korper and Lieb' (a legacy which is clearly evident within disability studies). It is the emphasis upon the phenomenology of the body as 'lived experience' and the inner sensations of the subjective body (*Lieb*), which is of great value in the development of a sociology of pain (Bendelow and Williams 1995). One can make a similar suggestion in relation to a sociology of impairment.

A sociology of pain

The starting point for those seeking an alternative to the biomedical model of pain is that all pain is subjectively meaningful and therefore culturally meaningful. There is no pain that is genuinely biological. Pain always has meaning, always is 'socially informed' (Csordas 1993: 3; Jackson 1994) and it informs the social. Thus, there is a need for a more sophisticated model of pain; one that locates individuals within their social and cultural contexts, which allows for the inclusion of feelings and emotions (Bendelow and Williams 1995) and which captures the complex ways in which pain as a carnal property is culturally produced. The case for a sociology of impairment can be made on similar grounds. The social model has to be reworked to incorporate all the complexities of being disabled (Crow 1996). Giving impairment a sociological agenda would facilitate such a move (Paterson and Hughes 1999).

A sociology of impairment

The pain of impairment

Much of the debate about the reintroduction of impairment into disability studies centres on the claim that the social model ignores the pain associated with some conditions. A phenomenological approach to the body offers an obvious theoretical point of departure for discussing such concerns. However, there is also the possibility of having a condition which is not (biologically) painful. It is the latter situation which is explored here since, although equally valid, the former has more to do with considering the issue of pain than impairment. Moreover, having a condition that is not (biologically) painful is often regarded as an issue used to combat the incorporation of impairment into the social model. The current calls for the integration of impairment into the social model represent a demand for disability studies to develop a sociology of pain rather than a sociology of impairment.

Dys-appearance

The work of Drew Leder (1990) provides a most obvious point of departure for applying the idea of *Korper* and *Lieb* to the experience of impairment and disability. From a phenomenological standpoint, he describes how in everyday life our body 'disappears' from awareness, it is 'taken-for-granted': 'While in one sense the body is the most abiding and inescapable presence in our lives, it is also essentially characterized by absence. That is, one's own body is rarely the thematic object of experience' (Leder 1990: 1).

However, this everyday customary mode of bodily *disappearance* tends to be profoundly disrupted in the context of factors such as pain and disease (Bendelow and Williams 1995). Here the body becomes ever-present in experience, albeit in a dysfunctional manner. In other words, in contrast to the disappearances that characterize ordinary functioning, the body, in the context of pain, dys-appears. That is to say: 'The body appears as a thematic focus of attention, but precisely in a dys-state' (Leder 1990: 84).

Leder illustrates this argument through a phenomenological approach to pain as a lived and embodied experience. Here he stresses the sensory intensification which pain summons, factors which together produce the peculiar grip it has over our attention. Yet as Leder also observes, pain, like any other experiential mode, cannot be reduced merely to these immediate sensory qualities, rather, it is ultimately a matter of being-in-the-world. As a result, pain re-configures our lived space and time, our relations with others and ourselves (Bendelow and Williams 1995).

Leder's analysis has obvious value when discussing the criticism that the social model of disability denies the embodied experiences of pain and affliction which are integral to the lives of many people with impairments (Morris 1991; Crow 1996). This complaint is met with the retort that pain is an issue for medicine not politics, and that the disability movement is not in the business of tackling pain but of tackling oppression. However, pain is clearly more than a physical sensation, and one cannot sever the bodily experience from the social experience, pain from politics. Engagement with Leder would facilitate a sociological approach to pain as a (possible) constituent of impairment (Paterson and Hughes 1999).

The embodied experience of impairment: reworking Leder

On the other hand, Leder's analysis requires some reworking in order for it to be applied when discussing the embodied experience of having impairment which is not (biologically) painful. In this case, one must assess whether the body is prevented from being phenomenologically absent from view by a form other than its biological 'dys-state'. One can argue – applying Leder – that the disablist and disabling socio-spatial environment produces a vivid but unwanted consciousness of one's impaired body. Here, the body undergoes a mode of 'dys-appearance' which is not biological but social. For example, in the context of the ubiquitous disabling barriers of the spatial environment, one's impaired body 'dys-appears' – becomes unceasingly present in experience. When one is confronted by social and physical inaccessibility one is simultaneously confronted by oneself; the external and the internal collide in a moment of simultaneous recognition. The body of a person with speech impairment 'dys-appears' when faced with (socially produced) embodied norms of communication. Since these norms largely reflect the carnal information of non-disabled people, the relationship of disabled people to them is one of significant disadvantage. The dys-appearance of the impaired body is structured by this disadvantage. Exclusion from and disruption to communication is not therefore a matter of the ability of an impaired person to communicate, but about conventions and norms of communication which are (a priori) hostile to non-conforming forms of physicality (Paterson and Hughes 1999). In fact, non-disabled people are produced by the norms of communication and the conventions of interactions which reflect their carnal peculiarities.

Norms of communication require what Goffman (1963: 35) called 'shared vocabularies of body idiom'. Yet these vocabularies and the 'idiom' that they constitute are not and cannot be shared because corporeality is not homogeneous. Goffman's conceptual apparatus fails to recognize that 'shared vocabularies of body idiom' are constituted by hegemonic non-disabled bodies, so the 'botching' of communication is not necessarily a problem of 'self-presentation', but one of carnal alienation. One must address critically the processes that constitute the conventions of communication, rather than, as Goffman does, take them for granted. If one takes 'body idiom' as given and one is judged in relation to its conventions (that is, on the basis of one's social performance), then disabled people are bound by the very logic of the argument to be found to be incompetent. But if one takes the view that the norms and conventions which constitute 'body idiom' are existentially rooted in and informed by a specific hegemonic form of carnality, then a radical interrogation of the *Lebenswelt* from the perspective of the impaired body becomes possible.

Embodied social world

Unlike in the case of pain where the body-subject reacts to a change in the body as object, the context described here is a fully intercorporeal and intersubjective phenomenon. It is intensely personal, but at the same time enmeshed in a wider structure of discrimination and oppression which in our contemporary narcissistic culture is profoundly aesthetic (Lasch 1980). It is crucial to understand the nature and level of analysis implied by a phenomenological sociology of impairment. Impaired carnality 'dys-appears' in the context of intercorporeality and intersubjectivity because it is not recognized or valued in *res extensa*, that is in the physical, cultural and social world. Conversely, non-impaired carnality is 'taken-for-granted' because it is acknowledged and endorsed in *res extensa*.

From a phenomenological viewpoint, *res extensa* is an extension of our physical/psychical selves out into the world. The world becomes embodied because it is our 'projects' that sculpt our surroundings. Nick Crossley's (1995) appropriation of Merleau-Ponty's 'Phenomenology of Perception' (1962) leads to a 'carnal sociology of the body'. This suggests that *res extensa* is carnally formed and informed. Norms, values, conventions, buildings, even time and space are carnally informed, shaped and structured by bodily activity. However, the information that is imprinted onto the world is dominated by non-disabled bodies, by a specific hegemonic form of carnality which excludes as it constructs.

A politics of time

The body of a person with speech impairment 'dys-appears', both functionally and aesthetically, when faced with (socially produced) embodied norms of communication. Embodied norms of communication are oppressive to people with speech impairment. This suggests a need for a politics of time as 'opposed' to the social model's typical politics of space. Disability studies has – as yet – failed to turn its attention to a critical politics of time and the importance of this with respect to experience and embodiment. Both time and proprioception are central to communication, indeed central to success in the *Lebenswelt*. Both are structured and coded and the codes interpenetrate to form an 'idiom' of timing and movement which combine as 'carnal performance'. These codes of movement and timing are based on a carnal order which is informed primarily by non-impaired bodies. It is these 'hegemonic' bodies which are culturally formative of the codes and idioms which constitute the norms of timing and movement. The scripts for communication, timing and proprioception are therefore predisposed to the exclusion of people with impairments. It is not the exclusion from the spatial environment (which has been the central concern of the social model) which is at issue here, but ostracism from opportunities to participate in the day-to-day, sensate minutiae of the lifeworld. In this system of 'codification' the impaired body-as-subject consistently and continuously has the propensity to 'dys-appear'.

A radical sociology of impairment seeks to problematize not the performance of bodies but the rules and conventions of intercorporeality which provide the benchmark for judgements about performance (Paterson and Hughes 1999). For example, 'social competence' is accorded to bodies which perform to the 'gold standard' norms of speech, timing and movement and denied to those which do not. The traditional therapeutic approach to this subject would be to focus on the (carnal) performance of the impaired person. The goal would be to determine ways in which she could re-manage her performance to restore orderly interaction. She would be able to reveal (communicate normally) her 'social competence' and so be included in the interaction. An interactionist approach would concentrate on non-disabled people's reaction to disabled people's presentation of 'social competence'. Its 'mission' is to encourage non-disabled people to grant the attribute of 'social competence' to bodies which do not perform 'normally'. It is a plea which acknowledges the 'otherness' of the disabled person's (carnal) performance but nevertheless seeks the non-disabled person's patronage of 'orderly' interaction: 'yes, she is "abnormal" but please include her anyway'.

However, taking a carnal sociological approach, one can argue that 'social competence' is formed and informed by non-impaired carnality. It is the production of 'failures' of intercorporeality rather than disruption to the interaction order which is the theoretical focal point. The 'social competence' of people with impairments is masked, not because of their carnal performance, but because the 'protocols' of competence are devoid of their carnal information. It is not disabled people's performance or the reaction to their performance which needs to be modified to prevent their exclusion, but the scripts from which non-disabled people judge and bestow 'social competence'. Such an approach sparks a radical praxis for inclusion, a struggle to carnally re-inform the codes of timing and proprioception which shape participation in the lifeworld (Paterson and Hughes 1999).

Interrogating the *Lebenswelt* (everyday world)

The context of impairment as dys-appearance

I will now illustrate the idea of impairment as 'dys-appearance' by examining some experiences of being disabled as a person with speech impairment. This method is used by Robillard (1996). He presents two specific incidents: a botched encounter in a 'shopping mall' and estrangement at a party, in order to demonstrate how verbal and non-verbal norms of communication curtail his possibilities for participation and produce anger in and at the social order. It is important to remember that norms of communication and norms of intercorporeal interaction are a reflection of the carnal needs of non-disabled actors.

I intend to focus on the conventions of interaction and intercorporeality rather than the spatial environment as a context for impairment as 'dys-appearance'. In the context of a social environment saturated with disablist images, attitudes and behaviour and devoid of carnal information that reflects my corporeal status, I am perpetually 'reminded' of my body. These incidents can be major or minor – sometimes depending on how I feel or their frequency that day – ranging from being stared at or sidestepped in the street, condescended to, mistaken as drunk, to being called disablist names. The body as corporeality indicates that how one feels about one's body, indeed, how one experiences it, is temporarily/spatially-specific, and there is rarely a constant in the ways in which one reflects upon one's body and how, in turn, one's body is received (Imrie 1996). Of course, such examples are in no way unique (see material from Sutherland 1981 to Keith 1996). It is often suggested that disabled people are 'hypersensitive' about non-disabled people's responses, reading disablism in social interactions where there may not be. Disabled people may be 'hypersensitive' about discrimination and prejudice but this is precisely because of their lived experience of a world which is devoid of their carnal information.

Carnally informed orders of time

Conversation is categorized into differing types (small talk, chat, discussion, etc.) and each has an allotted duration of participation. These norms of duration are exclusively informed by and reflect the carnal needs of people without speech impairment. Everyday chance encounters provide good examples of how carnally informed orders of time work to exclude me from opportunities to communicate. Instances of 'polite conversations' (for some reason frequently occurring in lifts) or 'chit-chat' in a corridor often become exclusionary situations for me because they do not demand (in terms of convention) prolonged interaction. For example, if an individual initiates small talk in a lift, it is an impossible situation because I have no time to speak before one of us reaches our destination and has to exit. The opportunity to communicate is constrained not only by the travelling time of the lift, but because the duration norm of this particular communication is not commensurate with my carnal needs. I do not enter the conversation because it will be cut short or result in one or both of us missing our floor, or worse still, the communication may end in the 'improper' situation in which the doors would have to be kept open by manual means. Such outcomes would stray outside the conventions of communication and so I am policed by these conventions into an unsatisfactory interaction. My options are reduced to a smile or a nod of the head, and I am 'reminded' of my body. These everyday 'codes of conduct' (which favour the corporeal status of non-disabled people over my own) encourage complicity with the oppression of disabled people. Hence, there is an interplay of micro- and macro-relations of power. Oppression and prejudice become embodied and become part of the experience of everyday life. In turn, the disadvantaged corporeal status of impaired bodies cannot be understood outwith the wider material and social position of disabled people.

The judging of social competence

An integral element of the 'dys-appearance' experienced by disabled people is the everyday reality of condescension – being perceived as the 'eternal child'. On occasions when I'm out with non-disabled companions they are very frequently asked 'Is this your brother?' The implication is that I am 'unable' to form social relationships outside the family and that non-disabled people could not possibly be accompanying me out of any other reason than 'family duty'. I am an incompetent player in the game of social interaction and hence I require 'baby-sitting', to be 'accompanied by a responsible adult'. The next story is a slightly different example of this patronizing attitude, but again it is based on the assumption that I am 'socially dead'. A friend and I once entered pub and went to wait at the bar. A women turned to my friend and said 'I really admire you'. The implication is that I am not an active social agent. I cannot give anything, but can only take from a social relationship, and my companions must be congratulated for their selfless acts of escorting me out into the 'real world'. I am objectified and so 'reminded' of my body by being judged as socially inarticulate, being denied the attribute of 'social competence'.

Instantaneous, infantalizing judgements are commonplace reactions to disabled people and are primarily based on aesthetic 'evidence'. In everyday life, the application of this form of judgement is profoundly oppressive: just as obesity is taken as a sign of lack of self-control (Turner 1984: 150) so the movement and speech of my body is automatically regarded as symptomatic of 'social incompetence'. As ethics (judgement) have become increasingly aestheticized in the postmodern world (Featherstone 1992, 1995; Maffesoli 1996) 'tyrannies of perfection' have played a more central role in the formation of intercorporeal encounters.

Conclusion

I have attempted to argue that disability studies' structuralist account of disability is essentially weak as a vehicle for analysing negotiations in the *Lebenswelt*, whilst individual models reduce competence to 'personal abilities'. Within the *Lebenswelt*, oppression is not simply produced by structural barriers, it is a question of intercorporeal norms and conventions, it is about the extent to which 'competence' is negotiated in the everyday world and how this negotiation hinges on carnal factors.

The oppression produced by the norms and conventions of intercorporeal intersubjective relations is illuminated by a reworking of Leder's concept of 'dys-appearance'. This provides a means of discussing the embodied experience of impairment as an intercorporeal phenomenon.

From a phenomenological standpoint, the non-impaired body – in a world which is a product and reflection of its carnal needs – is customarily 'unaware' of itself until it is confronted by pain. This experience can be characterized as a mode of bodily *disappearance*. In contrast, the impaired body is stunned into its own recognition as a consequence of the disablism which permeates everyday life. The suggestion that the physical, cultural and social environment is carnally formed and informed by bodily activity facilitates a crucial understanding of the nature and level of analysis implied by a phenomenological sociology of impairment. Impaired carnality 'dys-appears' in the context of intercorporeality and intersubjectivity because it is not recognized or celebrated in social space: It actively presents a challenge to the norms and conventions which inscribe it as 'abnormal'. The objectification marked by 'dys-appearance' is, in itself, a manifest form of oppression.

Acknowledgements

I am grateful to Len Barton for giving me permission to publish arguments which appear in an earlier form in the journal *Disability & Society*, 1999, Vol. 14.

References

Abberley, P. 1987. 'The Concept of Oppression and the Development of a Social Theory of Disability', *Disability, Handicap & Society*, 2: 5–19.

Abberley, P. 1993. 'Disabled people and "normality"', in Swain et al. *Disabling Barriers – Enabling Environment*. London: Sage.

Abberley, P. 1997. 'The Limits of Classical Social Theory in the Analysis and Transformation of Disablement – (Can This Really be the End; to be Stuck inside of Mobile with the Memphis Blues Again?'), in L. Barton and M. Oliver (eds) *Disability Studies: Past, Present and Future*. Leeds: The Disability Press.

Barnes, C. and Mercer, G. 1996. 'Introduction: Exploring the Divide', in C. Barnes and G. Mercer (eds) *Exploring the Divide: Illness and Disability*. Leeds: The Disability Press.

Bendelow, G. and Williams, S. 1995. 'Transcending the Dualisms: Towards a Sociology of Pain', *Sociology of Health & Illness*, 17: 139–65.

Campbell, J. and Oliver, M. 1996. *Disability Politics: Understanding our Past, Changing our Future*. London: Routledge.

Campling, J. 1981. (ed.). *Images of Ourselves – Women with Disabilities Talking*. London: Routledge & Kegan Paul.

Crossley, N. 1995. 'Merleau-Ponty: the Elusive Body and Carnal Sociology', *Body & Society*, 1: 43–63.

Crow, L. 1996. 'Including All of Our Lives: Renewing the Social Model of Disability', in J. Morris (ed.) *Encounters with Strangers. Feminism and Disability*. London: The Woman's Press.

Csordas, T.J. 1993. 'Somatic Models of Attention', *Cultural Anthropology*, 8: 135–56.

Donzelot, J. 1979. *The Policing of Families*. New York: Pantheon.

Featherstone, M. 1992. 'Postmodernism and the Aestheticization of Everyday Life', in S. Lash and J. Friedman (eds) *Modernity and Identity*. Oxford: Blackwell.

Featherstone, M. 1995. *Undoing Culture*. London: Sage.

Finkelstein, V. 1980. 'Attitudes and Disabled People: Issues for Discussion'. New York: World Rehabilitation Fund.

Finkelstein, V. 1996. 'The Disability Movement has Run out of Steam', *Disability Now*, February: 11.

Goffman, E. 1963. *Behavior in Public Places: Notes on the Social Organisation of Gatherings*. New York: The Free Press.

Habermas, J. 1975. *Legitimation Crisis*. Boston: Beacon Press.

Hales, G. (ed.) 1996. *Beyond Disability: Towards an Enabling Society*. London: Sage.

Hughes, B. and Paterson, K. 1997. 'The Social Model of Disability and the Disappearing Body: Towards a Sociology of Impairment', *Disability & Society*, 12: 325–40.

Imrie, R. 1996. *Disability and the City*. London: Paul Chapman Publishing.

Jackson, J. 1994. 'Chronic Pain and the Tension between the Body as Subject and Object', in T.J. Csordas (ed.) *Embodiment and Experience: The Existential Ground of Culture and Self*. Cambridge: Cambridge University Press.

Keith, L. 1996. 'Encounters with Strangers', in J. Morris (ed.) *Encounters with Strangers. Feminism and Disability*. London: The Woman's Press.

Lasch, C. 1980. *The Culture of Narcissism*. New York: Abacus.

Leder, D. 1990. *The Absent Body*. Chicago: Chicago University Press.

Lyon, M.L. and Barbelet, J.M. 1994. 'Society's Body: Emotion and the Somatization of Social Theory', in T.J. Csordas (ed.) *Embodiment and Experience: The Existential Ground of Culture and Self*. Cambridge: Cambridge University Press.

Maffesoli, M. 1996. *The Time of the Tribes*. London: Sage.

Merleau-Ponty, M. 1962. *The Phenomenology of Perception*, trans. Colin Smith. London: Routledge.

Morris, J. 1989. *Able Lives: Women's Experience of Paralysis*. London: The Women's Press.

Morris, J. 1991. *Pride against Prejudice. Transforming Attitudes to Disability*. London: The Women's Press.

Oliver, M. 1983. *Social Work with Disabled People*. London: Macmillan.

Oliver, M. 1990. *The Politics of Disablement*. London: Macmillan.

Oliver, M. 1992. 'Changing the Social Relations of Research Production?', *Disability, Handicap & Society*, 7: 101–15.

Oliver, M. 1996a. 'Defining Impairment and Disability: Issues at Stake', in C. Barnes and G. Mercer (eds.) *Exploring the Divide: Illness and Disability*. Leeds: The Disability Press.

Oliver, M. 1996b. 'A Sociology of Disability or a Disablist Sociology', in L. Barton (ed.) *Disability and Society: Emerging Issues and Insights*. Harlow: Longman.

Oliver, M., Zarb, G., Silver, J., Moore, M. and Salisbury, V. 1988. *Walking into Darkness: The Experience of Spinal Injury*. London: Macmillan.

Paterson, K. and Hughes, B. 1999. 'Disability Studies and Phenomenology: The Carnal Politics of Everyday Life', *Disability & Society*, 14.

Robillard, A.B. 1996. 'Anger in-the-social-order', *Body & Society*, 2: 17–30.

Shakespeare, T. 1994. 'Cultural Representations of Disabled People: Dustbins for Disavowal?', *Disability & Society*, 9: 283–301.

Shakespeare, T. and Watson, N. 1995a. *Habemus Corpus. Sociology of the Body and the Issue of Impairment*. Aberdeen: Quincentennial Conference on the History of Medicine.

Shakespeare, T. and Watson, N. 1995b. *The Body Line Controversy: A New Direction for Disability Studies?* Hull: Disability Studies Seminar.

Shakespeare, T. and Watson, N. 1997. 'Defending the Social Model', *Disability & Society*, 12: 293–300.

Shilling, C. 1993. *The Body and Social Theory*. London: Sage.

Sutherland, A. 1981. *Disabled We Stand*. London: Souvenir Press.

Turner, B. 1984. *The Body and Society: Explorations in Social Theory*. Oxford: Basil Blackwell.

Turner, B. 1992. *Regulating Bodies: Essays in Medical Sociology*. London: Routledge.

Turner, B. 1996 (second edition). *The Body and Society: Explorations in Social Theory*. London: Sage.

Turner, T. 1994. 'Bodies and Anti-bodies: Flesh and Fetish in Contemporary Social Theory', in T.J. Csordas (ed.) *Embodiment and Experience: The Existential Ground of Culture and Self*. Cambridge: Cambridge University Press.

Upias 1976. *Fundamental Principles of Disability*. London: Union of Physically Impaired against Segregation.

Wendell, S. 1996. *The Rejected Body. Feminist Philosophical Reflections on Disability*. New York and London: Routledge.

Young, I. 1990. *Justice and the Politics of Difference*. New York: Princeton University Press.

Zarb, G. 1992. 'The Road to Damascus: First Steps towards Changing the Relations of Disability Research Production', *Disability, Handicap & Society*, 7: 125–38.

6 The Body and Death

Clive Seale

Introduction

The fact that our bodies bring us our deaths as well as our lives is a fundamental influence on the kind of social life that we make together. The capacity to turn away from death is a primary motive for the construction of the human social bond, seen most obviously at fateful moments that involve death, in which unusual efforts may be made to restore fractured bonds. But careful examination also reveals that everyday life is permeated with such resurrective practice, through which members routinely confirm their mutual orientation towards life in the face of death. A sociological account of the body must therefore account for this basic and ever-present message from our material life in the world.

My argument in this chapter is that social and cultural life is a human construction which helps people to turn away from the inevitability of death, contained in the fact of our embodiment, and to turn instead towards life. In this first section of the chapter, in the interests of clarity and emphasis, I will give a short account of how I came to these views, skimming over some of the detail and references which I provide in later sections. First, though, it is worth noting that, in broad terms, my argument has been touched on before by sociologists or social thinkers, though it is an insight which has been underdeveloped, particularly in the contemporary sociology of the body. Thus Illich made the point in *Limits to Medicine* (1976: 205):

> We cannot fully understand the deeply rooted structure of our social organisation unless we see it as a multi-faceted exorcism of all forms of evil death.

Berger, whose phenomenological account of the social construction of reality (Berger and Luckmann 1971) goes furthest towards accounting for everyday life in the manner I am suggesting, recognized the importance of death in social life in *The Sacred Canopy*, an account of religious life:

> Death presents society with a formidable problem not only because of its obvious threat to the continuity of human relationships, but because it threatens the basic assumptions of order on which society rests. (Berger 1973: 32–3)

Ernst Becker, however, who was not primarily concerned with the development of sociology, but with extending psychoanalytic theory to incorporate social life, provides the fullest account of the influence of death on our mode of life when he proposed in *The Denial of Death* that:

> society is and always has been ... a symbolic action system, a structure of statuses and roles, customs and rules for behavior, designed to serve as a vehicle for earthly heroism ... a mythical hero-system in which people serve in order to earn a feeling of primary value. (1973: 4–5)

As well as structuring one's life so as to understand it in terms of an heroic personal mythology, Becker argued that the psychoanalytic concept of transference describes an important mechanism for generating feelings of value in the face of its ultimate negation by death, involving as it does a fascination with admired figures. In my work (Seale 1998) I have tried to develop these views about the centrality of death in order to discover their implications for an understanding of basic parameters of everyday, embodied social life. While this began from an interest in how sociology might illuminate the experience of dying and bereavement, it has developed into an account of how the study of death can illuminate social theory.

As I studied people's experience of death and bereavement I began to see that this could be extended to produce a broader understanding of fundamental features of social life. I could see that embodiment dictates basic parameters for the construction of culture, the key problem for which is contained in the fact that bodies eventually die. On the one hand, this threatens to make life meaningless, but on the other hand, as Becker argued, it is a basic motivation for social and cultural activity, which involves a continual defence against death. Through a variety of practices, both routine and extraordinary, the threat to basic security about being in the world posed by knowledge of mortality, is transformed in human social activity into an orientation towards continuing, meaningful existence. At the same time – and this was not recognized adequately by Becker, who retains a somewhat macho North American cultural perspective – the cultural forms made available to members of different societies to overcome the problem of death vary greatly. This was made clear to me by a study of the anthropological literature on death-related practice, which (unlike sociology until very recently) has long been preoccupied with accounts of mortuary ritual. For the sociologist, an understanding of cultural variation helps us perceive the degree to which our own constructions of death, dying and bereavement as well as broader issues concerning the formation of self-identity are, in fact, specific to the conditions of late modernity and, indeed, are influenced by the conceptions of particular social groups.

All this may be a little mysterious without further expansion of these ideas to show how I have reached these conclusions. I will do something to satisfy these needs here, but would also refer interested readers to a fuller account which I have published elsewhere (Seale 1998). My argument, then, is based on the contribution which the study of dying and of bereavement can make to social theory. Such study is of value in throwing into stark relief the divide between nature and culture that is normally hidden from view in everyday life. This divide is made fragile by the temporary reversals and inversions that occur in marginal situations and fateful moments, chief amongst which are close encounters with death.

This exposure then allows us to examine the roots of the social bond, which I have come to believe is too often taken for granted in social theory, a gap which will be shown in the section that follows this. With the help of Scheff (1990) I began to see that studies in conversation analysis (CA), which until then I had regarded as a somewhat obscure and over-technical obsession with dubious broader relevance, could in fact provide a snapshot of the creation and maintenance of basic social bonds. CA shows the continual creation and recreation of intersubjective understanding that allows us to recognize each other as accountably human beings. Yet I could also see that CA and ethnomethodology in general commonly failed to examine the basic motivations that lead humans to construct this bond together, which require an understanding of inner emotional life that is anathema to the somewhat behaviourist observational discipline that CA has become (Silverman 1996).

Finally, through study of the sociology of emotions, a field which developed around the same time as contemporary sociology of the body, I came to see that what I thought of as 'embodied emotionality' – that is, emotions expressed through and with the body – is of crucial importance in understanding why humans are motivated to participate in social life. This is done through the assertion of common membership of imagined communities, in which social bonds are created and sustained.

Elaborating the argument

As I explored this line of thinking at first I looked for social theory that would help in understanding the place of embodiment and mortality in social life, and found some useful leads to follow, though all were ultimately somewhat limited for my purposes. For example, Foucauldian analysis of the social construction of the body and of human subjectivity in discourse has been an important and productive theme in social theory. Foucault's own studies of medicine (1973), psychiatry (1967), penal regimes (1977) and sexuality (1979, 1986) provide a model for the view that bodies and minds, and the divisions between them, are the product of a variety of historically- and culturally-specific discourses. Power is seen as pervading all human relations, operating through a variety of characteristic techniques in contemporary social life, including population surveillance, the promulgation of norms of behaviour, and the examination of people by experts so that they are encouraged to confess themselves to be subjects within the governing discourses of their day.

Reflected in the work of Armstrong (1983), Nettleton (1992) and Rose (1989), for example, this line of thinking has proved highly productive in understanding the regulation of bodies within discourses of medicine, psychiatry and psychology. But as Giddens (1982) observes, followers of the Foucauldian approach to the social construction of bodies and selves have at times presented an over deterministic and disembodied analysis of human agency. Discourses are assumed to be all-pervasive, and people are assumed to be made unproblematically 'docile' by disciplinary regimes. These limitations are strikingly similar to those pointed out in relation to functionalist sociology (Wrong 1961). Although notions of discourse and representation are important in understanding the resources available to people in making sense of their lives and deaths, I wanted an understanding of this that would allow for human agency to a greater extent. Additionally, I found the avoidance, or 'bracketing out' of ontological debate in these writers disappointing, since this seemed to me to provide no possibility of viewing the body as having an independent material existence, ultimately outside the play of discourse, yet nevertheless deeply influential on people's relationship to discursive representations.

I found phenomenological perspectives (for example, Berger and Luckmann 1971) more satisfying in showing the involvement of human agency in the construction of culture, and in understanding this involvement as in part motivated by the problem of death. Their work is almost entirely devoted to showing how humans create meaningful worlds from a mass of otherwise undifferentiated experience. Like Durkheim, they view society as a human product which continually acts back upon its producer. Berger (1973: 14), for example, describes how, in outpourings of human being into the world ('externalization'), reality is produced, hardening and thickening into 'facticity' as social institutions are constructed in a process of 'objectification'. These entities, which are originally human products, are then reappropriated by people in a process of 'internalization', providing a socially shared stock of knowledge and practices with which to navigate the self through society.

Particularly appealing for my purposes was their account of the role of conversations and of language in maintaining an intersubjective version of reality. In crisis or 'marginal' situations, such as those engendered by a death, reality sustaining conversations are forced to become particularly 'explicit and intensive' (Berger and Luckmann 1971: 175). In these various ways, society provides a type of 'sheltering canopy' that defends against experience which would otherwise reduce the individual to a 'howling animality' (Berger 1973: 63). These ideas were linked to an analysis of the role of ritual in repairing damage to the social bond, though their account of ritual did not extend to the rituals of everyday life, for which I had to look elsewhere.

Limiting the usefulness of their work, too, was my perception that in their emphasis on agency, these writers appeared to commit the opposite fallacy to that of the Foucauldians, underemphasizing the extent to which discourses and objective structures influenced and constrained subjectivity as well as bodily experience. Although the work of Csordas (1993) within this tradition is interesting in incorporating a more developed account of the role of the embodiment within a phenomenological account, it does not seem to me to overcome this problem of imagining an excessive capacity for self-determination.

A variety of resolutions of the structure–agency problem have been attempted within social theory, and space precludes analysis of these here. In Seale (1998) I give an account of them, some of which incorporate a more embodied conception of the human subject. In particular there is Turner's sociology of the body (Turner 1992) and Bourdieu's development of the idea of a socially determined *habitus* (Bourdieu 1977). But within the confines of this chapter it is appropriate to focus on just one of these solutions, contained in Giddens' (1984) idea of structuration.

I was interested in this because it allows us to understand language as a medium for the appropriation of cultural scripts. I began to see that people could be understood as literally talking themselves into communities. Such narrative reconstruction of personal biography becomes particularly important at what Giddens calls 'fateful moments' such as those that often accompany dying or bereavement. Giddens' distinction between practical and discursive consciousness was interesting as it enabled me to see a continuity between the themes made explicit in more discursive moments occasioned by unusual events (as occur in mortuary rituals, or in the stories told by bereaved individuals), with the more routine events of everyday life, in which ontological security is barely disturbed as members negotiate their places in daily social life using skills of which they are hardly aware.

Giddens' work is rather notable for the absence of the body, and I was also aware of the view that his model of the reflexive formation of self identity in late modernity (Giddens 1991) was regarded by some as underplaying the role of emotions, so clearly it could not be seen as a complete solution to the problem I had set myself. All these social theorists had something to offer, but none on their own was enough. At the same time it was clear to me that social theory at this relatively context-free level could be no more than a general guide for an enquiry into how people actually experience their bodies, minds and social relations, a stock of sensitizing concepts that would enable, rather than restrict me in reaching a deeper understanding of the subject at hand.

In fact, these more general themes in social theory provided a framework of ideas within which more specific studies of illness, dying and bereavement could be placed, which then led to a reflection back on the adequacy of the more general accounts of social life. In particular, a series of studies of the narrative reconstruction of self-identity amongst the chronically ill were helpful in seeing how the problem of dying and bereavement might be understood. This perspective is seen, for example, in the work of the American anthropologists Kleinman (1988), Good (1994) and Frank (1995), and also in British work, exemplified by studies by Bury (1982), Gareth Williams (1984) and others on the experience of illness. The common theme of these studies is expressed in the titles of two important early contributions to this genre: 'Chronic Illness as Biographical Disruption' (Bury 1982) and 'Loss of Self: A Fundamental Form of Suffering in the Chronically Ill' (Charmaz 1983).

Chronic illness is found in these studies to be disruptive at many levels beyond the purely physical. First, it is disruptive of the taken-for-granted routines that Giddens stresses as both cause and consequence of a basic sense of security about being in the world. Physical restrictions lead to an inability to maintain previous social contacts, or to modifications in the form they take, usually in the direction of increased dependency or loss of reciprocity. Notions of time change, so that they no longer synchronize with the time-scales of other people, who may find a period short which, to a sufferer, appears interminable. Fears about others' tolerance can lead to the construction of discrediting versions of the self and to an experience of stigmatized identity, with resultant humiliations of information control, passing and covering in bids to normalize appearance in certain settings. Pain, in particular, alienates the self from the body, so that it appears like a separate and strange thing, asserting a 'dualism' between mind and body that in most normal circumstances are experienced as one (Simon Williams 1996), leading people to feel at times that their bodies have 'betrayed' them. With the help of these studies I began to understand illness as a potential 'fall from culture', to use Hilbert's (1984) words. Medicine, and other cultural scripts, were then stories or narratives which helped sufferers reconstruct the social bond as they aligned their understanding of their personal biographies with these communally constructed narratives.

In my survey of literature that might help me understand the place of death in social life, I then stumbled across the work of Thomas Scheff (1990, 1997) who, like Goffman, argues that maintenance of a human social bond is reflected both in large-scale ritual events and in the micro-rituals of everyday interaction. Scheff understood that minor currents of exclusion and inclusion underlie the smallest conversational exchange, generating feelings of pride and shame in the flux and flow of membership negotiations. At the root of these negotiations, then, lay our emotional lives, which provided the motivation for the construction of social bonds.

Scheff (1990) observes that fundamental social bonds are continually at risk at the routine level of everyday interaction, where people may manipulate claims to membership for momentary strategic advantage (perhaps to assert distinction), or through unconscious disturbance so that misunderstandings and distorted communication takes place. Social bonds are also disrupted at moments of major personal or general social change, such as described in 'life-events', 'fateful moments' or social revolutions. It is at this point that a variety of repair mechanisms may be wielded, ranging from restatements of communication, psychotherapeutic repair or societal reconstruction. Here, then, was a place for ideas about narrative reconstruction, developed in the study of illness, in the context of a much broader theory of the elemental bonds of social life. Indeed, Scheff's ideas help to explain why narratives of the self characteristically contain justifications, excuses and rationalizations for 'bad' behaviour as the self is presented in a morally acceptable fashion. Such reconstructions depict social bonds as intact (when they are in fact broken) or justifiably in tatters due to the bad behaviour of others, restoring pride and guarding against shame, and maintaining the legitimacy of the speaker's claim to membership of an imagined moral community.

This view of the ritual qualities of everyday life incidentally led me to question social commentators who mourn the 'decline' of ritual in the move from tribal or traditional societies to modern and late modern societies. This is a recurrent theme in journalistic discussions of death and bereavement, whereby we are routinely told of the 'decline' of mourning ritual, and more often than not exhorted to resist the supposed 'denial' of the 'taboo' topic of death, for which various aspects of modern social organisation are usually blamed (for example, hospitals, medical care, and so on). Clearly, allegiance to large-scale formal ritual is more problematic in a society where many of these compete, and a sense of scepticism about the truth value of any grand narrative is pervasive. Yet human social life is fundamentally ritualistic at the everyday level in the sense described above, an insight which is of importance in understanding how people experience dying and bereavement.

The final part of this puzzle lay in the role of the body, for I could see that the emotions involved in ritual activity arose from bodily sensations and desires, but this was not a topic which Scheff had considered. For this, I had to turn back to an earlier strand of 'social constructionist' writing, though this was a very different tradition from that of Foucault, being exemplified by the work of Mary Douglas who, in her work on laughter (1975), for example, uses the question of whether dogs laughed to present a view of the body as communicating to and from the social environment, a physical channel of meaning, laughter being a bodily interruption in social discourse. Cultures vary a great deal in the threshold at which laughter is considered appropriate, and the degree of bodily 'abandon' that can be shown. Sarbin (1986), in a volume on emotional life edited by Rom Harré, presents an account of emotions as metaphors used for outward movements of the body; people are not 'seized' or 'taken over' by emotions although they may, in their discursive explanations, suggest that this is how it felt: emotions, rather, are located in personal repertoires which dictate when particular displays are appropriate. The concept of 'embodied emotionality' seemed appropriate to me in describing this link between the body and emotional life, an idea that is intended to be somewhat reminiscent of Bourdieu's idea of *habitus*. As well as laughter, it seemed to me that a variety of events that involve the body, such as weeping, pain or breathlessness, some of which medical thinking reifies as 'symptoms', could be understood as the body's communicative interjection into social life, highly implicated in the membership negotiations accompanying the construction of human social bonds.

Three concepts

By the end of this Cook's tour of various social theorists, as well as more empirically grounded work, I felt that it was possible to envisage an account of our social lives that recognized the importance of the body and its death as central facts which both constrained and motivated our interactions. To this end, I have been able to formulate three organizing concepts which assist in understanding a variety of observable and recurrent features of social life. These are the idea of imagined community (derived and somewhat modified from the work of Anderson 1991); revivalism (derived from Walter 1994) and resurrective practice, which was mentioned earlier.

The first of these is expanded in scope in comparison with Anderson's original usage, where it referred to the sense of community derived from participation in nationalistic ideals, promoted by the existence of print media. I retain this, but suggest that membership of a variety of imagined communities is available to people in late modernity, for example that which is constructed in medical knowledge, in the governmental promotion of normal behaviour, by life insurance systems and in psychological discourse. I retain, too, Anderson's insight that 'nothing connects us affectively to the dead more than language' (1991: 145).

The second concept, revivalism, follows Walter in referring to the ideas promoted by certain late modern social movements such as hospice care that incorporate a critique of the modern way of death, which is perceived to involve a taboo. The revivalist alternative proposes an elevation of the (supposedly) private experiences of dying and bereavement, so that these are brought into the field of public discussion, as they are in psychological knowledge. Thus, revivalist psychological discourse enables individuals in late modernity, faced with bereavement and death, to engage in practices (such as psychotherapy) that involve claims to membership in an imagined human community of anonymous others.

This is an example of the third concept, that of resurrective practice. I intend this to refer, though, both to practices of a formal and organized nature for which there exists an established expertise and to the fine details of everyday conversation, since these have in common an affirmation of the social bond in the face of its dissolution. Resurrective practice restores a sense of basic security fractured by death, but is also a routine feature of daily life. It is therefore intended to capture the notion that social life involves the organized turning away from death and towards life. Resurrective practice enables us, for example, to place our biographies within imagined communities of others who share similar stories of the self, perhaps those orchestrated by revivalist social movements. The idea, though, retains a sense of agency and choice, as in structuration theory, where it is clear people often have a choice (albeit constrained at times by objective structures, or by bodily limitations), can draw on a variety of discursive representations as resources, and can choose to join a variety of imagined communities.

The idea of resurrective practice arose in particular from consideration of anthropological studies of mortuary ritual. These described attempts to transform death into hope, life and fertility through a variety of practices which combine to 'kill' death and resurrect optimism about continuation in life in spite of loss and certain knowledge of one's own future death. Durkheimian analyses of the mortuary rituals of tribal or traditional societies (for example, Hertz 1960) show how this is achieved by symbolic means. In modern societies, nationalist ideologies have often been successful in transforming the meaning of individual deaths into heroic acts that sustain the fictive immortality of particular social groups, bonded together in an imagined community. Another means for sustaining personal security about being in the world (ontological security) is, paradoxically, the triumphant killing of other people, both in actuality and in acts of symbolic violence, exclusion and stigma, since this gives a sense of mastery over death.

Yet, as Elias (1978, 1982) has shown, these violent and stigmatizing means for killing death are decreasingly available in the civil society of late modernity, where restraints on interpersonal violence are strong and the values of tolerance and sympathy are promoted as desirable social virtues. Implicated with this pacification of civil society are psychological versions of self-identity which can be said to offer a religion of the self, with associated rites such as psychotherapy. Psychological and other revivalist discourse can help people, faced with the fateful moments of death and loss, to restructure narratives of self identity and transform the event of death into a positive experience. This brings us full circle to the ideas of structuration theory and notions of narrative reconstruction at fateful moments through the appropriation of cultural scripts, which enable us to affirm a secure social bond in the face of its potential dissolution.

A case study

My work then became to apply these ideas to particular instances of social life. Because my work arose in the context of studying dying and bereavement, examples come from these areas, but I hope that these ideas may prove useful in considering other areas of social life. Because, though death so effectively threatens social bonds, it is an ideal site for perceiving processes that are normally taken for granted, so it is appropriate to begin there. Initially, I could see these general processes at work in the stories told by bereaved people (Seale 1995a and b), but I have also applied them to media representations (Seale 1998). An illustrative example from this latter study will assist in seeing how behaviour at fateful moments can be interpreted as moments of resurrective practice. The example has the additional benefit of being a media representation, demonstrating the role of these in providing exemplary guidance to people seeking to understand their own biographical situations.

The broadcast media constitute one area of representation offering cultural scripts to people approaching death, playing a significant part in generating an imagined community and in writing the cultural scripts that many people appropriate when facing their own death or bereavement (see Seale 1995b). However, analyses of the role of the media in representing forms of dying are relatively rare. Although media portray death in a number of ways (including, most obviously, violent deaths in fictional and news programmes), I focus here on a particular genre of heroic, confessional death that draws on similar themes to revivalism. Through a case study of one such confessional death, that of Dennis Potter the British television playwright, I demonstrate the construction of the aware dying role as a drama of inner adventure. In this discourse certain rhetorical devices – such as the juxtaposition of opposites – are routinely used to generate an authoritative voice, based on the demonstration of special status as a liminal being, as well as transforming the experience of dying into an opportunity for growth. The parallels with symbolic transformations of death into fertility in mortuary rituals are evident. The method which I use for this analysis is, broadly speaking, that of discourse analysis (Potter and Wetherell 1987).

I begin with extracts from the interviewer, Melvyn Bragg's preface in the booklet which the Channel 4 television company produced with the programme:

> Two or three weeks ago Michael Grade, the chief executive of Channel 4, rang me to say that a mutual friend of ours, Dennis Potter, was dying of cancer. After trying to absorb this we decided to ask Dennis if he would do one last interview. He agreed... Dennis wanted to be interviewed in a television studio. The best time for him was about 9–9.30 in the morning, and that, a week or two ago, was when we did it. (Channel 4 1994: 3)

Contained within the preface is a rhetorical device which the interview repeatedly uses, that of ironic understatement in references to Potter's impending death, the effect of which is to invite the reader (or viewer) imaginatively to dwell on these glimpses of the void over which Potter's life is poised. The phrase 'After trying to absorb this...' immediately followed by a description of action (issuing an invitation) is an example. There is no dwelling on the distressing emotions appropriate to a 'friend' told such news: the reader is expected to fill these in from common-sense understandings about typically appropriate behaviour, thereby imaginatively participating in the construction of the text. Cancer is thus depicted, by implication, as striking this man down in the midst of active social participation, just as the text itself is subjected to potential assaults of unrestrained feeling that in fact are never allowed to develop too far. In fact, the interview is a skilful dramatic performance jointly produced by both parties to the interview.

At various points in the interview normality is juxtaposed ironically with understated moments of abnormality to achieve this effect in the viewer. For example, Potter appears in a suit (rather than in bedclothes), seated in a chair (rather than lying down), in a television studio (rather than at home or hospital), occasionally sipping a drink, which we learn is a 'flask' rather than a glass of water. In the middle of the interview Potter says 'Can I break off for a second? I need a swig of that, there's liquid morphine in that flask' followed, in the written text, by '*(Intermission)*'. An 'intermission' of this sort had in fact occurred earlier on, but had not been 'explained' in this way, yet retrospectively it can be seen to have prefaced the later, more explicitly signalled intermission. This is also a device suggestive of a growing crescendo of bodily stress created by the interview. In the preface we learned that the 'best time' for Potter is in the morning, and during the interview he explains that he is too tired to work by the evening. By the end of the interview we are presented with a man who is physically exhausted by a marathon of effort: 'That'll have to do. I'm done. I need that thing [the flask] again' (1994: 21).

The presentation of the interview as a precarious performance of 'business as usual', covering this crescendo of stress is signalled by Bragg's first question, which follows a preliminary statement by Potter (which might in other circumstances have been edited out as extraneous material by programme makers) to the effect that he will need his 'flask [only] if there's any spasm, so I should put it out of sight'. To this opening indicator of Potter's suffering, Bragg juxtaposes a blandly 'normal' opening question: 'How long have you been working on this new thing?' referring to Potter's current writing of a television script. There is a striking and deliberate contrast between the normality of the question and the abnormality of the situation. Potter's depiction of his sip of morphine as a 'swig' also achieves this effect, juxtaposing the normality of 'swigging' perhaps wine or water, with the potential alternatives of 'taking' or 'having' or 'giving myself' a medication that remain unchosen common-sense descriptors.

The majority of the interview is devoted to Potter's account of his life and achievements, Bragg inviting him to reflect on themes within his work, assess the broader context of his achievements as a playwright, and explain the reasons for particular directions he took at various points in his artistic development. In this respect the interview follows the usual format of the highbrow arts programme interview and indeed of public obituaries. Yet at various points, in addition to the implicit hints at an underlying story of bodily suffering and disintegration outlined above, there is explicit talk about the experience and meaning of the illness. At these moments Potter is able to place himself firmly within the script offered by revivalist discourse on heroic death. For example, he presents his current situation as one of intense creative activity, a race against his bodily decline to achieve an ultimate moment of artistic fulfilment by completing two plays before he dies:

> I've been working [since the news of cancer] flat out at strange hours, because I'm done in the evenings, mostly because of the morphine, also the pain is very energy sapping. But I do find that I can be at my desk at 5 o'clock in the morning, and I'm keeping to a schedule of pages, and I will and do meet that schedule every day [p. 4]…. All I hope is that I've got enough days to finish it… When I go flat out I go flat out, and believe me with a passion I've never felt – I feel I can write anything at the moment. I feel I can fly with it, I feel I can really communicate what I'm about, and what I feel, and what the world ought to know. I have a vocation, a passion, a conviction about it… The histology of it [the cancer] suggests that I should already be dead, but I know what's keeping me going. (1994: 20, 21)

He explains a new sense he has of his character:

> as a child I know for a fact I was a coward… [but now I] find out that in fact, at the last, thank God, you're not actually a coward – I haven't shed a tear since I knew…. I haven't had a single moment of terror since they told me…(1994: 5, 21)

He also describes the altered state of his perception of everyday objects in the world, brought on by his awareness of imminent death, and his state of acceptance:

> Things are both more trivial than they ever were, and more important than they ever were, and the difference between the trivial and the important doesn't seem to matter – but the *nowness* of everything is absolutely wondrous. And if people could see that – there's no way of telling you, you have to experience it – the glory of it, if you like, the comfort of it…(1994: 5)

Potter, therefore, quite explicitly embraces the revivalist role of dying in full awareness. The interview's major purpose is to present Potter as possessing, by virtue of his contact with death, a uniquely elevated authority. This is indicated by his demonstration of rights appropriate to a liminal space, where he is able to overturn conventional forms, reminiscent of the right of the medieval court jester to ridicule the king without punishment. For example, he refers to his smoking of cigarettes during the interview, initially by joking 'I take it mine's the seat with the ashtray' (significantly, also not edited out as extraneous by the programme makers). Later, the following interchange occurs, giving a display of bravado as a condemned man:

> *Dennis*: You don't mind this cigarette? I have always smoked, but...
>
> *Melvyn*: Why should I mind?
>
> *Dennis*: Well people do nowadays - you get so bloody nervous smoking.
>
> *Melvyn*: It's all right, I'm a very passive smoker...
>
> *Dennis*: [In the train] there is one bit for smokers, and if I see people sitting there without a cigarette, I love to say: 'You do know this is a smoking compartment, don't you?'....Of course now I'm virtually chain smoking because there's no point in not... I like cream, like cholesterol. I can break any rule now. But the cigarette – well, I love stroking this lovely tube of delight. Look at it. *(Laughing)*
>
> *Melvyn*: I've packed in. Now stop, I'll be smoking again in a minute. (1994: 8–9)

Here we see an inversion of the 'normal' attitude towards smoking, demonstrating Potter's embrace of his death. Juxtaposition of opposites is repeatedly used to display Potter's marginal status between life and death. Thus, the delivery of his diagnosis was on St Valentine's Day, he tells us, 'like a little gift, a little kiss from somebody or something'. He contrasts his status as a liberal with a joking expression of racism: 'as a border person I always hate the Welsh – inevitably, because I was brought up to. *(Laughs)* Yet many of my friends are Welsh. But the Race Relations Act cannot touch me here – I'm a border person, and that's the way it is' (1994: 6). The admixture of the 'trivial' and the 'important' in an experience of 'nowness', seen earlier, is another example.

The special authority gained by his contact with death, demonstrated by these jokes and inversions, is used to present commentaries on the deficiencies of the living and to present projects for restructuring the world he will leave behind. For example, he castigates the 'pollution' of the British press and political life by the dominance of the media tycoon Rupert Murdoch, joking that he calls his pancreatic cancer 'Rupert' and he gives a lengthy critique, encouraged by the like-minded Bragg, of the 'commercialization' of the television industry by the import of a managerialist ethos. However, he reserves his final act of authoritative restructuring until the last, presented to coincide with the peak of the underlying crescendo of physical stress dramatized in the interview. At the end of the interview he makes a personal appeal to the controllers of Channel 4 and the BBC, saying that the hope that this wish might be granted is 'what's keeping me going'. He wants one of the plays he is writing to be shown on one channel, and then repeated on the next the following week, and that this should happen in reverse order for the second play. Boundaries between the rival channels, otherwise jealously maintained, are therefore to be broken down in an affirmation of essential unity, which Potter describes as 'a fitting memorial'. His wish was in fact granted after he died as people participated in this ritual act to mourn his passing, testimony to this authoritative display of rhetorical power.

Potter's death is analogous to the actions of a shaman or priest, presiding over the mortuary rites of some dead culture hero, who gains personal authority to restructure and guide the moral life of mourners by virtue of his special contact with the spirits of the dead. Like the Indian Aghori, who derive their special powers – such as the ability to fly – from physical contact with putrefying bodies, designating them as marginal beings (Parry 1994), so Dennis Potter indicates that 'I feel I can fly with it'. He sings, in a sense, his own funeral elegy and creatively transforms his death into an inspirational event.

Conclusion

The resurrective practice which Potter performs in the face of his own death draws on revivalist scripts to place himself at the forefront of an imagined community, in which personal insight is valued above 'denial', a secular 'facing' of death is preferred to religious illusions, and individuals are implicitly ranked on their fortitude in doing the above things. Potter is claiming an heroic place within this community through this public performance of his own dying, and no doubt has contributed to the aspiration of others to die in a similar fashion. This is not an isolated event, and I give accounts of a number of similar confessional deaths in Seale (1998). It represents a particular mode of dying, preferred by people in higher social classes as a sign of distinction, and particularly characteristic of death from cancer (which itself suggests the role of bodily events on constraining the choices that people can make).

The case study illustrates some more general themes that were raised in the earlier part of the chapter. If we study the process of dying (and bereavement) this is a particularly fertile site for observing events that in fact permeate general social life. Potter's claim, made through a narrative reconstruction of his personal biography, is that of secure membership within a community (albeit as a 'leader' for the moment), as a person who appropriately and morally affirms the value of intact social bonds, discharging his responsibilities as he sees them even at such a time of intense personal strain, and in the face of personal physical dissolution. His pride in the successful performance of this is obvious. It is, in fact, an extreme version of what we all do for most of our time on this earth, though normally in much more minor and routinized ways, until some disruptive event occurs that requires repair. At such times we may be constrained in the kinds of cultural scripts or resources we can employ, but we are impelled to make these choices rather than descend into the 'howling animality' that Berger and Luckmann (1973) describe, since this is what makes us human.

Finally, if I could just restate my main theme: an adequate sociological understanding of the role of embodiment in social life requires a recognition that our bodies give to us both our lives and our deaths so that social and cultural life can, in the last analysis, be considered as a human construction in the face of death.

References

Anderson, B. 1991 (second edition). *Imagined Communities. Reflections on the Origin and Spread of Nationalism*. London: Verso.

Armstrong, D. 1983. *The Political Anatomy of the Body: Medical Knowledge in Britain in the Twentieth Century*. Cambridge: Cambridge University Press.

Becker, E. 1973. *The Denial of Death*. New York: Free Press.

Berger, P.L. and Luckman, T. 1971 (first published 1966). *The Social Construction of Reality*. Harmondsworth: Penguin Books.

Berger, P.L. 1973. *The Social Reality of Religion*. Harmondsworth: Penguin Books. (First published in 1967 as *The Sacred Canopy*).

Bourdieu, P. 1977. *Outline of a Theory of Practice*. Cambridge: Cambridge University Press.

Bury, M. 1982. 'Chronic Illness as Biographical Disruption', *Sociology of Health and Illness*, 4 (2):167–82.

Channel 4. 1994. *An Interview with Dennis Potter*. London: Channel 4 Television.

Charmaz, K.C. 1983. 'Loss of Self: A Fundamental Form of Suffering in the Chronically Ill', *Sociology of Health and Illness*, 5 (2): 168–91.

Csordas, T. 1993. 'Somatic Modes of Attention', *Cultural Anthropology*, 8 (2): 135–56.

Douglas, M. 1975. 'Do Dogs Laugh?', in Douglas, *Implicit Meanings*. London: Routledge and Kegan Paul.
Elias, N. 1978. *The Civilizing Process Volume I: The History of Manners*. Oxford: Blackwell.
Elias, N. 1982. *The Civilizing Process Volume II: State Formation and Civilization*. Oxford: Blackwell.
Foucault, M. 1967. *Madness and Civilization: A History of Insanity in the Age of Reason*. London: Tavistock.
Foucault, M. 1973. *Birth of the Clinic*. London: Tavistock.
Foucault, M. 1977. *Discipline and Punish*. London: Allen Lane.
Foucault, M. 1979. *History of Sexuality. Volume I*. London: Allen Lane.
Foucault, M. 1986. *History of Sexuality. Volume II*. London: Allen Lane.
Frank, A.W. 1995. *The Wounded Storyteller*. Chicago: University of Chicago Press.
Giddens, A. 1982. *Profiles and Critiques in Social Theory*. London: Macmillan.
Giddens, A. 1984. *The Constitution of Society. Outline of a Theory of Structuration*. Cambridge: Polity Press.
Giddens, A. 1991. *Modernity and Self-identity: Self and Society in the Late Modern Age*. Cambridge: Polity Press.
Good, B.J. (1994) *Medicine, Rationality and Experience*. Cambridge: Cambridge University Press.
Hertz, R. 1960 (first published 1907). *Death and the Right Hand: A Contribution to the Study of the Collective Representation of Death*. Glencoe, IL: Free Press.
Hilbert, R. 1984. 'The Acultural Dimensions of Chronic Pain: Flawed Reality Construction and the Problem of Meaning', *Social Problems*, 31(4): 365–78.
Illich, I. 1976. *Limits to Medicine; Medical Nemesis: The Expropriation of Health*. Harmondsworth: Penguin Books.
Kleinman, A. 1988. *The Illness Narratives: Suffering, Healing and the Human Condition*. New York: Basic Books.
Nettleton, S. 1992. *Power, Pain and Dentistry*. Buckingham: Open University Press.
Parry, J.P. 1994. *Death in Banares*. Cambridge: Cambridge University Press.
Potter, J. and Wetherell, M. 1987. *Discourse and Social Psychology: Beyond Attitudes and Behaviour*. London: Sage.
Rose, N. 1989. *Governing the Soul: The Shaping of the Private Self*. London: Routledge.
Sarbin, T.R. 1986. 'Emotion and Act: Roles and Rhetoric', in Harré, R. (ed.) *The Social Construction of Emotions*. Oxford: Blackwell.
Scheff, T. 1990. *Micro Sociology, Discourse, Emotion and Social Structure*. Chicago: University of Chicago Press.
Scheff, T. 1997. *Emotions, the Social Bond, and Human Reality. Part/Whole Analysis*. Cambridge: Cambridge University Press.
Seale, C.F. 1995a. 'Dying Alone', *Sociology of Health and Illness*, 17(3): 376–92.
Seale, C.F. 1995b. 'Heroic Death', *Sociology*, 29 (4): 597–613.
Seale, C.F. 1998. *Constructing Death: The Sociology of Dying and Bereavement*. Cambridge: Cambridge University Press.
Silverman, D. 1996. *Discourses of Counselling: HIV Counselling as Social Interaction*. London: Sage.
Turner, B.S. 1992. *Regulating Bodies. Essays in Medical Sociology*. London: Routledge.

Walter, T. 1994. *The Revival of Death*. London: Routledge.
Williams, G.H. 1984. 'The Genesis of Chronic Illness: Narrative Reconstruction', *Sociology of Health and Illness*, 6: 175–200.
Williams, S. 1996. 'The Vicissitudes of Embodiment across the Chronic Illness Trajectory', *Body and Society*, 2 (2): 23–47.
Wrong, D.H. 1961. 'The Oversocialized Conception of Man in Modern Sociology', *American Sociological Review*, 26: 183–93.

7
The (Im)possibilities of Living as People with AIDS: Incorporating Death into Everyday Life

Brian Heaphy

Introduction

The body has become a primary focus for reflexively constructed narratives of the self in late modern worlds (Giddens 1991; Shilling 1993; Mellor and Shilling 1993). The stories we tell ourselves about 'who we are' are increasingly centred on a concern with our bodies. Because of this, encounters with illness and death can pose a significant threat to the self. This is compounded by the growing absence of collective meanings around death in secular societies (Mellor and Shilling 1993). In short, there are limited resources available to individuals in late modern societies for making sense of the (inevitable) demise of their own bodies. This has particular implications for those who are 'chronically' or 'terminally' ill (cf. Bury 1997). It also has implications for an increasing number of the outwardly 'healthy' who have been identified as being at risk of illness or death (cf. Beck 1992). Faced with serious illness – or with the risk of serious illness – many individuals have little choice but to attempt to incorporate an acute awareness of their own mortality into everyday life. In this chapter I employ an analysis of personal narratives of PWA (people living with AIDS and/or HIV) to explore key dilemmas encountered in such an endeavour. I also indicate the ways in which this is both a highly personal *and* political task.

The personal narratives referred to in this chapter are drawn from interviews with 28 men and eight women living with AIDS (AIDS and/or HIV). The interviews were undertaken in 1993 and 1994 for a study of the implications of AIDS for everyday living and changing selves (see note 1). Personal stories, Plummer (1995) suggests, live in the flow of power: 'The power to tell a story, indeed not to tell a story, under the conditions of one's own choosing is part of the political process' (Plummer 1995: 26). By researching these the aim is to understand the dynamics that shape the story and the consequences of telling a particular story under specific circumstances. As Heaphy, Donovan and Weeks (1998) put it:

> The research then becomes concerned with what can be said, why it is said now and not at other times, and the effects of telling a particular story in a particular way. This is what Plummer (1995) calls the 'pragmatic connection', by which stories can now be examined for the roles they play in lives, in contexts, in social order. Hence, the concern is with the role a certain kind of story plays in the life of a person or society. (Heaphy et al. 1998: 467)

Personal narratives of living with AIDS contain many stories that are explicitly about bodies. In this chapter, however, I focus on stories of 'testing', 'reskilling' and 'relating' where the concern with the body is often more implicit. These provide significant insights for the everyday politics that PWA engage in. Narratives of testing, reskilling and relating are structured by 'received wisdoms' that tie AIDS to death, and are underpinned by a concern with the decline of the body. They reveal a variety of impulses that encourage PWA to be silent and invisible as the possessors of problematic bodies. I argue that these impulses must be understood in terms of broader dynamics relating to the management of death in Western societies. Viewed from this perspective, the politics of living with AIDS cannot be separated from the politics of the body – and more particularly from the politics of dying.

Testing stories

Testing narratives concern the circumstances through which individuals come to test HIV positive, or are diagnosed as having AIDS-related illnesses. They represent a key moment in narratives of living with AIDS. Testing stories provide insights for the 'truths' about AIDS that individuals come to diagnosis with, and emphasize the extent to which diagnosis is marked by a sense of life being irretrievably altered. The experience of diagnosis is shaped by various factors, including: the circumstances and contexts which bring individuals to test; personal expectations of what testing will reveal; and prior knowledge and experience of AIDS (see also Adam and Sears 1996). These, in turn, are structured by individuals' perceptions of the extent to which they are 'at risk'.

A key factor in determining the impact of diagnosis is the extent to which individuals understand diagnosis to be consistent with their lifestyles or 'who they are'. In the accounts of non-drug-using heterosexual women, for example, there is much emphasis placed on the extent to which they had assumed AIDS to be related to illicit drug use, promiscuous sexual behaviour, and particularly homosexuality and male bisexuality (cf. Patton 1990, 1993; Boulton et al. 1991). Particular challenges are faced by these women in understanding how 'the impossible' could have happened, and in making sense of their new positioning in relation to discourses of risk and deviance (O'Sullivan and Thomson 1992; Adam and Sears 1996; Crawford, Lawless and Kippax 1997). Consider Diana's account:

> It was a shock, my God it was a shock. I was with my previous partner for ten years, right? I got rushed in with pneumonia in June and the nurse scratched her finger on the [needle], and asked me to have a test done, and I said 'Yeah, go for it'. I've never slept around, never used drugs, never put myself at risk. No hassle. Came back in two weeks and I was HIV. And I said 'No, you've made a mistake', and they said 'No, we haven't'. And that was it.

For women like Diana, an AIDS diagnosis can result in the crumbling of key certainties that were taken for granted. It can require considerable reflection on the nature of a partner's (hetero)sexuality, on the extent to which 'normal' sexual lives are risky, and on popular 'truths' about AIDS (cf. Boulton et al. 1991). It can also imply a significant rewriting of the personal narrative of 'who I am' – particularly as it problematizes the extent to which they can continue to see themselves as 'normal' women.

For gay men, in contrast, diagnosis can serve as confirmation of the dominant truths and realities about 'who gets AIDS'. Even amongst those who do not particularly expect a positive diagnosis, and who have introduced safer sex into their lives, diagnosis is likely to be greeted with a sense of being 'unfortunate' or 'unlucky' (cf. Lipp 1991). As Paul S.P. recounts:

> I didn't feel particularly exposed. But, I've always been a bit of a fatalist and thought, you know 'If it happens, it happens and that's that'. That isn't to say that really from about 1987 or so I no longer had unsafe sex, as it were. Excepting one or two occasions after that, and which one in particular may have been what infected me, I don't know.

Popular conceptions which link homosexuality with AIDS are reinforced by both popular and local gay community knowledges (Adam and Sears 1996: 1–2). Few gay men can feel confident that they are HIV negative (Adam and Sears 1996: 2). They are therefore likely to have given considerable thought to the possibilities and implications of a personal diagnosis. Also, as gay men are already positioned as deviant in some respects (cf. Sharrock 1997), the implications of diagnoses for disruption of biographical narratives would appear less extreme than they are for women. These factors can lessen the blow to 'the self' in some ways. They do not, however, *neutralize* the crisis effects of diagnosis. This is due to the perceived inevitabilities that are attached to AIDS. As Simon indicates, a key inevitability relates to its 'terrible' consequences:

> I think that was my biggest horror. What on earth am I going to do now? I'm going to go round, you know, telling people, this terrible thing and I'll be like the grim reaper? You know, and I don't want to be. I think that was the main thing.

For both men and women, a primary aspect of the crisis that AIDS represents is related to its perceived implications for the body. Diagnosis is understood to have 'inevitable' consequences for illness and *radically shortened life expectancy* (Carricaburu and Pierret 1995; Adam and Sears 1996). For both the ill and the asymptomatic, diagnosis introduces the *real* possibilities of death into life. These possibilities can become 'the background to everything else that happens' (Lipp 1991: 10). It is in these respects that diagnosis can be particularly disruptive at the level of self (Pollak, Paichler and Pierret 1992; Carricaburu and Pierret 1995; see also Bury 1982, 1997). An AIDS diagnosis introduces the inevitability of the demise of one's body into narratives of the self that tend to be built around an exclusion of questions of mortality (Mellor and Shilling 1993). The disruption that takes place relates to stable certainties that the individual has taken for granted. For some PWA, this can include the certainty of one's 'normality'; for the majority it includes the 'taken for grantedness' of the *ongoing* normality of everyday life.

Narratives of reskilling

In the literature on living with AIDS there is considerable concern with the 'coping' and 'survival' strategies that PWA develop. I would argue that a focus on PWA 'reskilling' is more appropriate (cf. Giddens 1991). The notion of reskilling can allow for a more *dynamic* sense of what is at stake in responding to an AIDS diagnosis (see Heaphy 1996 for a detailed account). It is a process through which individuals (and collectives) attempt to regain a sense of control in the face of crisis (Giddens 1991). For PWA it can involve seeking out (expert and local) resources for making sense of the implications for the body, and familiarizing oneself with the various courses of action that are possible. It can also entail negotiating questions related to the self and identity, including 'Who am I now?'; 'What can I become?'; 'What is it to be a PWA?' (Heaphy 1996).

The focus on reskilling conjures up a sense of active agents, and provides insights for the issues of power at stake in efforts to develop ways of living with AIDS. There are a multiplicity of (often competing) knowledges that can be employed in reskilling, including medical, alternative, therapeutic, and self-help knowledges. These have much to say to PWA about who they are now and what they are to become. They offer a diversity of ways of understanding the new situation and a range of possibilities for action. They provide empowering *and* limiting visions of the possibilities of living with AIDS (Heaphy 1999). In short, they can be conceptualized as resources that have critical implications for self-understandings and self-identities (cf. Giddens 1991). For the purposes of this chapter I focus on two key forms of expert resources that can be accessed by PWA in their reskilling endeavours: knowledge within the AIDS clinic, and counselling and therapy.

The clinic

Of the various resources that are available to PWA, relationships with medical practitioners are particularly important. The clinic is a primary source of knowledge on the virus and syndrome, and on the implications for the individual's body. Depending on the individual's state of health, and how long they are assumed to be infected, various trajectories are offered. These range from the 'optimistic' to the 'pessimistic'. Drug trials and medical intervention are often presented as holding out some hope (Anderson and Weatherburn 1998). But, in the end, the tendency is to be open about the extent to which there is no 'final' solution. In line with broader constructions that tie AIDS to illness and death (see Erni 1994), expert knowledge within the clinic confirms that what is ultimately at stake is the decline of the body:

> And we find the attitude of the medical staff, although medically they're trying to do their best, but I think they're really a pessimistic bunch. I mean I felt quite freaked. I mean, 'I said what's the prognosis,

> what's happening?' She said, 'Well, you're talking in terms of five years...' But, that seemed to be, she told me to make my will out. (Rose)

The clinic can also be the source of more 'common-sense' knowledge on how to approach *living* as a PWA. This often concerns the need for caution in disclosure, and the value of silence regarding one's HIV status. As Linford recounts:

> He told me not to worry about it, and if I need to discuss it, if I need to know anything about AIDS or the virus or whatever...he would like to discuss it with me...and he said the important thing is to tell the people you know who will accept the fact that you're HIV positive, but don't go and tell anyone you don't know, be very careful of who you tell and I said yeah...He said there were people out there who don't understand the virus.

This quotation highlights key information that can be imparted to PWA about their situation. In the first case, limited disclosure is offered as an 'appropriate' strategy for living with AIDS in everyday life. This is a theme that recurs throughout accounts of interactions with a variety of AIDS experts, where *silence* and *invisibility* are central survival strategies that are offered to PWA. Second, if the message is that people in everyday life 'don't understand the virus', it is also that the clinical practitioner has privileged access to the 'truth' of AIDS. This sanctions the clinic itself as the 'appropriate' space where individuals can learn and speak about their situation.

Knowledge within the clinic shores up the notion that AIDS is primarily medical: it is 'about' illness and death, and 'about' problematic bodies. AIDS is also presented to the PWA as being medical in that it is 'about' sexual health, and is a 'sexually transmitted disease' (see Patton 1985). While the clinic cannot provide *the* solution, it offers the vague possibility of a future solution, and in the meantime offers the promise of 'health management' through observing the individual's body over time. Efforts can be made to assist the individuals in managing their own bodies – particularly in terms of sexual and reproductive 'health'. This can involve incitements (and reminders) to live 'appropriate' sexual lives and to avoid particular sexual practices (Henderson 1991; Heaphy 1996). It can also involve making explicit expert concerns with the (moral) choices that PWA make with regard to their bodies (see Henderson 1991; Heaphy 1996). This is evident in June's account of informing her doctor of her pregnancy:

> She didn't like it. She ask me about a termination and I said, 'No, I want to keep the baby'. She didn't like it.

In the end, interactions within the clinic can provide PWA with an understanding of the various ways in which they are the possessors of problematic bodies: they are the possessors of 'incurable' bodies, but are also problematic as vectors of transmission. While the PWA is often informed that a lack of understanding in everyday worlds can make public existence dangerous – the individual is also reminded that he or she presents a danger to others as the agent of death.

Counselling and therapy

In the narratives of many PWA, a particularly valuable 'expertise' is provided by those who are concerned with the emotional and psychological aspects of reskilling – counsellors and therapists. Counselling and therapy are often identified as key resources that can 'make a difference' (Lipp 1991; for an argument *against* therapy in this context, see Adam and Sears 1996). As Paul W.N. puts it:

> I suppose it made me realize that I'm not dead yet. I've still got a life to live whether I've got a terminal disease or not... It's like – life is for living. I can't walk around, you know, sort of doing the drama queen bit. 'I'm dying!' – you know.

In reskilling narratives, the value of therapy is often framed in terms of the extent that it enables AIDS to be 'put in its place'. Therapy can encourage some PWA to challenge the notion that AIDS and the possibility of death should be the central focus of their lives. This potentially allows individuals to plan ahead 'as if' they were not faced with questions of illness and death, and to acquire a sense that AIDS is marginal to who they 'really' are:

> ...I think that once I'd sorted out other things in my life... once all that was sorted out, and I began to value myself, the HIV thing, I think, all fell into place. (Simon)

Therapy can assist in 'bracketing out' the immediacy of questions of illness and death. It can assist PWA to get on with their lives with a feeling that they have 'dealt with', or are dealing with, AIDS. For many PWA it plays a crucial part in reintroducing the possibility of survival and 'going on' (Lipp 1991; see also Sherr 1996). For some it also provides a more dynamic sense of the possibilities of 'living'. Yet, in doing this, therapy reinforces the assumed *impossibility* of incorporating an acute awareness of death *into* everyday living. As such it can only ever offer PWA a temporary solution. This is evident in Georgina's account, where it is clear that therapy cannot erase the problems associated with AIDS:

> I had a real crisis in my third year... I'd had enough. I thought, 'Well, I've done that now. I've done living with HIV now and haven't I coped well.' And it's like 'I don't want to do it any more...' [Laughs]. And at that point I went up to twice a week [in therapy] because I just couldn't... didn't know whether I was going to be able to hold on to my life and I felt very depressed and I felt quite suicidal as well, actually.

AIDS can be conceptualized as an *ongoing* set of crisis moments: there can be no final 'solution' or 'resolution' to the problem of living as a PWA. As Lipp (1991: 10) notes, part of the experience of living with AIDS can be of 'constantly waiting for something to happen' (see also Pollak et al. 1992; Carricaburu and Pierret 1995). Once its inevitability has been sharply introduced, the reality of death cannot simply be bracketed out by the individual. While this may be successful as a very temporary strategy, the fragile nature of the body is always waiting to return. Hence, as Georgina indicates, living as if the 'real' or 'certain' possibility of death had not been introduced into life cannot be wholly effective.

Therapy can offer a sense that there is a life – a future – to be lived through assisting the PWA to put the question of death aside. But therapy also fails the PWA in this regard: it has limited value as a resource for imagining the possibilities of more fully incorporating an acute awareness of death *into* life. It is not an empowering vision of living *as* a PWA that is on offer, but the temporary possibility of living as if the individual was not. In a manner that is consistent with the advice provided within the clinic, it offers a strategy for living that encourages 'denying' the reality of one's position.

Narratives of relating

Relationships sustain and enable particular ways of understanding one's situation as a PWA. They have much to say to the PWA about 'what' she or he is, and provide a sense of how it is possible to be in everyday life. While family and friendship relationships can offer crucial resources in the form of love, care and support (see Callen 1990: 75–6), there are various impulses that encourage silence within these. Fear of rejection is a most obvious one, and is well founded for some (Cameron 1993; Adam and Sears 1996). As Alan recounts:

> They were bad, they were just bad about it... And they were just absolute bastards, and that affected me a lot. The way they handled me was so bad, and I never realized my family was so prejudiced, really prejudiced.

Many PWA, however, have stories of acceptance to tell – particularly those who have negotiated strong relationships over time with biological family, families of choice (cf. Weeks, Donovan and Heaphy 1998) and friends (Heaphy, Weeks and Donovan 1999a). But in the most accepting of networks, disclosure about the various dilemmas and challenges that PWA face in day-to-day living can be limited. As Diana recounts:

> You wear these masks don't you? They [relatives] say to me 'How do you sleep at night?' and I say 'I knock myself out with sleeping pills'. But there are times when I do go to bed and rock myself to sleep. But that's only because I'm there on my own and nobody sees me. Then I get up in the morning, here I am again – singing. And people get upset, and I say 'Don't get upset. If I can cope with it, you cope with it – you know. I can't carry everybody at the same time'. But I do, yeah. I'd like to be more open about it. But there again, how can you be more open about it with your family?

In their accounts of relating, PWA suggest a variety of reasons for silence in day-to-day living. These include the desire to protect oneself from negative reactions, the desire to protect loved one's from the 'tragedy' (cf. Hays, Magee and Chauncey 1994), and the immediate and ongoing emotional labour that disclosing can necessitate (see also McCann and Wadsworth 1992). Narratives of relating also suggest that AIDS can introduce an 'uneasiness' into accepting relationships. This is most obvious when friends or significant others discontinue contact over time. It is also evident where PWA and their significant others do not know how to 'get it right' in their interactions. Various tensions can exist: between overestimating and underestimating the 'burdens' that are being carried; between caring for and patronizing each other; between being supportive and being invasive; between reciprocity and dependence (see Hays et al. 1994). These tensions can concern not knowing 'what to do' and 'what to say'. They suggest that many PWA and their significant others do not have easy access to an appropriate 'way of being' in the face of the personal 'tragedy' of AIDS. They are also consistent with the situation that 'the dying' and their loved one's face in their encounters (Elias 1985).

Sexual relationships

Narratives of disclosure within sexual relationships are especially revealing of a diversity of dynamics at play that can *limit choice* with regard to disclosure, and present disincentives to existing openly as PWA. These represent important limitations for envisaging possible ways of being *as* PWA. It has been noted that there are particularly powerful incentives for heterosexual women not to disclose in sexual relationships. HIV positive women are faced with the task of renegotiating and transforming some of the meanings of heterosexual encounters in their efforts at negotiating safer sex (Crawford et al. 1997).

Crawford et al. (1997: 7) argue that because women cannot rely on men to share their understandings (see also Jackson 1996; Holland et al. 1998) tensions can arise between disclosing HIV status to enable safer sex (and to face rejection and violence); to insist on condom use (which may appear 'insulting' and result in violence); or to engage in unprotected sex. There can also be material consequences of disclosure for those women who are dependent on male partners (Wilton and Aggleton 1991). For some women, like June, a further risk is that disclosure potentially blocks off the possibility of intimacy:

> After you tell them about diagnosis they find it difficult to relax. If you tell them, they always have that in mind.

It has been suggested that the position of gay men in relation to disclosure within sexual relationships is significantly different from that of heterosexual women (Crawford et al. 1997: 1). AIDS has been a collective crisis for gay communities (Heaphy et al. 1999a), and has facilitated a collective reinvention of sexual lives based on the ethic of safer sex (cf. King 1993; Patton 1993; Weeks 1995). Also, as same-sex relationships tend to be marked by reciprocity, negotiation and a lack of 'appropriate' roles, there would appear to be considerable potential for PWA to work out 'ways of being' in these (cf. Blasius 1994; Heaphy et al. 1999b).

Viewed in this light, disclosure within sexual relationships would appear to be a relatively unproblematic issue for gay PWA. But the narratives of gay PWA would suggest that the situation is more complex than this. On the one hand, these narratives indicate that the ethic of safer sex does offer significant opportunities for living sexual lives. On the other hand, they also indicate strong impulses towards 'passing' within sexual encounters.

In terms of casual sexual relationships, the dominant narrative amongst gay PWA is one of non-disclosure. Disclosure becomes an issue in ongoing relationships. Reasons for not disclosing include: the barrier that can be created to physical intimacy (the risk that it will 'be a turn-off'); the pressures to become over-intimate (that it will necessitate conversations that are inappropriate for the stage of the relationship); and the risk of rejection (based on fear of transmission). As Nigel indicates, non-disclosure may be a 'rational' course of action to take:

> I mean, I've heard people, even when it comes down to kissing, worrying about whether they can catch it. And I feel like, I feel bad doing that with them. Even though that's a thing they should face up to themselves.

Even if disclosure does not lead to obvious rejection, many PWA remark on the pressures that HIV negative men experience, who may initially feel that they have to 'pretend to be OK'. In their ongoing interactions, however, some HIV negative partners can confirm the problematic nature of the PWA. As Simon recounts:

> ...we were talking about stuff and then he said 'I've been thinking anyway,' he said 'It doesn't really make any difference about', you know, 'you being positive'. And I said 'Well, why should it?'... He said 'No, I was thinking – at least you won't go with anybody else.'... And I thought 'Oh, God! Is that all [you think] of me?' But, you know, 'At least you won't go off with anyone'.

For some gay men living with AIDS, a way around the dilemmas outlined above has been to limit their sexual relationships to others living with AIDS (see also Adam and Sears 1996: 78). While this may be an effective strategy for some, as a form of *self-segregation* it must be understood to be a strategy developed in light of the extent to which relationships with HIV negative gay men are sometimes seen as 'too risky'. The risks can relate to infection and rejection, but also that reactions to disclosure will reveal much to the PWA about how they are perceived. As Enright (1996) has suggested: 'For most of us who are positive, HIV becomes something we try to live with; for most negative guys, it's something we will die from' (Enright 1996: 40).

I have detailed elsewhere how gay community 'norms' of safer sex have (inadvertently) allowed for the construction of gay men living with AIDS as *failed* community members (Heaphy 1999; see also Ward and Jones 1996: 6). As 'the infected' they are revealed as having failed at safer sex (Ward and Jones 1996; see also Rooney and Taylor 1997). As such, it has been implied that they represent a danger 'from within' to gay communities. In light of this, it is not so surprising that the narratives of gay PWA indicate that the predominant tendency within sexual relationships is, in the first instance, towards silence. As Rooney and Taylor (1997) note with regard to their study of gay PWA:

> The evidence from this study is that negative or untested [gay/bisexual] men can be, hostile, rejecting and even violent to men who disclose as HIV positive. (Rooney and Taylor 1997: 61–2)

While gay community knowledge has enabled some new possibilities for relating in the age of AIDS, it does not provide gay PWA with the resources necessary for relating *as* those who are living with AIDS. While there are different dynamics at play, the challenges facing gay men living with AIDS are, in significant respects, similar to those facing women with AIDS: to imagine 'new' ways of relating that can incorporate the 'realities' of their lives. In terms of the broad spectrum of relationships that PWA have, the challenge is to imagine and negotiate ways of living that can allow for and incorporate the 'realities' of AIDS and death. For PWA this implies resisting 'social death' in the face of powerful incentives and impulses to silence and invisibility.

The politics of living with AIDS

Narratives of testing, reskilling and relating provide a sense of the dynamics that inform the 'possibilities' and 'impossibilities' of living as PWA. Testing stories are accounts of crisis moments that are disruptive at the level of self. Reskilling narratives provide insights for the existence of resources that can be employed in responding to this crisis. But they also indicate the ways that key 'expert' resources can encourage particular (in Foucauldian terms disciplinary) self-understandings which encourage silence and invisibility. From narratives of relating it is also clear that the various consequences of disclosure can provide incentives for the *social death* of 'the PWA' (silence and invisibility *as* those living with AIDS) in everyday living. In interactions with various experts, and within intimate relationships, those living with AIDS are widely encouraged to live *as if they were not*. In the remainder of this chapter I argue that these incentives must be understood from the perspective of operations of power as they relate to the management of the problematic body in modern societies. This reveals that politics of living with AIDS cannot be separated from the politics of body – and more particularly from the politics of dying.

To attempt to imagine the possibilities of living with AIDS is to encounter key problems relating to living and dying in late modern worlds. PWA are among the increasing numbers of 'the dying' that have been identified in the endeavour to conquer the causes of death (cf. Bauman 1992: 137–42). Medical technologies have, however, allowed for the identification of a 'problem' to which they have yet to provide any final solutions. In such circumstances many PWA may have little choice but to attempt to become 'expert' in their own illnesses to varying degrees (cf. Beck 1992). But, as a central dilemma faced in living with AIDS is to imagine the possibilities of constructing a life with an acute awareness of death, they also have no choice but to contemplate (and attempt to become 'expert' in) the meaning of death. As Georgina recounts:

> [It's brought up questions] like 'What's the meaning of all of this?' Yes, quite a lot. And sometimes I wish that I was able to find some kind of spiritual meaning because it becomes hard when you don't.

Death and the demise of the body are ultimately *the* issues at stake in living with AIDS. They are also key issues at stake in the *politics* of living with AIDS. Theorists of power and AIDS highlighted the importance of understanding AIDS as a historicised phenomenon (see Weeks 1990, 1993). They have also drawn our attention to the extent to which the histories of the regulation of sexuality (and gender and race) can tell us much about the politics of AIDS (Patton 1990; Weeks 1990; Blasius 1994). These histories can, it is widely suggested, explain 'the burdens' (of stigma) that PWA must face in living their everyday lives. While this position has shaped much of the thinking on politics and power in the realm of AIDS, in bracketing out the question of death it has also blocked off a fuller understanding of operations of power in this realm. To understand these we must also consider the implications of recent histories of the management and control of 'the dying' in the West.

The experience of death has become increasingly individualized in Western worlds (cf. Elias 1985). As Mellor and Shilling (1993) suggest, an ever-increasing reduction in 'the scope of the sacred', also has profound implications for the lack of public legitimations of the reality of the social world in the face of death (Mellor and Shilling 1993: 413; cf. Berger 1990). Coupled with the emphasis that is increasingly placed on the body as a focus for self-meaning and self-worth (Giddens 1991; Mellor and Shilling 1993), these dynamics can make death particularly disturbing for those who encounter it at close hand. This can explain the crises that individuals experience in facing the decline of their own bodies (Mellor and Shilling 1993: 414). It can also explain the reluctance, as described by Elias (1985), of the living to come into contact with the dying.

Elias (1985: 68–91) points out that death is a problem in encounters between the living and those broadly perceived to be on the path to death, including 'the aged'. In their interactions with each other, both 'the living' *and* 'the dying' have difficulty in knowing how to behave towards each other. As both have limited resources for managing the situation, the search for an appropriate way of being in this situation 'falls back on the individual' (Elias 1985: 26). This can shed light on some of the 'uneasy' interactions between PWA and those they encounter. It can also provide insights into the relationship between what has been termed 'the sequestration of death' (see Giddens) and silencing and invisibilising impulses that encourage the *social death* of PWA (silence and invisibility *as* those living with AIDS).

The sequestration of death refers to the processes through which the problem of dying is hidden from view to protect our socially constructed realities (Shilling 1993; cf. Berger 1990). This does not mean that we do not constantly 'talk' or represent death (see Armstrong 1987; Shilling 1993:188–92). What is at stake are the places deemed appropriate for the dying to exist in, and the question of *who* is the appropriate speaker on death. In normal everyday lives individuals do not expect (or desire) to have everyday 'normal' interaction with those perceived to be on the path to death (Elias 1985). As Shilling (1993) notes in a discussion of the dynamics at stake:

> Unable to confront the reality of the demise and death of their own bodies, the self-identities of individuals are often made insecure by the presence of death in other people's bodies... While

> the *discussion* of death occupies a form of public space... hospitals can be seen as the institutional expression of the modern desire to sequester *bodily* evidence of sickness and death away from the public gaze. (Shilling 1993: 190; original emphasis)

The sequestration of death also refers to the processes through which the dying are allocated appropriate places to speak (the clinic, and therapists' consultation rooms), and who it is who has the authority to represent – or tell the story of – the 'realities' of the dying, and to speak on their behalf. As Bauman suggests: 'it has been put in custody of selected specialists boasting scientific credentials' (Bauman 1992: 152; and quoted in Shilling 1993: 189). In the end, both the *inappropriate existence* and the *inappropriate voices* of the dying are experienced as highly problematic by 'the living'. The introduction of these into everyday life is threatening to the sense of reality – of 'the way it is' – that the living operate with. The tendency is therefore to attempt to keep them at bay.

As those who are popularly understood, and understand themselves, to be on an *inevitable path to death* (cf. Erni 1994), the dilemmas and challenges of PWA can include those facing the dying. Viewed from this perspective, many of the dilemmas outlined in narratives of sensitising, reskilling, and relating can be understood to be beyond questions to do with 'the politics of stigma' as they are usually framed in analyses of AIDS. Put another way, it is not *only* constructions of PWA as deviant in relation to sexual (and drug) practices and identities that are at stake.

As with 'the dying' the presence of the PWA in the everyday life can be experienced as highly problematic by others: through audibly and visibly existing they bring home the (always hovering) existence of death to others. For both PWA, and those they encounter, this can facilitate a return for 'the trained emotion of shame, that makes us numb when we meet death face to face' (Bauman 1992: 129). At its most extreme these encounters can cause a very real sense of panic and crisis (most evident in negative and violent reactions to disclosure). Encounters with PWA bring home the realization that 'that could be me'. This can be compounded by a general awareness of the transmissible nature of HIV (that get translated into beliefs about its 'contagious' nature) that accentuate just how *easily* 'that could be me'. This brings up an important point about the implications of the ways in which AIDS has been constructed as being about both sex *and* death. If the body becomes increasingly central to the project of the self in late modern worlds, sexuality has also become 'a focus for considerable personal emotional investment' (Mellor and Shilling 1993: 422). The tie between sex and death is potentially deeply disturbing. As Mellor and Shilling note:

> AIDS tells people not only that the meaning they have invested in their sexual relationships cannot protect them from the reality of death, but that the very focus of their investment can be the channel through which death now enters their life. (Mellor and Shilling 1993: 423)

As those who carry death in their bodies, individuals living openly with AIDS run the risk that they can facilitate a 'crisis' for others. This is particularly the case in sexual encounters where 'death' can be transmitted with ease and pleasure. It is from this perspective that we can understand the broad impulses that can work to keep PWA silent and invisible in everyday interactions – everyday life is not deemed an appropriate or desirable place for the problem of death. It is also from this viewpoint that we can make sense of the ways in which the endeavour to live with AIDS is at once a highly personal *and* political challenge. To do so is to challenge a particularly powerful story in modern worlds: that the operation of everyday life requires that the 'reality' of death – and the presence and voices of the dying – *must* be held at bay.

Conclusion: crisis and opportunity

The personal narratives of PWA indicate that close encounters with AIDS can facilitate crises. These are related to – and accentuate – the lack of resources available for incorporating the inevitability of death into everyday life. But while living with AIDS is 'about' crisis in many respects, it also offers an opportunity: to challenge received wisdoms relating to the 'impossibility' of incorporating death into life. As Elias (1985: 42–5) indicates, this is not an *essentially* impossible task (as is implied by Giddens 1991: 49). It is, however, an enormously difficult one in societies where we are increasingly deprived of meanings for making sense of the deterioration of our bodies. This is compounded by silencing and invisibilizing impulses at play that encourage us to keep the problem of death at bay. The ultimate effect is that the search for meaning in the face of death falls back onto the individual. This is problematic because 'the construction of meaning around death is an essentially social, communal phenomenon' (Mellor and Shilling 1993: 423).

Two political tasks arise for those individuals who, like many PWA, are concerned with developing new ways of living *with* death: to resist the broad impulses that can encourage the social death of 'the dying' (silence and invisibility *as* the dying), and to generate resources for developing a sense of *how* it might be possible to do 'the impossible'. Resisting social death through speaking and visibly existing is a precondition for the formation of radically new ways of existing (cf. Blasius 1994). In doing so individuals facilitate crises for hegemonic notions of 'how it is' or 'how it can be'. As Bourdieu (1977) indicates, such crises can act as developers for 'stimulating knowledge and sites from which to speak' (Mort 1994: 201). As such, resisting social death is also a precondition for the development of resources that are necessary for transforming visions of how it is possible to live (cf. Bourdieu 1977: 168–9).

What are the implications for the resources that might be employed in negotiating the possibilities of living *as* PWA? In the first case, developing new ways of living requires a critical interrogation of knowledge formations that play a hegemonic role in shoring up the 'naturalness' of established forms of existence. In the realm of AIDS, this implies critically evaluating the role of medical and therapeutic knowledges as *the* appropriate resources for living with AIDS. These tell us 'how it is' and 'how we can be' in the face of death. In doing so they suggest that dying is an unpolitical process.

Second, in challenging this sanctioned expertise, and the incitements produced to silence and invisibility, PWA can become actively involved in creating resources – particularly in the form of personal narratives. From Plummer's (1995) work it is clear that personal stories (as they are spoken *and* performed) have a powerful role to play in the kind of culture-building that making 'new' lives requires. Stories, he argues, gather people around them and attract audiences who themselves become story-tellers. In telling their tales PWA are generating resources for making sense of living *and* dying. In listening to these we can understand that dying is more than personal 'tragedy' – it is an endeavour that is deeply intertwined the politics of body.

Note

1. There have been notable medical developments in realm of AIDS since these interviews were undertaken. Put briefly, 'combination drug therapies' have

been heralded as major developments in the treatment of AIDS. These do not provide a medical solution to AIDS, but do appear to offer significant possibilities in terms of longer periods of survival. While the value of these therapies are debated (and contested), they have given some new hope to many PWA. It is likely, therefore, that the present-day stories told by PWA would differ in some ways from those told in 1993–94. While I would not want to claim that the analysis offered here could be provided of the stories that PWA might presently tell, I would argue that the issues highlighted are still very much of relevance to the current situation of PWA (see Heaphy 1999).

References

Adam, B.D. and Sears, A. 1996. *Experiencing HIV: Personal, Family and Work Relationships*. New York: Columbia University Press.

Anderson, W. and Weatherburn, P. 1998. *The Impact of Combination Therapy on The Lives of People with HIV*. London: Sigma Research.

Armstrong, D. 1987. 'Silence and Truth in Death and Dying', *Social Science and Medicine*, 24(8): 651–7.

Bauman, Z. 1992. *Mortality, Immortality and Other Life Strategies*. Cambridge: Polity.

Beck, U. 1992. *Risk Society: Towards a New Modernity*. London: Sage.

Berger, P. 1990. *The Sacred Canopy: Elements of a Sociological Theory of Religion*. New York: Anchor Books.

Blasius, M. 1994. *Gay and Lesbian Politics: Sexuality and the Emergence of a New Ethic*. Philadelphia: Temple University Press.

Boulton, M., Schramm Evans, Z., Fitzpatrick, R. and Hart, G. 1991. 'Bisexual Men: Women, Safer Sex and HIV Transmission', in P. Aggleton, G. Hart and P. Davies (eds) *AIDS: Responses, Interventions and Care*. London: Falmer Press.

Bourdieu, P. 1977. *Outline of a Theory of Practice*. Cambridge: Cambridge University Press.

Bury, M. 1982. 'Chronic Illness as Biographical Disruption', *Sociology of Health and Illness*, 8(2): 137–69.

Bury, M. 1997. *Health and Illness in a Changing Society*. London: Routledge.

Callen, M. 1990. *Surviving AIDS*. New York: Harper Collins.

Cameron, M. 1993. *Living With AIDS*. Newbury Park, CA: Sage.

Carricaburu, D. and Pierret, J. 1995. 'From Biological Disruption to Biographical Reinforcement: The Case of HIV-positive Men', *Sociology of Health and Illness*, 17 (1): 65–88.

Crawford, J., Lawless, S. and Kippax, S. 1997. 'Positive Women and Heterosexuality: Problems of Disclosure of Seropositive Status to Sexual Partners', in P. Aggleton, P. Davies and G. Hart (eds) *AIDS: Activism and Alliances*. London: Taylor and Francis.

Dollimore, J. 1998. *Death, Desire and Loss in Western Culture*. London: Penguin.

Elias, N. 1985. *The Loneliness of Dying*. Oxford: Blackwell.

Enright, S. 1996. 'Acting Positively on Sex', in Health First (eds) *A Report from a Conference about Sex and HIV Positive Gay men and Bisexual Men*. London: Health First.

Erni, J.N. 1994. *Technomedicine and the Cultural Politics of 'Curing' AIDS*. Minneapolis and London: University of Minnesota Press.

Giddens, A. 1991. *Modernity and Self-Identity*. Oxford: Polity Press.

Hays, R.B., Magee, R.H. and Chauncey, S. 1994. 'Identifying Helpful and Unhelpful Behaviours of Loved Ones: The PWA's Perspective', *AIDS Care*, 6(4): 379–92.

Heaphy, B. 1998. 'Silence and Strategy: Researching AIDS Narratives in the Flow of Power', in R. Barbour and G. Huby (eds) *Meddling with Mythology: AIDS and the Social Construction of Knowledge*. London: Routledge.

Heaphy, B. 1996. 'Medicalisation and Identity Formation: Identity and Strategy in the Context of AIDS and HIV', in J. Weeks and J. Holland (eds) *Sexual Cultures: Communities, Values and Intimacy*. London: Macmillan.

Heaphy, B. 1999. 'Reinventing the Self: Identity, Agency and AIDS'. Unpublished PhD thesis. University of the West of England, Bristol.

Heaphy, B., Donovan, C. and Weeks, J. 1998. '"That's Like my Life": Researching Stories of Non-heterosexual Relationships', *Sexualities*, 1(4): 453–70.

Heaphy, B., Weeks, J. and Donovan, C. 1999a. 'Narratives of Love, Care and Commitment: AIDS and Non-heterosexual Family Formations', in P. Aggleton, G. Hart and P. Davies (eds) *AIDS: Family, Culture and Community*. London: Taylor and Francis.

Heaphy, B., Donovan, C. and Weeks, J. 1999b. 'Sex, Money and the Kitchen Sink: Power in Same-sex Couple Relationships', in J. Seymour and P. Bagguley (eds) *Relating Intimacies: Power and Resistance*. London: Macmillan.

Henderson, S. 1991. 'Care: What's in it for Her?', in P. Aggleton, G. Hart and P. Davies (eds) *AIDS: Responses, Interventions and Care*. London: Falmer Press.

Holland, J., Ramazanoglu, C., Scott, S., Sharpe, S. and Thomson, R. 1998. *The Male in the Head: Young People, Heterosexuality and Power*. London: Tufnell Press.

Jackson, S. 1996. 'Heterosexuality as Problem for Feminist Theory', in L. Adkins and V. Merchant (eds) *Sexualizing the Social: Power and the Organization of Sexuality*. London: Macmillan.

Keogh, P., Beardsell, S., and Sigma Research. 1997. 'Sexual Negotiation Strategies of HIV-Positive Gay Men: A Qualitative Approach', in P. Aggleton, P. Davies and G. Hart (eds) *AIDS: Activism and Alliances*. London: Taylor and Francis.

King, E. 1993. *Safety in Numbers*. London: Cassell.

Lipp, J. 1991. 'Living with HIV and AIDS', *Dulwich Centre Newsletter*, 2: 5–16.

McCann, K. and Wadsworth, E. 1992. 'The Role of Informed Carers in Supporting Gay Men with HIV-related Illness: What Do They Do and What Are Their Needs?', *AIDS Care*, 4 (1): 25–34.

Mellor, P.A. and Shilling, C. 1993. 'Modernity, Self-Identity and The Sequestration of Death', *Sociology*, 27(3): 411–31.

O'Sullivan, S. and Thomson, K. (eds) 1992. *Positively Women: Living with AIDS*. London: Sheba Feminist Press.

Patton, C. 1985. *Sex and Germs: The politics of AIDS*. Boston, MA: South End Press.

Patton, C. 1990. *Inventing AIDS*. London: Routledge.

Patton, C. 1993. 'With Champagne and Roses', in C. Squire (ed.) *Women and AIDS: Psychological Perspectives*. London: Sage.

Plummer, K. 1995. *Telling Sexual Stories: Power, Change and Social Worlds*. London: Routledge.

Pollack, M., Paichler, G. and Pierret, J. 1992. *AIDS: A Problem for Sociological Research*. London: Sage.

Rooney, M. and Taylor, S. 1997. *Sexual Health Promotion Needs of HIV Positive Gay Men*. London: Health First.

Sharrock, C. 1997. 'Pathologizing Sexual Bodies', in A. Medhurst and S. Munt (eds) *Lesbian and Gay Studies: A Critical Introduction*. London: Cassell.

Sherr, L. 1996. 'Tomorrow's Era: Gender, Psychology and HIV Infection', in L. Sherr, C. Hankins and L. Bennett (eds) *AIDS as a Gender Issue: Psychosocial Perspectives*. London: Taylor and Francis.

Shilling, C. 1993. *The Body and Social Theory*. London: Sage.

Ward, P. and Jones, J. 1996. 'The Phase That Dare Not Speak Its Name', in Health First (eds) *A Report From a Conference About Sex and HIV Positive Gay men and Bisexual Men*. London: Health First.

Weeks, J. 1990. 'Post-modern AIDS?', in T. Boffin and S. Gupta (eds) *Ecstatic Antibodies: Resisting AIDS mythology*. London: Rivers Oram Press.

Weeks, J. 1993. 'AIDS and the Regulation of Sexuality', in V. Berridge and P. Strong (eds) *AIDS and Contemporary History*. Cambridge: Cambridge University Press.

Weeks, J. 1995. *Invented Moralities: Sexual Values in an Age of Uncertainty*. Cambridge: Polity Press.

Weeks, J., Donovan, C. and Heaphy B. (1998) 'Everyday Experiments: Narratives of Non-Heterosexual Relationships', in E. Silva and C. Smart (eds) *The 'New' Family?* London: Sage.

Wilton, T. and Aggleton, P. 1991. 'Condoms, Coercion and Control: Heterosexuality and the limits to HIV/AIDS Education', in P. Aggleton, G. Hart, and P. Davies (eds) *AIDS: Responses, Interventions and Care*. London: Falmer Press.

8

Dormant Issues? Towards a Sociology of Sleep[1]

Simon J. Williams

> *The bed, you must remember, is the symbol of life ... There is nothing good except the bed, and are not some of our best moments spent in sleep?*
>
> (Guy de Maupassant, n.d.: 682)

> *The sleeper is never completely isolated within himself* [sic], *never totally a sleeper...never totally cut off from the intersubjective world... Sleep and waking, illness and health are not modalities of consciousness or will, but presuppose an 'existential step'.*
>
> (Merleau-Ponty 1962: 162)

> *The notion that going to sleep is something natural is totally inaccurate.*
>
> (Mauss 1973: 80)

Introduction

It is by now a well-rehearsed argument that, until quite recently, sociology has been almost exclusively concerned with matters of life rather than death. As the cessation of life itself, death was seen as at best peripheral and at worst irrelevant to the sociological enterprise. Yet death now, sociologically speaking, is 'big business', spanning a diversity of corporeal themes and socio-cultural issues from the existential dilemmas of the reflexive self (Mellor and Shilling 1993) to the 'public invigilation of private grief' (Walter et al. 1995), and from the 'sequestration of experience' (Giddens 1991) to the postmodern deconstruction of 'immortality' itself (Bauman 1992).

Given this reversal in the sociological fortunes of death – a trend that reflects and reinforces the broader 'revival' of death in Western culture (Walter 1995) – it is all the more remarkable that a similar transformation has not occurred in relation to another crucial, albeit neglected, aspect of our embodiment – one that consumes approximately a third of our total lives. I am, of course, talking about sleep. Like death, sleep is a central aspect of social life, yet its sociological import, by and large, has been neglected as a central topic of investigation. Even the most cursory scan of the literature reveals a dearth of work on the sociological consequences and significance of sleep. Instead, the field is dominated by medical and psychological research on the problems and sequelae of sleep disturbance, and psychoanalytic and phenomenological literature on the process and meaning of dreams and dreaming. Literature too abounds with references to sleep and dreaming, from Shakespeare to Montaigne, Shelley to de la Mare, Milton to Cervantes, yet its sociological significance has yet to be recognized.[2]

Reasons for this sociological neglect are manifold, but three in particular warrant further discussion. First and foremost, we have the general argument that sociology, as the study of society and the geometry of social forms, is primarily concerned with waking rather than sleeping life. To investigate the latter, according to this line of reasoning, is at best a marginal and at worst a futile sociological exercise. At first glance this seems a reasonable enough assertion. Sleep, after all, is a highly personal, privatized experience in contemporary Western society; a liminal, unconscious, aspect of bodily being and an 'asocial', 'inactive' form of corporeal 'activity'. Even on its own terms of reference, however, a moment's thought reveals the limitations of this position as sociologically untenable.

Sleep is fundamental to any given society or group (i.e. a 'functional' prerequisite), permeating its institutions as well as its embodied agents, its beliefs as well as its practices, its rituals as well as its mythologies, its spatio-temporal arrangements as well as its discursive and culturally constituted boundaries. The fact that sleep, as a temporal, embodied state, is 'lived through' and presupposes an 'existential step' (cf. Merleau-Ponty above) further underlines it sociological relevance. Even if sleep itself, as Taylor (1993: 464) comments, is not an entirely social practice, the language within which it is discussed and the cultural constraints on its meanings, motives and methods are indeed genuine sociological concerns.

A second possible reason for this neglect is that the study of sleep is best suited to the disciplines of biology, psychology or, in the case of dreams and dreaming, psychoanalysis. Certainly, as discussed below, sleep involves a biological process of replenishment, rejuvenation and repair. Psychoanalytic perspectives on dreams and dreaming – what Freud saw as the 'royal road to the unconscious' – appear equally entrenched features, for better or worse, of Western culture and contemporary society (see, for example, Freud 1976 [1953]; Murray 1965). Seen in this light, the 'what' and 'why' questions of sleep and dreaming, as unconscious mental and physical processes, are perhaps best left to such disciplines. This does not, however, as Taylor (1993) rightly argues, rule out the possibility of other more interesting sociological questions to do with the *'how'*, *'when'* and *'where'* of sleep – i.e. its connection with the broader socio-cultural and historical order, including disciplinary technologies and strategic configurations of power/ knowledge – from being posed. In this respect, the key sociological problematic becomes one focused on the *'doing'* of sleep rather than 'being asleep' (ibid.: 464).

Dreams themselves, however, become sociologically significant, not simply in terms of the archetypal imagery and symbolic associations that ritualistically unite and divide us – cf. Durkheim's notion of 'collective effervescence' in *Elementary Forms of Religious Life* (1961 [1912]) – but also through the (proto-)professionalization of our innermost thoughts and desires in the (post-)therapeutic climate and narcissistic culture of our times – what Rose (1989) appositely refers to as 'governing the soul'. In this case, the sociological focus is more upon the *use* of dreams and dreaming, both individually and collectively, socially and culturally, politically and therapeutically, than the psychological process as such. These issues, in turn, relate to the more general problem of human embodiment in social theory today, including a critical reconsideration of seemingly ossified conceptual forms such as mind and body, biology and culture, reason and emotion, conscious and unconscious, human and machine. Previously banished to the margins of sociological thought and practice, the 'mindful' (Scheper-Hughes and Lock 1987), emotionally 'expressive' (Freund 1990) body now occupies centre-stage, as traditional sociological questions are translated into a new, more corporeal frame of reference; one which, hitherto, has not properly incorporated the social significance of sleep, dreams and dreaming (Williams and Bendelow 1998).

Closely connected to these first two points, a third possible reason for this neglect concerns the problem of 'sociological imperialism': a professionalizing process in which sociologists seek to extend their empire still further, arrogating power and transgressing disciplinary boundaries under the all encompassing banner of 'the social'. Perhaps the most recent expression of these concerns – concerns frequently voiced in relation to sociology's alleged 'assault' on the medical citadel (Strong 1979) – relates to the newly evolving sociology of emotions. Sociological commentary on the emotions, according to Craib (1995), displays the same sensitivity and understanding as psychoanalytic discussion of society (i.e. none at all); a problem compounded, he maintains, when the having of *something* important to say is confused with having *everything* to say.

These, to be sure, are important points. Yet in no way do they preclude the possibility of a sociology of sleep from flourishing. Like emotions, sleep is a multi-faceted phenomenon. A proper grasp of this most complex of topics, therefore, demands just such an interdisciplinary effort: to claim otherwise, quite simply, is disciplinary hubris. Seen in this light, territorial battles and disciplinary border skirmishes merely serve to distract us still further from the real (sociological) task in hand. Whilst, as we shall see below, the sociological aspect of sleep has not totally escaped the notice of its embodied practitioners, there may certainly be advantages in bringing these scattered insights together in a new, more integrated way. Indeed, whilst possible objections of the kind mentioned above may doubtless be raised, it would be hard to find a sociologist who did not see sleep as a socially significant topic, worthy of further investigation and debate.

It is within this context and against this theoretical backdrop that the rationale for this chapter emerges. Sleep, I shall argue, is a prime example of the 'socially pliable' body, one which displays a high degree of malleability in relation to changing socio-cultural and historical forms. More generally, sleep constitutes a central social resource, linked as it is to issues of time and space, agency and identity, and providing, in the process, a key sociological indicator of societal development, from incest taboos to the 'civilizing of bodies', and from power relations to the institutionalized division of labour and the rationalization of work and leisure in late capitalist societies (Aubert and White 1959a and b). Key questions here include the following: What is the sociological significance of sleep and how should it be studied? What light can a sociology of sleep shed on mind/body, biology/society, structure/agency divides? How are we to conceive of temporality, spatiality and intentionality in this context? To what extent can the sociological study of sleep furnish us with new insights into more macro-oriented processes of power and surveillance, discipline and control? It is to questions such as these that I now turn in the hope of fleshing out more fully the contours of this hitherto largely 'dormant' sociological enterprise.

Biology/society: the *habitus* and beyond

Bodies, as Frank (1991) argues, are the foundation of both discourses and institutions as well as being their product. Discourses, in other words, are embodied and social institutions cannot be understood apart from the real, lived experiences and actions of bodies. The grounding of social theory must, therefore, be the problem of human embodiment: only from this basis can theory put selves back into bodies and bodies (whether sleeping or waking) back into society. Sleep, like emotions, lies at the heart of these corporeal concerns, and it is from here that sociologists, as embodied practitioners, must themselves proceed to more familiar sociological terrain regarding questions of social order and control, regulation and resistance.

Without sleep, waking life – the staple diet of sociology to date – would be impossible. Indeed, as I have argued, the very notion of waking life assumes a vast area of uncharted sociological terrain (i.e. sleep and embodiment, energy and rest) which informs and underpins even the most mundane of tasks. Our embodied actions in the world, in other words, including our skills as competent social agents, are crucially dependent on the sleep, energy and rest which our non-waking life provides as a biological means of rejuvenation, replenishment and repair. As a physiological function, sleep results either when neuromuscular fatigue cuts down corticol excitation, or when for physiological reasons still not fully understood, both the cortex and the wakefulness centre of the brain become inactive after a few days (Aubert and White 1959b: 5). This is not, of course, to suggest that sociologists focus their attention on these biological processes and imperatives *per se*. Rather, what is most important here, sociologically speaking, is the affordances they afford, the accordances they accord, for the conduct of everyday social life. Seen in these terms, these physiological substrates, and their relationship to everyday waking life, constitute necessary components of a broader sociological analysis of the social significance of sleep, energy and rest.

This, in turn, points to the socially pliable nature of human biology (i.e. its 'completion' by culture), and the tilting of the balance from unlearned to learned forms of behaviour. There is apparently no specific physiological mechanism linking human sleep with darkness or the astronomical cycle of day and night. The pattern of human sleep cannot, therefore, be explained in primarily physiological terms. Indeed, a wide range of sleep behaviour is physiologically possible: something which indicates very directly that many of the taken-for-granted features of sleep have less to do with physiological necessity than with socio-cultural determination. Sleep, in short, is more than a straightforward biological activity, it is also, in large part, a motivated act, bestowed with symbolic value and moral significance, and necessitating, like all other activities, the adoption of a prescribed socio-cultural role (Aubert and White 1959a and b).

That this is so is ably and amply demonstrated by Marcel Mauss. In his classic paper 'Techniques of the Body', Mauss seeks to capture the 'ways in which from society to society men [*sic*] know how to use their bodies' (Mauss 1973 [1934]: 70). Body techniques, he argues, display three fundamental characteristics. First, as the name implies, they are *technical* in that they are constituted by a specific set of bodily movements or forms: 'The body is man's first and most natural instrument.' Second, they are *traditional* in the sense that they are learnt or acquired by means of training and education: 'There is no technique and no transmission in the absence of tradition'. Finally, they are *efficient* in that they serve a definite purpose, function or goal (e.g. walking, running, dancing or digging) (Mauss 1973: 75).

A key concept here for Mauss is the *habitus* (i.e. our more-or-less ingrained socio-cultural relation to the body and its movements).[3] There is, he argues, no such thing as a 'natural way' for the adult; to claim otherwise is 'totally inaccurate'. Rather, in every society; 'everyone knows and has to know and learn what he [*sic*] has to do in all conditions' (Mauss 1973: 85). If this is true of body techniques in general, then it is particularly true of sleep and sleeping. Mauss himself, for example, recounts how the war taught him to 'sleep anywhere' – on horseback, standing up in the mountains, on heaps of stones – yet never was he able to 'change bed without a moment of insomnia': only on the second night could he quickly get off to sleep (Mauss 1973: 80). Indeed, all sorts of different ways of sleeping are practised throughout the world. Members of some societies, for example, have nothing to sleep on except the 'floor', whilst others have 'instrumental assistance'. There are also people with pillows and those without; people with mats and those without; populations which lie very close together in a ring, with or without a fire, in order to sleep; and those, such as the Masai, who can sleep on their feet (Mauss 1973: 80).[4] These arguments and insights extend to other techniques of the body such as rest. Members of certain societies, for example, take their rest in what, through Western eyes, seem very 'peculiar positions'. The whole of Nilotic Africa and part of the Chad region all the way to Tanzania (formerly Tanganyika), for instance, is populated by men who 'rest in fields like storks. Some manage to rest on one foot without a pole, others lean on a stick' (Mauss 1973: 81).

All in all, this suggests a view of sleep and rest as what, for want of a better term, may be referred to, in embodied terms, as an 'active' socio-cultural and historically shaped form of corporeal 'inactivity'. Far from belonging to the realm of biological 'givens', sleep, in other words, bears the imprint of time and the marks of culture. The Navaho, for example, believe that evil is brought by stepping over a sleeping person, whilst amongst the Bedouin Rwala, a 'culprit' cannot be killed by an avenger whilst sleeping, lest it bring similar vengeance on the latter's own head! (Aubert and White 1959a: 54). Here we return to the distinction, introduced earlier, between being asleep and doing sleep. Sleep, as I have suggested, is a social role, displaying a high degree of plasticity in relation to changing socio-cultural and historical forms. It is here, at the intersection of physiological *need*, environmental *constraint* and socio-cultural *elaboration*, that the *emergent* nature of sleep as a sociological process is most readily apparent. This in turn raises other important questions concerning the relationship between sleep, temporality and intentionality, issues to which we now turn in the next section.

Temporality and intentionality: from dreams to death

Sleep, as alluded to above, is a temporally bounded activity; one that displays considerable socio-cultural variability. Whilst the minimum amount of sleep that is physiologically needed cannot be specified – the best estimate being approximately eight hours, age variations notwithstanding – it is generally the case that in most societies our physiological need for sleep is less than the social time accorded it (Aubert and White 1959a). There also appears to be no physiological reason why sleep should occur at night-time, and whilst other environmental factors such as temperature and relative humidity are important constraints,[5] a wide range of adjustment to these factors is indeed possible. A considerable amount of training, for example, is involved in getting children to sleep at night-time and to fit into 'appropriate' (i.e. adult-determined) sleeping patterns. That sleep tends to occur most commonly at night-time, therefore, represents a complex mixture of social and environmental processes: a time when, traditionally at least, isolation and quiet are more easily obtainable, and when a diminution in vision and temperature induces a need to be indoors – factors which become increasingly redundant due to technological developments which do away with these environmental and physical constraints on our ancestors (Aubert and White 1959a).

An encounter with sleep, as Aubert and White note, represents a qualitative break in time-concepts between night and day, placing a formidable social barrier between two successive days and the social activities they encompass. As such, it opens up the opportunity for a 'fresh start': 'a communion rite in which minor sins and cares are washed away' (1959a: 53). Sleeping also provides what they appositely refer to as a 'temporal resource', enabling us to get more or less out of the day, depending on our particular circumstances. Thus whilst I may decide to forgo sleep and 'burn the midnight oil' for a week in order to finish this chapter, others, through boredom or involuntary detention (e.g. the prisoner), may choose instead to 'sleep the time away' in order to hasten its passage. In a different vein, caregivers frequently complain about their loss of sleep when those, such as old people with dementia, turn 'night into day'.

Night-time is also, of course, a time for 'surreptitious' activities of various kinds, from crime to sex, cultural innovation to black magic, werewolves to vampires. Night, as Alvarez notes, has always been a time of fear: 'Predators move unseen under the cover of darkness and all animals, man [*sic*] included, are most vulnerable to their enemies when they sleep' (1995: 22). If, as Goffman (1961) argued in an essay on paranoid logic, normal appearances are the most troubling of all, then this is particularly true of the people one encounters and the places one inhabits late at night. Night-time, in short, constitutes a time of danger and vulnerability, feeding on our poor visibility and transforming even the most innocent of day-time gestures (i.e. a stranger asking us the way) into suspicious, potentially menacing acts (e.g. a possible mugger, killer, rapist, etc.). On the other hand, it can also be a time of great festivity and celebration, from the spectacular illumination of the night sky by fireworks to Midnight Mass, and from New Year's eve to the midsummer solstice (Alvarez 1995: 14).

If night-time constitutes one key temporal dimension of sleep, then dreams and dreaming constitute another. Like night-time itself, dreams leave us similarly vulnerable: 'those otherworldly visitations when secret fears and desires come drifting to the surface' (Alvarez 1995: 22). In this respect, the physical conquest of 'outer darkness' (e.g. the advent of electricity, street lighting, etc.),[6] has now been replaced by the gradual illumination of 'inner darkness' (i.e. the 'darkness inside the head') through disciplines such as pyschoanalysis. Thus when Freud, defining the aim of psychoanalysis, said '"Where there was id, there shall be ego", he was echoing, in his own way, God's first edict "Let there be light"' (Alvarez 1995: 22).

In dreams, the conscious sequencing of time, common to waking life, is suspended if not reversed; condensed, displaced and overdetermined by unconscious mental processes which defy rational ordering or logical temporal form. Whether or not dreams become viewed as evil and irrational expressions of human nature, or are valued as intrinsically 'good' – furnishing insights into past, present and future events is a socio-culturally defined matter. In some cultures, as Aubert and White (1959b) note, they are connected with supernatural and spiritual dimensions of social life, or are used, through the invocation of sleep spirits, to induce sickness and nightmares in others. Stories of medieval legends abound concerning those who have gone to sleep and have been – or are to be – awakened many years later, often with new insights and wisdom. The Greek poet Epimenides, for example, is said to have fallen asleep in a cave when a boy, and not to have awoken for 57 years, when he found himself possessed of all wisdom. Similarly, legends associated with King Arthur, Charlemagne and Barbarossa, and stories such as the Seven Sleepers of Ephesus, Tannhausser, Ogier the Dane and Rip Van Winkle, not to mention Sleeping Beauty, attest to the temporal dimensions of sleep, the symbolic significance of the sleeper, and the magical properties of dreaming. In our own times, however, psychoanalytic interpretations notwithstanding, the validity, reliability and responsibility of dream life have tended to be played down if not denied (accorded little legitimacy). The dreams of people in the Western world are, in other words, 'relatively unsocialized events in contrast to the heavy socialisation of primate man [*sic*] in his role as sleeper' (Aubert and White 1959b: 4. See also Woods 1947).

Here, questions concerning the temporality of sleep merge imperceptibly with other more general issues of intentionality regarding the roles of sleeper and dreamer, and the social functions which these activities perform both within and between societies. Unlike death, sleep is a 'temporally bounded' activity which is 'lived through', so to speak (Taylor 1993). Consequently, there are many ways in which it can be talked about and used (both appropriately and inappropriately) in the contexts of everyday waking life. On the one hand, for example, lack of sleep or tiredness may be used as an excuse (legitimate or otherwise) for derelictions of interactional duty, the 'incompetent' performance of practical tasks, or to bring a tedious evening politely to a premature close – 'Sorry, I have to get up early in the morning.' It may even, as is common these days, provide the basis for a social event itself – as in children's so-called 'sleep-over' parties. On the other hand, we may choose, consciously or otherwise, to avoid, ignore or insult somebody through sleep or tiredness – the unsuppressed yawn, for instance, or the feigning of sleep in a boring lecture. Fellow travellers may also become rather too intimate when sleep renders their normal modes of corporeal propriety problematic (e.g. drowsy, rocking, heads that come to rest, however unwelcomely, on other passengers' shoulders). Here we have a primal sociological scene and unfolding drama of which even Goffman himself would have been proud: one where sleeping in public places is acceptable, if not condoned, but where certain standards of bodily decorum, deference and demeanour still apply, even with one's eyes closed!

To these discussions of temporality and intentionality, we may add the intimate associations, both past and present, between sleep and death itself: the ultimate finality. Discussion of death, for example, is often expressed through the language of sleep (e.g. the 'big sleep', 'rest in peace') in a way that transforms its finality into something altogether more liminal and less threatening – a discursive twist which both resonates with and reinforces the notion that the dead are merely slumbering passengers on the way to 'another' or 'better' place, the status of which remains uncertain to us earthly mortals (Taylor 1993). As Shelley put it:

> How wonderful is Death
> Death and his brother sleep!
> One pale as yonder man and horned moon
> With lips of lurid blue,
> The other glowing like the vital morn,
> When throned an ocean's wave
> It breathes over the world:
> Yet both so passing strange and wonderful.
> (Percy Bysshe Shelley, *The Deamon of the World*)

Death, in other words, is not so much denied as deferred: a 'life-strategy' in which mortality itself is 'deconstructed', 'tamed' or romanticized through the idiom of sleep and the discourse of dormancy (Illich 1975; Aries 1976; Kellehear 1984; Bauman 1992).

These symbolic associations, in turn, have been seized upon, marketed and sold by the leisure and entertainments industries. Indeed, from Walt Disney's production of *Sleeping Beauty* to Oliver Sacks'

Awakenings, and from *Sleepless in Seattle* to *Nightmare on Elm Street*, dormancy has become a media spectacle and a box office hit: an 'obscenity', in Baudrillard's (1988) terms, in which 'all becomes transparence and immediate visibility' and everything is exposed to the 'harsh and inexorable light of information and communication'. Here we glimpse the complexity of contemporary society, on the one hand, continuing trends towards the privatization or sequestration of all 'natural' bodily functions, on the other hand, pushing towards their 'all-too-visible' (i.e. obscene) public exposure as the latest form of media hype. Viewed within this context, modernist concerns with corporeality are slowly but surely giving way to postmodern concerns with hyper-reality (i.e. images without grounding). It is to these broader sociological issues that we now turn through a focus on the 'institutionalization' and 'social patterning' of sleep.

The 'institutionalization' and 'social patterning' of sleep: a broader sociological agenda

Historical insights into the social organization of sleep and sleeping arrangements, including the bed and the use of the bedroom, can be gleaned from many different sources (see, for example, Wright 1962; McIlvane 1972). Attempts to weave them into a sociological frame of reference, however, have perhaps been most successfully achieved, albeit indirectly, through the work of the historical sociologist Norbert Elias (1978, 1982) in his two-volume study of *The Civilising Process*; particularly his analysis of manners in the bedroom (see also Gleichmann 1980; Mennell 1989). In the Middle Ages, for example, the sleeping/waking cycle of the individual was relatively undisciplined and unruly. People often slept in the daytime, and in any place which was convenient. Sleeping, in other words, was at this time a relatively 'public', undifferentiated, matter and the physical space within which it occurred was shared, not infrequently, with (many) others: in the upper classes, the master with his servants, or in the other classes, men and women in the same room, often with guests staying overnight (Mennell 1989). Erasmus, for example, in *De Civilitate Morum Puerilium* (1530), instructed his readers:

> If you share a bed with a comrade, lie quietly; do not toss with your body, for this can lay yourself bare or inconvenience your companion by pulling away the blankets. (cited in Elias 1978: 161)

People, we are told, slept naked and the sight of the fleshy human body was a common occurrence, especially in bath-houses. This 'unconcern' for nakedness, as Elias observes, slowly disappeared in the sixteenth century, progressing more rapidly in the seventeenth, eighteenth and nineteenth centuries – first in the upper classes and much more slowly in the lower classes. Garments to be worn in bed, for example, were gradually introduced from the Renaissance onwards. To have to share a bed was also, by the eighteenth century, quite exceptional (for the upper classes) and consequently details of how to behave if the need arose were largely left unspoken. La Selle, for instance, in *Les Règles de la Bienséance et de la Civilité Chrétienne* (1729) writes: 'You ought neither to undress nor go to bed in the presence of another person' – the tone becoming appreciably stronger in the later 1774 edition.

The upshot of these developments, as Elias (1978: 163) observes, is that the bedroom has become one of the most 'private' and 'intimate' areas of human life, and sleeping, like most other bodily functions, has been increasingly shifted 'behind the scenes' of social life: what Giddens (1991) refers to as the 'sequestration of experience'. Here too, in much the same way as with eating:

> ... the wall between people, the reserve, the emotional barrier erected by conditioning between one body and another, grows continuously. To share a bed with people outside the family circle, with strangers, is made more and more embarrassing. Unless necessity dictates otherwise, it becomes usual even within the family for each person to have his [*sic*] own bed and finally – in the middle and upper classes – his own bedroom ... *Only if we see how natural it seemed in the Middle Ages for strangers and for children and adults to share a bed can we appreciate what a fundamental change in interpersonal relationships and behaviour is expressed in our manner of living.* And we recognize how far from self-evident it is that *bed and body should form such psychological danger zones as they do in the most recent phase of civilization'*. (Elias 1978: 168; my emphasis)[7]

Moving more fully into the public sphere, a key feature of work and institutional social life, as the above discussion suggests, concerns the spatio-temporal ordering of the sleeping/waking cycle: from the prison to the factory, the military barracks to the (boarding) school, the hospital to the hotel (cf. Goffman 1961; Foucault 1979). The socio-culturally prescribed and historically variable role of the sleeper, in this respect, however 'privatized' it may have become, is indeed central to any given society. Indeed, without these 'institutional arrangements' society would, quite simply – given an ever-more complex division of labour and specialization of functions – be impossible. Sleep, in other words, and its social organization through the sleep role, is a *functional prerequisite*. Some cultures, for example, as we have seen, have elaborate collective rituals and symbolic practices surrounding the symbolic significance of dreams and the portents they provide; others do not. Some, partly for climatic/environmental reasons, have institutionalized the siesta – thereby allowing people to rest during the hottest part of the day – others have not. At a more concrete level, buildings themselves are often described and evaluated, in their very architecture if not their function, in units of measurement predicated on sleep and rest. When searching for a house, for instance, one of the first things one stipulates is that it has to have one, two or three bedrooms; hospital capacity and throughput are also measured in terms of beds and bed-days, and hotel rates are calculated on a bed and breakfast basis (i.e. number of nights stayed). Even on the roads, motorists are told to 'take a break – tiredness kills'!

Sleep, as consequence of these very developments, has become something of a 'leisure pursuit' in late Western society (Taylor 1993). Asked what they intend to do with their weekends, vacations or retirement, many people cite sleeping as both an 'acceptable' and 'desirable' pastime. This, in turn, is linked to the attainment of a certain level of socio-economic development: members of a hard-working subsistence economy, for example, are more likely to define sleep as necessary respite from exhausting physical labour than a leisure pursuit (ibid.: 468). Perspectives on and commonsensical definitions of sleep, in other words, are likely to differ according to social location, context and function. Plenty of sleep before an important job interview, exam or strenuous bout of physical exercise may, for instance, be considered a necessity (ibid.: 468). It is also instructive, given the intimate links between leisure and pleasure, to reflect here on the intriguing cultural overtones and symbolic associations between sleep and sexuality in contemporary Western culture. It is now commonplace, for example, to describe (illicit) sexual liaisons through the 'discourse of dormancy' (e.g. 'She's sleeping with him', 'He's sleeping with her', 'They're sleeping together') – which, of course, in most cases, is a fairly inaccurate description of what actually occurs! (Taylor 1993). Carnal activity, in other words, is dressed up as corporeal inactivity, naked desire as mortal slumber.

Meanwhile, a whole sleep and rest 'industry' has grown up, supplying us with everything from (sexy) nightwear and pharmacological aides, to the ultimate bed where a 'silent night' is more or less guaranteed. In Greater London, for example, the number of beds purchased in any one year is estimated to be around 321,000, whilst the total time spent in bed in a week by Greater Londoners amounts to a staggering 371,200,000 minutes (Hind 1997). There is also the intriguing question as to whether or not we are actually sleeping less these days. It is certainly true that there are more all-night facilities and services – from nightlines to nightclubs and from 24-hour supermarkets to round-the-clock television – and it can be argued that this is due to market needs for ever more consumption. Increasing urbanization and noise pollution, not to mention the problems of caffeine, may add to these dilemmas, with knock-on consequences for sleep, health, neighbourly relations and efficiency, both at work and elsewhere.

These issues are particularly well illustrated in relation to the modern hospital. Indeed, the modern hospital is *par excellence* a microcosm of the 'dormant' or 'sleeping society'. Even the quickest of strolls though its wards and corridors, its theatres and pharmacies, its staff quarters and laundry rooms, reveals the sociological significance of sleep. First, we have the role of sleep itself as a 'therapeutic tool': a 'natural' cure or healing process, whereby we sleep our way through illness (i.e. 'sleep it off'). Second, we have the spatial organization of sleep, embodied through the physical regimentation of beds, linen and other accessories on the wards. Third, closely allied to issues of space, we have the temporal ordering of the sleeping–waking cycle, including infamous early morning starts and 'lights out' orders in this most 'total', of total institutions.[8] Fourth, we have the public monitoring and surveillance of sleep on the wards and intensive care units, together with the problems of sleep that hospitalization itself bring for patients themselves. Fifth, we have what may be termed the 'pharmacology of sleep' in the shape of anaesthetics, sleeping tablets and a variety of other sleep-inducing drugs and therapeutic aides: factors which may not simply 'ease' the problems of 'sleeping sickness', but also serve as powerful disciplinary means to render bodies truly passive and docile.[9] Closely allied to this, we have the 'instrumentation' of sleep, including sleep clinics/laboratories with multidisciplinary personnel and a panoply of electrical equipment, graphs and digital images designed to 'measure' things such as REM and brain activity whilst asleep – i.e. electrophysiological monitoring techniques, clinical observations, etc. (see Alvarez 1995: chapter 3). Sixth, we have, of course, the problems of long hours and shift-work for hospital staff themselves, including medical mistakes and their iatrogenic consequences. Seventh, we return to the links, common in popular culture, between sleep and death: from patients dying in their sleep to the ethical dilemmas which the medical imperative to sustain life at all costs creates for patients in comatose or (near-)vegative states. Finally, at the broadest, most general level, what we have here is a clear expression of the 'professionalization' or 'medicalization' of sleep; one which, like all professionalizing strategies, may or may not be in our own best interests.

Underpinning these institutional issues, are broader questions of power, surveillance and control. Sleep, as I have suggested, particularly through its (cultural and symbolic) associations with night-time, leaves us vulnerable. In this respect, the balance of power tips firmly in favour of those who remain awake vis-à-vis those who sleep. Whilst the general thrust of the civilizing process may indeed be towards increasing thresholds of shame and embarrassment towards the 'natural' body, and the removal behind the scenes of carnal activities and experiences such as sex, sleep and death, it is none the less the case that certain groups of people, such as children, the hospital patient, the prisoner, the homeless, have their sleeping as well as waking life monitored far more closely than others, at times and in circumstances far from their own choosing (cf. Elias 1978; Foucault 1979). Indeed, from the night-watchman to the hospital nurse, the monitoring of sleep and the 'policing' of the times within which it occurs is a central or 'core' feature of society. Sleep may also be 'withheld' in various ways, as a form of punishment, torture or interrogation; a process likely to wear down even the most recalcitrant and resistant of individuals. In short, sleep can profitably be analysed in terms of the observer/observed relationships, together with the broader power/knowledge dynamics and webs of surveillance and control it raises across the social spectrum (Taylor 1993): factors which, adapting Jamous and Pellioule's (1970) use of the term in a different context, are succinctly captured by the determinacy/indeterminacy ratio (i.e. a measure of the degree to which sleep patterns are set by self or others).

The fact that none of us is immune from the need to sleep, however, and that sleep, like illness and death, is ultimately no respector of status or hierarchy – what Philip Sydney appositely referred to as the 'indifferent judge' between the 'high' and 'low'; the 'poor man's wealth, the prisoner's release' – means that today, in Western society, the institutionalized role of sleeper ensures, in most cases, at the very least the following duties, rights and obligations – ones that resonate with certain features of the Parsonian 'sick role' (Parsons 1951).

Duties/obligations

1. To sleep at night and therefore to conform to the general pattern of sleep time, unless legitimate social circumstances, such as work arrangements, dictate otherwise.
2. To sleep in a bed, or similar device, in a private place, away from public view, in proper attire (i.e. pyjamas, night-dress etc.) – the latter is not an absolute requirement, and indeed, is increasingly being circumvented if not flouted.

Rights

3. Freedom from noise and interference from others, except in times of emergency.
4. Exemption from normal role obligations/conscious demands.
5. No loss of waking role status whilst asleep.

Beyond these general, if not universal, features of the sleep role, it is equally clear that sleep is 'socially patterned' in various ways according to a broader range of socio-structural and demographic factors. Age is an obvious example – babies, for instance, spend more time sleeping than adults. The amount of sleep required across the life-course, however, varies considerably due to the complex interaction of biological and social factors. Adults in the Health and Lifestyles Survey (HALS) – a study involving a sample of some 9,000 women and men aged over 18 – were almost evenly divided between those who claimed to sleep for 7–8 hours, those who 'usually' slept for less, and those who 'usually' had longer. Younger men and women were more likely to quote more than 8 hours, with the proportions sleeping less than 7 hours rising steeply with age – a factor confounded by health status.[10]

Gender is also important here. While tiredness and fatigue, as Ridsdale (1989: 486) comments, are part and parcel of the 'normal chaff' of daily life, studies suggest that females show an excess of tiredness over their male counterparts. Again, findings from the HALS are instructive here; 20 per cent of men and 30 per cent of women reported 'always feeling tired' in the month before interview (Cox et al. 1987). Experiences of tiredness were also found to vary in interesting ways *amongst* as well as between men and women themselves. Those under 39, for example, those without children, and those with children aged 6–16, were less likely to report 'always feeling tired' than those with younger children. Likewise, as the number of children increased, so did the proportion reporting tiredness (Cox et al. 1987). Similarly, Popay (1992) found that tiredness, particularly severe or chronic tiredness, featured as one of the most frequent symptoms or conditions referred to spontaneously by women in her study. As Brannen and Moss (1988) show, women's tiredness varies in both type as well as quantity: young babies and broken nights bringing one sort of tiredness; another, being at home full-time, centred on boredom and lethargy; trying to combine domestic and paid work, a third type, derived from physical and mental fatigue.

Similar points can be made in relation to class. Not only is the 'epidemiology' of sleep, energy and rest likely to vary, in more or less predictable ways, according to socio-economic factors, but so too is its very definition. Hunt et al. (1986), for example, in a large community survey, found a greater prevalence of sleeping problems – as measured on the Nottingham Health Profile (NHP) – amongst those from traditional manual working-class backgrounds. It may also be suggested, on the basis of these and other findings, that those in upper social class circles display, on average, a greater tendency both to retire to bed and rise later than their working-class counterparts: itself another key index of social power, status and privilege (i.e. the freedom or flexibility, expressed through the determinacy/indeterminacy ratio, to set one's own sleep pattern). Overcrowded housing conditions and problems of shift-work – the likelihood of which increases as one descends the social scale – underline these class-related issues, having a profound effect both on sleep patterns and sleeping arrangements. On the other hand, lack of sleep may serve as a mark of social distinction, as when the hurried business executive or the harrassed politician complains of 'feeling tired' or 'not needing much sleep', snatching a few hours here or there (i.e. 'power napping'), in a whirlwind life of international meetings and impossible deadlines.

The interaction between socio-economic status and factors, such as age and gender, serves to reinforce further these points, highlighting the rich and varied picture which the social patterning of sleep, energy and rest provides; one that may serve, in an analogous fashion to Durkheim's concept of anomie or Marx's notion of alienation, as a key contemporary indicator of social malaise and societal 'unrest'. Seen in this light, debates over social structure, including the inequalities and lay concepts literature on class and health, could usefully be extended through a sociological focus on sleep, energy and rest.

Little work has been done, to date, on the ethnic patterning of sleep, yet many of the above points apply equally well. Not only is the value, practice and significance of sleep likely to vary according to cultural group membership, but distinctive patterns of work and employment, together with problematic housing conditions suggest a complex picture: one which may be less about ethnic patterning *per se*, than the underlying socio-economic and material circumstances in which these minority groups live, and their implications for health (Smaje 1995). In the early postwar years of migration (the 1950s and 1960s), for example, many South Asian men, employed on a shift-work basis, shared beds on a 12-hour rotating cycle (Ratcliffe 1980). Similarly, in the current economic period, shift-work, especially in the manufacturing industry (e.g. textiles), is particularly prevalent amongst the Muslim community. Overcrowding (more than two people per room) is another striking feature of the Pakistani and Bangladeshi communities – suggesting that, civilizing processes to the contrary, the sharing of bedrooms, if not beds, is still commonplace in certain segments of contemporary Western society (Ratcliffe 1996a and b). These and many other issues raise significant sociological questions about sleep and rest, yet to date, as I have argued, we have little direct empirical evidence upon which to base these contentions. There is, in short, an urgent need for more empirical as well as theoretical work in this important and promising new area of research on the institutionalisation and social patterning of sleep.

Having sketched here, albeit briefly, what I take to be the main contours and parameters of a sociology of sleep, it is to a fuller set of reflections on their significance – why, that is, we should take these claims seriously – and the future research agendas they raise, that I now turn in the concluding section.

Discussion and concluding remarks

The study of sleep, as we have seen, meshes closely with 'core' sociological problematics – from the problem of social 'order' to the dilemmas of bodily 'control'. The fact that sleep, as a temporal resource, is 'lived through', and that the sleeper is never entirely 'cut off' from the intersubjective and intercorporeal world of which s/he is a part (cf. Merleau-Ponty's quotation at the beginning of this chapter), further underlines this sociological point. The argument here, in short, is for a sociological analysis of the material and socio-cultural circumstances, contingencies and consequences of sleep as an embodied activity (i.e. the *'doing'* of sleep and the social and cultural significance (or otherwise) of dreams and dreaming), rather than the more medico-centric or psychoanalytic focus on its whys and wherefores. The very nature of sleep, I venture, can fully be understood only when placed within the sociological meanings and contexts, actions and purposes of embodied agents across the spatio-temporal zones and boundaries separating day from night, the public from the private.

Like other aspects of our human embodiment (e.g. pain and emotions), sleep is an 'uncontainable' term in any one domain or discourse; something that lies ambiguously across the nature/culture, biology/society divide; transcending many former dichotomous modes of Western thought. As notions such as the body techniques, the civilizing process and the *habitus* suggest, the body is not a fixed or static entity, but a pliable set of significances which is 'open' to endless socio-cultural elaboration across time and space. This notion of human beings as 'unfinished creatures', 'completed' by culture, in turn suggests a (partially) 'socialized' view of biology itself; one which challenges former reductionist thinking and the spectre of socio-biologism. We need, in other words, as Shilling (1997) rightly argues, to recognize the significance for agency of a socially shaped form of embodiment; one that refuses to make the actor a mere construction or product of the social system (i.e. bodies as both shaped by and shapers of social structure). Rewritten and reread in this new, more open way, the biology/society equation becomes, in fact, far more complex, subtle and sophisticated: a position which demands and necessitates a *dialectical* rather than reductionist stance on sleep and sleeping.

A central issue here, as I have argued, is the notion of the sleep role. To be sure, the norms and expectations surrounding this role are likely to vary considerably, both historically and cross-culturally, yet the need to sleep is a universal feature of human embodiment, and in all societies, as we have seen, the role of sleeper is a central, if not sacred, one. This, coupled with the spatio-temporal organization of sleep, its social patterning, together with the broader questions of power and surveillance, discipline and control it raises – of which the observed/observed, determinancy/ interdeterminacy ratio are key indices and cross-cutting axes – suggest a viable and indeed challenging new area of sociological research and investigation.

More broadly, sleep, it can be suggested, provides a key indicator of societal development, an index of social organization, and a fruitful vantage point from which to revisit old sociological issues, as well as to develop new ones. From the state of civilized bodies to the social organization of time and space, and from the nature and status of incest taboos and family relations (Aubert and White 1959a) to the institutionalized division of labour, the sociological study of sleep furnishes us with invaluable insights into the contours and existential parameters of society, classical or medieval, feudal or industrial, (late) modern or postmodern.

What, then, of future research agendas in this important, yet embryonic, new area of sociological study? Certainly, as I have argued, there is a need to focus on the experience (i.e. phenonemological) as well as the representational (i.e. discursive/symbolic), the material as well as the cultural, the institutional (i.e. macro) as well as the individual (i.e. micro) aspects of sleep. Perhaps the most pressing issue, however, concerns the need to develop a coherent set of sociological concepts, adequate to the task in hand. The *habitus* and body techniques, as we have seen, provide a useful starting point here, as do associated notions such as the civilizing and sequestration of sleep, the sleep role and the determinacy/indeterminacy ratio. Much still remains to be done, however, in this relatively uncharted sociological terrain. This chapter, in this sense, provides a mere starting point, risks of 'sociological imperialism' notwithstanding.

One potentially fruitful area, alongside the sociology of the body, where many of these sleep-related issues might flourish is the sociology of health and illness. As we have seen, the links between sleep and health are readily apparent, shedding important new light on issues such as the inequalities debate; mediating between health and social structure, as well as being an important process in its own right. It is also possible that chronic fatigue, coupled with long-term sleeping problems, plays a contributory role in the very process of health selection itself; a topic hotly debated in medical sociological circles at present. This, coupled with the cultural and symbolic issues surrounding the body and sleep – the study of which would undoubtedly augment the lay concepts literature in significant new ways – and the importance of the hospital as a microcosm of the 'sleeping society', places the sociology of health and illness, at the heart of this (dormant) enterprise.

In raising these issues I have not, of course, sought to tackle the underlying methodological challenges they raise – to do so adequately would require another chapter in its own right. Suffice it to say that a number of interesting questions suggest themselves. Are existing research methods, for example, predicated as they are on the study of waking life, really up to the sociological task in hand? What particular methodological problems does the study of sleep pose for the sociologist, and to what extent can lessons be learnt from related areas of research such as the sociology of death and dying? Can people reliably or validly account, in waking life, for the taken-for-granted features and unconscious facets of their role as sleepers? More generally, given the complexity of these issues and the rudimentary nature of the concepts to hand, are quantitative or qualitative methods, or a combination of the two, the best way forward in the early stages of this dormant research programme?

There are no easy or simple answers to these questions, yet they are perhaps best seen as teething problems rather than insurmountable obstacles to the fully-fledged development of this most fascinating of areas: one which not only manages to distinguish itself successfully from other disciplinary claims, but also to contribute something genuinely new and important to this evolving field of interdisciplinary research. It is high time, in short, that somnolent sociologists, as embodied practitioners, stopped 'sleeping on the job' and fully 'woke up' to the significance of this important topic and neglected domain. In this respect, Milton's provocative question 'What hath night to do with sleep?' may serve as a useful point of departure and a promising platform from which to fashion other similarly challenging sociological questions concerning the nature of sleep within dormant society. But perhaps the last word in this literary vein should go to Cervantes who, in *Don Quixote*, expresses the matter in the following terms:

> Blessings on him who invented sleep, the mantle that covers all human thoughts, the food that satisfies hunger, the drink that slates thirst, the fire that warms cold, the cold that moderates heat, and, lastly, the common currency that buys all things, the balance and weight that equalizes the shepherd and the king, the simpleton and the sage.

Sleep, in short, previously banished to the margins of sociological thought and practice, is no mere 'dormant' issue.

Acknowledgements

Thanks to all those people, too numerous to mention, who shared with me their thoughts, views and opinions on this fascinating topic and who, in doing so, encouraged me to venture further into this largely unchartered sociological terrain. Special thanks to Tim Holt and Ruth Charity for enthusiastic support and some esoteric references, and to the editors of this conference volume for helpful comments on an earlier draft.

Notes

1. This is a revised version of an earlier chapter which appeared in Williams and Bendelow (1998).
2. Perhaps the classic text in this respect is Walter de la Mare's (1939) *Behold, This Dreamer*. London: Faber and Faber, comprising a wonderful collection of poems and passages in prose of reveries, night, sleep, dream, love dreams, nightmare, death, the unconscious, the imagination, divination, the artist and kindred subjects. See also Cosnett's (1997) intriguing exploration of 'Charles Dickens and Sleep Disorders'.
3. This notion of the *habitus* has a long history, dating back as far as Aristotle and Aquinas, through the work of Elias, to the contemporary writings of sociological figures such as Bourdieu, Maffesoli and others.
4. See also Johnson (1931) and Johnson et al. (1930) for other early work on bodily position in restful sleep.
5. Cf. the Spanish 'siesta' or Norway's proverbial 'long winter nights' and 'spring awakening' (Aubert and White 1959b: 13).
6. Street-lighting in London, for example, first began as a 'primitive enterprise' when, in 1694, Edward Heming obtained a licence to put lights outside every tenth house from 6 pm to midnight between Michaelmas and Lady Day, and to charge householders 6 shillings a year for the privilege of 'relative security'. Similar attempts began some 32 years earlier in France, instituted by a Parisian cleric, the Abbé Laudati (Alvarez 1995: 17–18).
7. For other interesting work on the history of the bed and the use of the bedroom, see Wright (1962), McIlvaine (1972) and Parsons (1972) respectively.
8. As Goffman observes, the central features of a 'total institution' can be described as the breakdown of the barriers ordinarily separating sleep, play and work – activities which normally occur in different places, with different co-participants, under different authorities. Within a total institution, all aspects of life are conducted in the same place, in the immediate company of a large batch of others, and in a tightly scheduled sequence; activities brought together into a single rational plan purportedly designed to fulfil the official aims of the institution (Goffman 1961: 17).
9. The number of sleeping pills swallowed per night in Greater London is estimated to be in the order of 522,250 + (Hind 1997).
10. This strong association between current health and current sleeping habits led Blaxter (1990: 127) to conclude that the use of sleeping habits as a 'voluntary' behaviour was unjustified.

References

Alvarez, A. 1995. *Night*. London: Vintage.

Ariès, P. 1976. *Western Attitudes towards Death and Dying: From the Middle Ages to the Present*. London: Marion Boyars.

Aubert, V. and White, H. 1959a. 'Sleep: A Sociological Interpretation I', *Acta Sociologica* 4 (2): 46–54.

Aubert, V. and White, H. 1959b. 'Sleep: A Sociological Interpretation II', *Acta Sociologica*, 4 (3): 1–16.

Baudrillard, J. 1988. *Selected Writings*, ed. M. Poster. Cambridge: Polity Press.

Bauman, Z. 1992. *Mortality, Immortality and Other Life-Strategies*. Cambridge: Polity Press.

Blaxter, M. 1990. *Health and Lifestyles*. London: Routledge.

Brannen, J. and Moss, P. 1988. *Mothers and Daughters: A Three Generational Study of Health Attitudes and Behaviour*. London: Heinemann.

Craib, I. 1995. 'Some Comment on the Sociology of Emotions', *Sociology*, 29 (1): 151–8.

Cosnett, J. 1997. 'Charles Dickens and Sleep Disorders', *The Dickensian*, 443 (93) (part 3): 200–4.

Cox, B.D., Blaxter, M., Buckle, A.L.F. et al. 1987. *The Health and Lifestyle Survey: Preliminary Report*. London: The Health Promotion Research Trust.

De la Mare, W. 1939. *Behold this Dreamer*. London: Faber and Faber.

de Maupassant, G. n.d. *The Complete Short Stories of Guy de Maupassant*. London: Blue Ribbon Books.

Durkheim, E. [1912]1961. *The Elementary Forms of Religious Life*. New York: Free Press.

Elias, N. [1939]1978. *The Civilizing Process: Vol. I: the History of Manners*. Oxford: Basil Blackwell.

Elias, N. [1939]1982. *The Civilizing Process, Vol. II: State Formations and Civilization*. Oxford: Basil Blackwell.

Foucault, M. 1979. *Discipline and Punish: The Birth of the Prison*. London: Tavistock.

Frank, A.W. 1991. 'For a sociology of the Body: An Analytical Review', in M. Featherstone, M. Hepworth and B.S. Turner (eds.) *The Body: Social Process and Cultural Theory*. London: Sage.

Freud, S. [1953]1976. *The Interpretation of Dreams*. Harmondsworth: Penguin.

Freund, P.E.S. 1990. 'The Expressive Body: A Common Ground for the Sociology of Emotions and Health and Illness', *Sociology of Health and Illness*, 12 (4): 452–77.

Giddens, A. 1991. *Modernity and Self-Identity*. Cambridge: Polity Press.

Gleichmann, P.R. 1980. 'Einige soziale Wandlungen des Schlafens', *Zeitschrift für Soziologie*, 9 (3): 236–50.

Goffman, E. 1961. *Asylums: Essays on the Social Situation of Mental Patients and Other Inmates*. Harmondsworth: Penguin.

Hind, J. 1997. 'London index: Beds', *London Evening Standard*. 3 October.

Hunt, S.M., McEwen, J and McKenna, S.P. 1986. *Measuring Health Status*. London: Croom Helm.

Illich, I. 1975. *Medical Nemesis*. London: Calder and Boyars.

Jamous, H and Pelliole, B. 1970. 'Changes in the French University-Hospital system', in J.A. Jackson (ed.) *Professions and Professionalisation*. Cambridge: Cambridge University Press.

Johnson, H.M. 1931. *Bodily Positions in Restful Sleep*. New York: The Simmons Company.

Johnson, H.M., Swan, T.H. and Weigand, G.E. 1930. 'In What Positions Do Healthy People Sleep?', *Journal of the American Medical Association*, 94: 2058–62.

Kellehear, A. 1984. 'Are we a "death-denying" society?', *Social Science and Medicine*, 18 (9): 713–30.
McIlvaine, P. H. 1972. 'The bedroom', *Human Factors*, 14(5): 421–50.
Mauss, M. [1934]1973. 'Techniques of the body', *Economy and Society*, 2: 70–88.
Mellor, P. and Shilling, S. 1993. 'Modernity, Self-identity and the Sequestration of Death', *Sociology*, 27 (3): 411–31.
Mennell, S. 1989: *Norbert Elias: Civilization and the Human Self-Image*. Oxford: Basil Blackwell.
Merleau-Ponty, M. 1962. *The Phenomenology of Perception*, trans. by C. Smith. London: Routledge.
Murray, E.J. 1965. *Sleep, Dreams and Arousal*. New York: Appleton-Century-Crofts.
Parsons, T. 1951. *The Social System*. London: Routledge and Kegan Paul.
Popay, J. 1992. '"My Health is Alright, but I'm just Tired All the Time": Women's Experience of Ill Health', in H. Roberts (ed.) *Women's Health Matters*. London: Routledge.
Ratcliffe, P. 1980. *Race Relations at Work*. Leamington Spa: Warwick District Community Relations Council.
Ratcliffe, P. 1996a. '"Race", Ethnicity and Housing Differentials in Britain', in V. Karn (ed.) *Employment, Education and Housing among Ethnic Minorities in Britain*. Ethnicity in the 1991 Census, Volume 4. London: HMSO.
Ratcliffe, P. 1996b. *'Race' and Housing in Bradford*. Bradford: Bradford Housing Forum.
Ridsdale, L. 1989. 'Chronic Fatigue in Family Practice', *Journal of Family Practice*, 29 (5): 486–8.
Rose, N. 1989. *Governing the Soul*. Cambridge: Polity Press.
Scheper-Hughes, N. and Lock, M. 1987. 'The Mindful Body: A Prolegomenon to Future Work in Medical Anthropology', *Medical Anthropology Quarterly*, 1 (1): 6–41.
Shilling, C. 1997. 'The (Un)socialised Conception of the (Embodied) Agent in Modern Sociology', *Sociology*, 31 (4): 737–54.
Smaje, C. 1995. *Health 'Race' and Ethnicity: Making Sense of the Evidence*. London: King's Fund.
Strong, P. 1979. 'Sociological Imperialism and the Medical Profession: A critical Examination of the Thesis of Medical Imperialism', *Social Science and Medicine*, 13A (2): 199–216.
Taylor, B. 1993. 'Unconsciouness and Society: The Sociology of Sleep', *International Journal of Politics, Culture and Society*, 6 (3): 463–71.
Turner, B.S. 1994. Preface, in P. Falk. *The Consuming Body*. London: Sage.
Walter, T. 1995. *The Revival of Death*. London: Routledge.
Walter, T., Littlewood, J. and Pickering M. 1995. 'Death in the News: The Public Invigilation of Private Grief', *Sociology*, 29 (4): 579–96.
Williams, S.J. and Bendelow, G. 1998. *The Lived Body: Sociological Themes, Embodied Issues*. London: Routledge.
Woods, R.L. (ed.) 1947. *The World of Dreams: An Anthology*. New York: Appleton-Century-Crofts.
Wright, I. 1962. *Warm and Snug: A History of the Bed*. London: Routledge and Kegan Paul.

Part III

Exploring Bodies: Time, Space and Leisure

9

Techniques of Neutralization, Techniques of Body Management and the Public Harassment of Runners

Greg Smith

Introduction

When people put on training shoes and go outside to run, they render themselves open to what Carol Brooks Gardner has identified as 'public harassment' – to multifarious types of 'abuses, harryings, and annoyances characteristic of public places and uniquely facilitated by communication in public' (Gardner 1995: 4). An early lesson that every runner must learn is how to conduct oneself when confronted with the whistles, catcalls, jokes, mockery, insults, derision and threat or actuality of physical attack originating from others using the same public space. In this chapter I shall examine some characteristic forms of self-management that runners[1] employ to deal with these abuses and annoyances. The conceptual basis for this analysis is provided by three classic sources: Marcel Mauss (1979) on body techniques; David Matza (1964, Sykes and Matza 1957) on techniques of neutralization; and Erving Goffman (1963, 1971) on the sociology of public places. From Mauss we can obtain an anthropological sensitivity to the symbolism of the comportment and motility of the human body; from Matza, an orientation to the function of words as social actions; and from Goffman, an observational method and a terminology responsive to the contextual, motivated character of embodied social action.

In this chapter I shall argue that while the notion of techniques of the body is a sensitizing concept that emphatically underlines what might be involved in the social construction of the human body, it can only take us so far. It must be augmented by an approach that brings into view the enactment or performance of body techniques (Crossley 1995).

When so expanded it is difficult to resist reference to such mental predicates as motives. In the case of the public harassment of runners it is necessary to consider the practical management of the runner's body alongside the justifications they give for acting as they do. Analysis of techniques of the running body therefore calls for a corresponding analysis of techniques of neutralization. The one requires and complements the other. These claims call first for theoretical explanation, then ethnographic elaboration. First, however, a note on method is required.

Method

The empirical basis for the chapter is a collection of 25 interviews with adult runners and race walkers (10 women, 15 men), supplemented by my own observations arising from more than three decades of participation in these activities. Interviews took place in a variety of locations, including respondents' homes and places of work, in car parks after road races and in club houses after training sessions. A simple schedule was devised, beginning with questions about the runner's sporting biography and current activities before focusing on their experiences of public harassment. I endeavoured to draw interviewees out about the specifics of their troublesome encounters with the non-running public. Interviews were taped and transcribed for analysis.

My identity as an active runner and race walker, visibly embodied in my appearance and evident in the cultural knowledge I displayed, was an essential resource in both securing agreement to interview and in conducting the interviews themselves.[2] When interviewing runners I was not a 'professional stranger' (Agar 1980) gathering data about a little-known tribe whose ways were utterly foreign to my own. Rather, I was a participant accumulating stories and recollections that I could match from my own experiences. In a very full sense, then, this was sociology 'from within'. The interviews, of course, provided me with a wealth of situations and a range of responses far beyond anything a single person could encounter. But throughout the interviews and the subsequent writing I was aware of the close interrelation of my own biography, the reported experiences of those whom I interviewed, and the conceptual tools selected to analyse features of the public harassment of runners. Without the lived experience of the topics this chapter investigates, I would not have known where to begin. But once begun, I quickly became aware that the materials I had elicited were readily amenable to interactionist sociological analysis.

Runners and public harassment

Although some interviewees reported physical assault or its threat (see Smith 1997: 63 for details) the most widespread (but not exclusive) form of public harassment runners face was delivered in the form of 'street remarks' (Gardner 1980) – the gratuitous evaluative commentary offered by a citizen to a passer-by. Street remarks clearly breach the 'civil inattention' rule that Goffman (1963) proposes is the mainstay of social orderliness and felt security in public places. The issue this chapter examines is the embodied sources of and solutions to runners' discomfiture when out training.

The perception of the extent of abusive commentary and the threat that it represented varied. Some runners reported that these incidents were relatively infrequent, a minor inconvenience that brought forth mildly quizzical or resigned responses ('it goes with the turf,' as one woman memorably put it). For others public harassment was a substantial annoyance. Many interviewees readily acknowledged that there are significant variations in how public harassment is experienced by different categories of person. Very generally, these differences crystallize into a pattern that can be described as a *gradient of harassment*. The likelihood and experience of public harassment is generally worse: for women than for men; for those on their own rather than those running in company; in summer than winter; in daylight than after dark; for beginning than more experienced runners; for race walkers than runners; for visibly heavier or slower runners. As became apparent through the interviews, runners tacitly understood the multifarious considerations that could make them the object of incivil attention. Runners have a close appreciation of the typical factors affecting the incidence and prevalence of their harassment by members of the public. It formed part of their practical knowledge in handling themselves in public and was for many a firmly ingrained part of their taken-for-granted, out-of-awareness cultural background – a kind of runners' *habitus*.

Techniques of the body: Mauss's conception of embodied instrumentalities

Very obviously, the body is the means or instrument for carrying out all the practical actions through which persons engage the world. Accordingly, the notion of body techniques (or 'techniques of the body') is a pivotal concept for an observational sociology of running.

In a 1934 lecture the French anthropologist Marcel Mauss devised the concept of 'body techniques' to describe 'the ways in which from society to society men [*sic*] know how to use their bodies' (Mauss 1979: 97). There is no 'natural' form to bodily actions, no panhuman, pre-cultural, universal or inherent shape to actions such as walking, swimming, spitting, digging, marching, even staring or giving birth. Rather, bodily actions are historically and culturally variable, acquired capacities that speak to culturally-specific memberships. According to Mauss the human body is our 'first and most natural instrument ... [our] first and most natural ... technical means'. When we engage the material world, for example when we drink, we employ 'a series of assembled actions, [which are] assembled for the individual not by himself alone but by all his education, by the whole society to which he belongs, in the place he occupies in it' (Mauss 1979: 104, 105). Sometimes the individual's society may not provide the relevant technique. Mauss tells how he taught a little girl with bronchial problems in a remote part of France how to spit. At four *sous* per spit she proved to be an adept learner!

Mauss's primary aim was to establish the cultural shaping of body techniques. He went on to identify a number of topics worthy of further investigation. Among these are gender and age differences, the effects of training, and the transmission and acquisition of these techniques. If we apply these ideas to running, we can see that as a body technique it varies quite conspicuously according to gender and age. Adult women in Western societies rarely run and when they do their movements are more restricted and inhibited than men's (cf. Young 1980). For adult men and women in such societies it is walking, not running, that is the usual mode of locomotion; children, in contrast, will frequently break into a run. Mauss also notes that body techniques can be more efficiently executed as a result of cultivation. In the case of running, repeated practice (known as 'training') can offset many of the effects of gender and age differences; Mauss's notion of trained accomplishment lies at the very heart of running as a sport and as a leisure activity. Through training it becomes possible to run further and faster and in the process modify the appearance and functioning of the body. Lastly, Mauss argues for close observation of socialization practices in order to learn more about how these techniques are acquired. In the case of running, Mauss observes changes evident in his own lifetime in the way children are taught to hold their arms (no longer in a high, across the chest position) and acknowledges the role of explicit, oral instruction in bringing about these changes.

Mauss's ideas have paved the way to a social constructionist interpretation of human embodiment. However, it is difficult to apply the concept of body techniques effectively in ethnographic research without further conceptual supplementation. In the metaphor of Wittgenstein's ladder, body techniques lift us to the level of a cultural understanding of embodied action, but once there it becomes necessary to seek other sources of guidance and illumination. One productive direction has been suggested by Nick Crossley (1995), who has sought to develop a theory of intercorporeality that links the embodiment-based phenomenology of Merleau-Ponty to the interaction sociology of Goffman. This chapter draws upon the interactional sensitivity of the Goffman end of the proposal.

Embodiment as interaction: Goffman

How are body techniques enacted in the actual situations of everyday life? Here the sociology of Erving Goffman (1922–82) can aid an appreciation of how body techniques feature in ordinary interaction. Goffman proposes that a special set of cultural understandings obtain whenever people are in the physical presence of each other. In situations of co-presence (social encounters), such when we are engaged in a conversation with a friend or are travelling on public transport, we have a pressing practical need to acquire information about others, about their status and identity, mood and orientation towards us, and so forth. Some of this information is given verbally by what people say to us, but other information is 'given off' or exuded by nonverbal conduct: their facial expressions, the stance they adopt, the disposition of their limbs, the tone of their speech. The cultural meanings associated with these gestures is not so much a language (the popular phrase 'nonverbal language' is at best a metaphorical usage) as an idiom: a standardized mode of expression. Hence the concept 'body idiom', which describes an institutionalized symbolism evident in 'dress, bearing, movements and position, sound level, physical gestures such as waving or saluting, facial gestures and broad emotional expressions' (Goffman 1963: 33). There is no time out from body idiom in any social encounter, for although

> an individual can stop talking, he cannot stop communicating through body idiom; he must say either the right thing or the wrong thing. He cannot say nothing. (Goffman 1963: 35)

Some elements of body idiom can be employed by the person to provide a gloss or explanation or critical comment on an untoward feature of the immediate social situation. Waiting on a street to meet someone the person may scan the surrounds or glance ostentatiously at a wristwatch in order to display graphically an innocent intent to passers-by. A pedestrian on a crossing may shake a head or wag a finger at a motorist who has only just managed to stop. These acts of 'body gloss' (Goffman 1971: 125) are identified as gestures that broadcast to anyone who cares to witness them our attitude towards some real or potentially threatening act.[3] In Goffman's perspective, then, the human body is the prime instrument of face-to-face interaction, an expressive entity capable of complex and nuanced communicative activity. Although the body was never a major analytic focus of Goffman's inquiries, his studies have proved a rich resource for constructionist analyses of embodiment.

As an illustration of this potential, consider how Goffman's focus on the specifics of interaction can serve to develop Mauss's notion of body techniques (Crossley 1995). Take the example of walking. Mauss (1979: 100, 102) recognizes that different groups acculturate a characteristic gait and posture in their members. He mentions the loose-jointed, hip-rolling *onioni* gait of Maori women, notes how as a small boy he was schooled to walk with his hands closed not open, and offers some plausible speculations about the impact of American cinema on French women's style of walking in the early 1930s. Goffman implicitly assumes a constructionist stance as his starting point for investigating how walking figures in face-to-face situations, such as making one's way down a busy city street or shopping mall. He shows how walking involves a range of cultural understandings about types of persons who may have to be managed or avoided (beggars, market researchers, pamphleteers), those to whom special care must be exercised (the frail, persons with white canes or guide dogs, toddlers), those who can be turned to for reliable directions (traffic wardens, police), those who want us to stop and listen and watch (buskers, mime artists), those who appear likely to threaten our persons and property. In walking down a street we must constantly monitor our own bodies and those of others in order to avoid collisions – less complicated when we are a 'single' (i.e. a solitary walker) than if we are a 'with' (accompanied by others with whom we must coordinate our progress). This involves scanning approaching pedestrians, but doing so in an unobtrusive and non-threatening way in accordance with the norm of 'civil inattention'. These skilled, embodied actions (and many others detailed in

Goffman 1963 and 1971) are body techniques at the micro-level of everyday social interaction.

Goffman's conceptual apparatus thus provides the basis for an analysis of the *exercise* or *performance* of body techniques (Crossley 1995: 146–8). These might best be termed body management techniques in order to emphasize the distance that Goffman has travelled from Mauss. In addition, Goffman provides a sociological demonstration of how a rigid mind–body dualism cannot be empirically sustained, since mind (e.g. the mundane practical intelligence required to walk down the street without mishap) is implicated in interactional conduct that is unavoidably mediated through the human body. In examining the exercise of body techniques we can come to see that mind and self are not ghosts in the machine of the body, resident in the upper portion of the skull, which somehow lie 'behind' action. Rather, mind and self are better understood as encoded in the ordinary enactment of body management techniques.

Techniques of neutralization

The notion that mind and self are encoded in ordinary action is consistent with the sociology of motives as it has developed since C. Wright Mills' (1940) pioneering work. By drawing upon this analytical tradition we can begin to open up the interview data and get some empirical purchase on the body management techniques of publicly harassed runners. Matza (1964; see also the earlier formulation of Sykes and Matza 1957) originally devised the concept of techniques of neutralization to describe the justifications that delinquents provide to account for their unlawful conduct. The concept has a broader applicability. When some act is called into question, these techniques serve to mobilize socially approved rhetorics that neutralize the act's questionable features. As Scott and Lyman (1968) point out, techniques of neutralization (or 'justifications') assert the positive value of a social act in the face of a claim to the contrary. Such contrary claims are commonly expressed in ridiculing street remarks directed to runners. Here are two descriptions of a scenario familiar to most runners:

> Teenage lads give you most grief when you're out. It's because there's a gang of them. If they weren't in a gang they wouldn't be any trouble – they've nothing really against runners... You can hear them all chatting and talking and when you approach they seem to

> go all quiet, and then you get the smart-arse who has to say something, who just can't keep quiet. (man aged 25)

> Young people are the worst, teenage types. When they're on their own they're no problem; it's when they're in groups of two or more they feel the need to pass comments as you run past. Often it's just 'Look at the state of that!' or 'Look at them tits!' or 'Look at that bum!' or things like that. Other times it's 'Get them knees up!' or 'Can't you go any faster?' ... Most of the time it doesn't bother me. (woman aged 35)

Passing motorists may slow down, 'beep' their horns in an endeavour to startle the runner, or their passengers may shout abuse through an open window. Beginning runners can find such treatment a significant source of discomfort, even threat. More experienced runners tend to become inured to the incivility but may still on occasion find it a cause of annoyance or unease. The overall effect, if not intention, of such street remarks is often to induce a sense of awkwardness and irritation, momentarily at least, at becoming the innocent target of another's discourteous conduct.

How do runners neutralize the moral and emotional freight of street remarks? Sykes and Matza's (1957) typology offers an initial guide to runners' responses to the offensive comments they encounter:

- *Denial of responsibility*. Some runners suggest that street remarks are the work not of responsible persons but of children and others whose puerile comments render them equivalent to children.
- *Denial of injury*. Street remarks are a form of teasing, a type of playfulness, and thus to be regarded more as a test of character than as a source of offence. A man of 33 said: 'They're just comments. Occasionally they can be irritating, but I wouldn't class them as insulting.'
- *Denial of victim*. Street remarks are merely verbal, doing no real damage to recipients – 'It's just water off a duck's back', said one man who had been running since the late 1970s.
- *Condemnation of the condemners*. Street remarks are voiced by people who do not understand running and who thus qualify themselves for sympathy. One runner suggested that they were uttered by people 'having a bad day' – 'If it'd been a Saturday and they were at a football match they would shout at the referee!'
- *Appeal to higher loyalties*. Runners reported that the physical and psychological benefits of running far outweighed the unease produced

by street remarks, which were regarded as part of the price to be paid for exercising in certain kinds of urban environments.

This typology, with its emphasis on the reasoning informing runners' treatment of street remarks, suggests a direction for the analysis of body management techniques. Yet an adequate analysis must show the mutual embeddedness of forms of practical reasoning about running and the practical management of the embodied action itself. Thus the next section attempts to make this linkage by means of an analysis of the typical strategies runners employ to deal with public harassment.

Public harassment and runners' body management techniques

I discuss runners' body management techniques in terms of four baldly stated strategies: (1) ignore 'ignorance'; (2) avoid 'trouble'; (3) talk back; (4) hit back. These techniques featured recurrently in the transcripts of the interviews. They can be placed on a continuum of response, from least to most confrontational.

Ignore 'ignorance'

The commonest response of runners to public harassment was simply to ignore it. Gardner (1980: 345) notes that 'blocking' or 'repressing' was a common reported response of women to street remarks in many kinds of public place. Runners of both sexes also adopt this tactic extensively. Interviewees repeatedly offered versions of the following traditional argument: Street remarks may be irksome, but they are the work of ignorant people, and to respond is both to dignify the original remark by lending it a significance that it does not deserve and to embroil the recipient in a 'no-win' situation. As one runner observed, 'Generally, it's just not worth responding because if you make a remark you just extend it and get more back.' A female runner elaborated:

> You tend to adopt different policies. Sometimes you think it's better to say nothing, not to respond to these comments at all. Other times you might say, 'Oh come on then, I bet you couldn't do anything,' or if it was particularly insulting you might tell them to fuck off or something, which I have done in the past. I find that that isn't the best one actually, because then they know they've got a response from you and you tend to hear another chorus coming from behind you and you think, 'Well why did I bother, what was the point in that?' (Woman aged 35)

A male runner reinforced this reasoning:

> It's best to bear in mind that it will stop when you get out of earshot in twenty or thirty seconds, depending on how fast you're running. It's over and done with and really isn't worth bothering about. I think that's the general rule for myself and most other runners I've been out with – just don't bother, it's not worth the candle. (Man aged 48)

Runners exhibit a keen awareness of the ever-present possibility of disadvantageous escalation if the slightest hint of a response was allowed to become evident. Underlying this pragmatic tactic there was a moral conviction: that a dignified silence conferred dignity on the silent respondent.

The practice of ignoring ignorant comments can become so ingrained in some runners that they simply do not hear – or perhaps more accurately, refuse to listen to – the street remarks addressed to them. One woman observed that, when she went out, she was so focused on her running that street remarks were heard as 'noises, not things that I internalize'. She continued: 'I would be very surprised if I could tell you what was said or who said it or what they looked like, because most of it doesn't register.' A notable feature of a number of the interviews was the poor recall of many runners of exactly what did get said to them when they were out running. The likeliest explanation for such reticence was runners' awareness of escalatory risks attendant upon response to street remarks. Thus, runners blocked out remarks at the moment they were uttered (or, in some cases, perhaps chose to report non-comprehension to the interviewer in order to avoid further questioning as to why they had not reacted to such a slur). In specific instances, of course, it may not be possible to discern whether the runner is actually failing to register a street remark or just appearing to ignore it. It may be impossible for the source of a street remark to separate the target's mind and body, recognition of a street remark and the behavioural display of that recognition (that is one great merit of the technique for runners). Doubtless in many cases actual not-listening is closely intertwined with a display of not paying attention to the incivil attention. In so far as the practicalities of accomplishing 'ignoring' were concerned, it seemed that the display of not-listening – the management of the shadow – was more consequential than its putatively real substance.

Avoid 'trouble'

Many runners are sufficiently irritated by street remarks as to avoid those places and times when they 'knew' difficulties might arise. One runner told me how his regular run, which went past a group of pubs popular with young people and known locally as a scene of frequent altercation and occasional violence, was amended on Friday and Saturday evenings in order to avoid 'groups of people getting drunk'. His reasoning was: 'Why attract trouble? You hear about trouble there every week so you just avoid it.' This example drew upon a spatially and temporally localized phenomenon well known to residents of what was a socially mixed part of Manchester. Pubs can also be the source of a certain amount of what runners may see as congenial teasing, especially in the more amiable atmosphere that was generated by drinkers gathered outside the premises when the weather permits. One interviewee sketched such a scene thus, noting that the runner provided a valuable talk topic (as might almost anything else): 'You get a group of lads outside a pub having a few pints. The conversation's lapsing and then you show up – you're manna from heaven! They're thinking, "Look at this prat coming along the road!"' One woman runner said she sometimes tried to avoid running past pubs on summer evenings and weekends because of the volley of comments she knew her person and activity would attract. 'But usually you're there and you think, Oh bugger!' Even on balmy summer's evenings, however, there was the possibility that a good-humoured hazard could degenerate into something that was simply a hazard.

Avoidance of particular places and times was significantly gendered: men were much more likely to venture 'off-road' as a single whereas women would attempt such routes only with another. Time was also gendered. Two men reported that as shift-workers they regularly ran in the middle of the night. Women, on the other hand, were much more disciplined about when they went out and cautious about running after dark. Temporal considerations figured in a decidedly contextual manner. Darkness might conceal threats and dangers, but it could also cloak the embarrassable runner. Several runners reported that as beginners they would go out very early in the morning or late at night to take advantage of their decreased visibility (especially to neighbours and acquaintances) at these times. (This is a tack also taken by runners whose appearance suggests they are not physically fit or whose appearance is bound always to miss the mark of the lithe athletic ideal, the mesomorphically healthy man, for instance, or large-breasted women who have discovered the limited effectiveness of sports bras.)

Another aspect of avoidance involved dressing unobtrusively. Again this appears to be significantly gendered.[4] Men tended not to see very far beyond the demands of practicality in selecting the clothing they ran in, whereas women were clearly influenced also by demands of modesty. One woman spoke of her 'running uniform' of tracksters and T-shirt: even on hot summer's days she would wear this costume. Several women said that they always wore T-shirts when training, preferably long and baggy and thus more concealing of chest and hips ('Why invite unwanted and unnecessary comments?' said one). Lighter, more exposing apparel, such as vests and crop-tops, seemed to be reserved for racing or trackwork. Two women suggested that while they 'dressed up' for their gym sessions ('it's like a night out with the girls'), they 'dressed down' to run in public. One elaborated that, 'When I'm running I don't want to draw attention to myself. I don't try to look glamorous while I'm running, whereas when I go to an aerobics class, yes, I look different. You dress up a little bit – you flaunt your body.' This runner expressed a wish 'to be accepted as a runner, not as a *female* runner.' Unfortunately, she added, 'a lot of men can't see that.' Sometimes, however, it was possible for the runner to intervene proactively in the process of harassment and redefine what is transpiring. Next I will discuss some of the defences, inversions and mitigations that runners could attempt.

Talk back

There was widespread support among runners for the view that silence, of ignoring ignorance was the best policy when faced with street remarks. In certain circumstances, however, the recipient's silence can be read by the interlocutor as a face-threatening act (Goffman 1967). This could place the recipient in a difficult position. The dilemma could be resolved by the tactic of 'minimal response' – a smile, a nod, a word or two. One woman formulated the issue as follows:

> I try not to have any more conversation than is necessary because I don't want to actually talk to them, or I don't want them to think that I want to talk, or want them to talk back to me more. I don't want to establish any relationship whatsoever.
> GS: You don't want to encourage them?
> No. But I don't want to snub them completely because at times I don't want to make them angry… (Woman aged 43)

This woman agreed that not reacting was the generally the best policy but that it could be damaging in some circumstances: 'Sometimes it works the other way. You get a bad reaction because you haven't reacted. Like, "Oh God it may never happen" or, "For God's sake, smile!"...and if you turn round and say what you want to say well then they completely, completely go for it.' As this suggests, the minimal response tactic was difficult to accomplish reliably and remained an intrinsically treacherous move.

Sometimes runners will venture a humorous response to those who taunt them. The potentially face-threatening aspect of a street remark can be neutralized by redefining the original remark in a humorous direction or by using a potentially insulting comment to make a statement that will – if only fleetingly – command respect. In response to the derisory comments offered by a group of youths that culminated in 'Can't you run any faster than that?' one male runner called back 'I only wish I could!' Face is not just saved but enhanced by the runner's presence of mind, which transforms an insulting comment into a joke (albeit a self-deprecating one) that could be shared with his detractors.

In these situations there was always the risk that even humour will prompt a worse response from the runner's detractors. Closure was often accomplished by the necessary brevity of the exchange: the runner was a moving target who was disappearing down the road should a third round be attempted. Sometimes more effective closure can be achieved if the runner could summon the resources to make an issue and take a stand, as in the following incident:

> The road a short distance from my house was crawling with workmen. It was a lovely hot summer's day. As I approached on the other side of the road I thought, I bet I get some comments from this lot. At my age you get blasé about it. I saw the first one who spotted me, and he drew me to the attention of his friend, and by the time I was opposite them the whole lot had stopped work. They shouted, 'Go on! Phworrr! Get your knees up, go on!' – all this business. So I just stopped dead in my tracks and weighed them, and they went quiet. I said, 'I'm sorry, you're all too young for me!' and carried on down the road. The next day I ran past again and got a nice, friendly, 'Morning, love!' (Woman aged 59)

A former schoolteacher, this runner was able to take advantage of her considerable interpersonal authority to secure closure of the exchange. This runner relished these situations, saying 'it's all part of the fun of running, to see if I can give better than I get.'

Children unaccompanied by an adult can be tenacious questioners in public places, masters and mistresses beyond their years of the arts of 'ceremonial deviance' (Cahill 1987). Runners may find that the tactic of ignoring their comments is not always easy to sustain since children can be very persistent and because their 'nonperson' status means that they need not be taken very seriously by others or themselves. On my runs into the university from home I usually carry a small bag in each hand containing personal effects, papers and the like. Passing through a working-class district that was beginning to acquire a rough reputation, I was quizzed regularly about the contents of the bags. I let the kids guess but did not disclose, since to do so would provide them the status of ratified participants in an encounter that would likely shift frame from civil inquiry to opportunity for insult. One example of this escalation occurred when I was race walking through the same area. A couple of boys about seven or eight years of age approached me: 'You exercising, mate?' I ignored them. They ran off and then returned. One said, 'Where have you come from?' I didn't want to say, so I gesticulated over my shoulder and told them, 'A long way back.' The kid's instant reply was, 'Then what are you doing around here?' He ran off. I laughed, because I knew that I was far too big to be threatened by the kid and because he would have given the same answer no matter what I had replied ('Borneo.' – 'Then what are you doing round here?'). But I felt disturbed by the hostile in-group attitudes the remark evinced.

These negotiations need not only involve the participants in a street remark encounter. They might be facilitated by events occurring behind the backs of runners. A woman spoke of persistent aggravation from a gang of lads on one part of her training route:

> One of them found out via his mother that I'd run a marathon. After that I didn't get any abuse from that particular gang. Rather it was 'Go on love, you're doing well, keep going.' They still used to shout, but it wasn't insulting. It was as if they had a grudging respect: 'See her, y'know the one that had that baby, she's run a marathon.' They'd obviously spoken about it, because after that I never got any trouble. (Woman aged 35)

Detractors' acquaintance with this woman's sporting achievement and her identity in the local community here served to effect a redefinition of the situation from public harassment to collective acclaim.

Sometimes exchanges between runners and their harassers can progress from negotiations to outright disputes. There is a fundamental conflict of interest between runners and dog owners that is regularly fought out in parks the world over. The opening terms of the dispute are standard: the runner is brought to a halt by an unleashed dog that is barking, leaping up at the runner, circling the runner's heels. The runner is concerned about the risk of being bitten, scratched, toppled or simply embarrassed when revealed in public as someone whose activities are being thwarted, and, of course, the runner is frustrated at not being able to run. The dog-owner gives assurances of the dog's benign intent ('It's only having a bit of fun, love, it won't hurt you') and often cannot see what all the fuss is about. The runner sees things differently:

> You ask the owner to get the dog under control and they say, 'It's alright, it's only playing.' But I don't want to play with it, I want to go for a run, thank you! (Man aged 47)

> They'll say, 'It only wants to play.' Yes, but I don't. I object to people on public roads and paths with dogs who come and interfere with what I'm doing. I'm not interfering with their activities, why should I have to stop? (Woman aged 59)

> Some people are very good. They'll see you coming and they'll call the dog to heel and they'll hang on to them till you pass. And there are other prats who will shout things like, 'Oh, it's only having a bit of fun, love, it won't hurt you', 'He's only playing.' No! No! He's got big teeth! He's bigger than I am! (Woman aged 41)

In such situations there may be an interpretive asymmetry so fundamental that rational debate cannot bridge the parties. Usually the runner makes an escape at the earliest opportunity. One runner suggested that some dog owners seem to express an attitude 'of dismay at having to call the dog off, as if they cannot quite understand why they have to.'

Negotiations around the management of dogs and runners in public places are sometimes hostile in tone. Runners report high levels of exasperation and frustration in these situations but rarely resort to physical conflict with dog owners (although dogs are occasionally kicked or struck in anger). However, there are situations where public harassment results in physical retaliation from the runner. Some instances are considered next.

Hit back

Ignoring jibes and heckling is the response of very many runners most of the time. Not listening and maintaining a dignified silence are common responses. Occasionally – very occasionally in my data – runners report instances of physically responding to a slight. Sometimes the context of the physical response is playful. A middle-aged male out running with a workmate recalled how they approached a teenaged couple one evening. The young man was sitting on a low wall with his woman friend leaning against him. As the runners approached the young woman straightened up and deliberately got in the runners' way in what they took as a show of bravado and cussedness:

> And I saw absolutely no reason for me to alter my running line so I just dipped my shoulder – I played rugby for twenty years before I took up running – and gave her a little nudge. Not particularly hard but just enough to off-balance her. She bounced into her boyfriend on the wall and grabbed him and the centre of gravity was such they both went flying over the wall. It was hugely amusing – they were both laughing themselves – I think it was a mutually understood thing that she had really got her comeuppance. It was really amusing, it wasn't unpleasant – poetic justice! (Man aged 48)

On rare occasion runners do hit back in anger. The same runner recalled how, when just past his fortieth birthday and a little sensitive to the evidence of his advancing years, he gave pursuit to a youth whose abuse had been particularly foul-mouthed and had focused on the runner's ageing appearance. When cornered the youth presented the excuse that it was his friend who was the real guilty party. The runner, whose 'rag was up' by now, recounts:

> I really gave him a damn good clout and said 'Well pass that on to your friend!' and added something like 'Some of these old buggers are a bit fitter than you might think and a bit more formidable than you might have thought.' Well, I hoped that taught him a little bit of a lesson. Having said that, I didn't run in the same area for a month or two afterwards!

Another man recalls running with his wife when he was 'in a very poor mood' (it was a few days after his mother's unexpected death). A passer-by made an offensive remark about his wife. The runner immediately stopped, grabbed the man responsible by the neck and suggested that should the remark ever be repeated he would throw him in the river. In this case an offensive comment directed at an intimate was an assault felt more keenly than one directed to self and was overlayed with notions of chivalrous defence. The husband of an international race walker of diminutive stature once told me of how she 'lost it' when barracked one night when they were out training, with the result that she pushed a young man, who stood more than a foot taller than herself, through a chip-shop window. The husband was quick to spirit away his still incensed spouse from the scene of the crime.

No doubt stories like these have apocryphal dimensions. They are certainly told with a great deal of glee. Vigilante logic is at work: lessons are taught and comeuppance delivered. Rather than dignified silence, there is justified revenge; instead of turning the other cheek, runners vent rage physically. Intolerance is met with intolerance. In these stories the runner is transformed into an avenging figure who, challenged by a provocation of significant proportions, felt justified in acting violently toward its source. Duly incited, the runner's violent act could come to be seen as an appropriate and deeply moral response. And the fellow runners to whom these tales are told will vicariously share the moment, appreciate very fully its contours and dynamics, and laugh. These are the legends that sustain a subculture.

Conclusion

In this chapter, I have tried to show that an adequate sociological analysis of the body management techniques of publically harassed runners requires attention to both the details of bodily enactment and to the practical reasoning informing that enactment. This is the sense in which body techniques and techniques of neutralization are each implied by the other. The body management techniques discussed above – ignoring ignorance, avoiding trouble, talking back and hitting back – might be regarded as strategies of resistance to the everyday intolerance faced by publicly harassed runners. As I have tried to indicate, they are strategies that contain significantly gendered components.

The preceding analysis of runners' strategies has been partial and partisan. Two important qualifications should be noted. First, although the chapter has concentrated upon incivilities directed at runners, it must be acknowledged that runners are not always model citizens who observe all the proprieties. Runners can inconvenience others and act as a nuisance in public places. Riders complain that runners may spook the horse; drivers, that they behave as if their vehicles were made of pillows; hikers, that they may be surprised and off-balanced; pedestrians, that men runners may use their speedy passage to pinch women's bottoms (Gardner, personal communication). Some runners interviewed owned up to running recklessly, especially in dense traffic. Weaving in and out of slow-moving traffic was a recurrent misdemeanour. Some admitted to running without due care and attention when they were going for a 'time': they conceded that fast running was conducive to the production of raised levels of aggression. One runner told me, 'when I used to run in a pack with a club we'd get cars cutting us up and we'd bang them on the bonnet or bang them on the roof and get into "verbals" with drivers.' Another spoke of running in a group along a popular seafront where the lead runner's advice to the oncoming, predominantly retired and elderly promenaders, was to 'get out of the fucking way'. A woman reported being stopped by a driver who proceeded to lecture her about running on the wrong side of the road. The dispute about the interpretation of the law was only concluded when she closed the encounter, telling him in no uncertain terms to mind his own business.[5] Runners may be more sinned against than sinning, but are not entirely blameless parties in uncivil interactions in public places.

A second qualification concerns the content of street remarks. A large proportion of the street remarks runners routinely receive are unambiguously offensive or carry pejorative connotations. On occasion, however, runners find themselves the recipients of gratuitous remarks from citizens that are genuinely encouraging and/or complimentary. A minimal supportive interchange (Goffman 1971) may be enacted. Runners report that they sometimes receive good-humoured comments – such as 'Keep it up!', 'You're brave!', 'Go on lad!', 'Nearly there!', 'Rather you than me!' and 'Come on, love, you're doing well' – that seem to require no more than a nod and smile in reply. These comments seem to originate predominantly from unacquainted persons in their middle years or older. Some were of visibly pensionable age, a crucial contextualizing consideration for remarks like 'Twenty years ago I might have beat you!' and 'I wish I could still do that.' In Goffman's terms, both old and young people are ritually profane persons whose profanity presumably allows them to issue gratuitous remarks easily to passers-by. However, that does not explain why the old are an unfailing source of encouragement to the runner and why the young are just as surely a tireless fund of ridicule. Perhaps the encouragement of the old derives from their lived experience of ritual sacredness and the significance of supportive interchange. Correspondingly, the ridicule of the young may derive from their incapacity to appreciate the ritual sacredness of persons as anything more than an externally imposed imperative.

Body techniques are also required for the proper management of supportive street remarks: smiles, waves, the return of greetings and so forth. This underlines once again how intricately normatively organized public spaces can be. In drawing upon the concepts of techniques of neutralization and body management techniques the preceding analysis has attempted to articulate the performative dimensions of running in urban social space. The chapter has shown some of the interrelations between interpretive skill, social competence and embodied action in a commonplace physical activity. People going out for a run do much more than merely run.

Notes

1. Except where otherwise specified, 'runners' is used as the generic to include runners and race walkers of a range of abilities. Aged between 21 and 59 at the time of the interviews, my sample included beginners with no more than a few months' experience of fun running to national age group record holders.
2. A similar claim is made by Monaghan (2001) in his ethnography of body-building subcultures. In this case, disclosure of sensitive information about drug-taking practices was made possible only because the researcher could manifestly lay claim to a body-builder identity.
3. These brief comments merely sketch a few aspects of Goffman's contributions to the sociology of embodiment. Goffman is rightly renowned for his studies of such eminently embodied phenomena as stigma and gender difference. Therefore it is not surprising that his thinking has figured in such major theoretical syntheses as Turner (1984) and Shilling (1993).
4. A conjecture worth testing in future studies is that the activity of running *polarizes* the gendered dimensions of conduct in public places. Therefore, compared to being in public in some more commonplace capacity, such as shopper or pedestrian, men were likely to feel more assured, confident, and robust (an '*armouring*' effect) when running, while women were likely to feel more apprehensive, uneasy and suspicious (an '*exposure*' effect). Viewed thus, running was an activity that magnified aspects of the gendered experience of public places.
5. An example of a runner harassing a member of the public from my fieldnotes: 'About ten miles through the London Marathon the field is passing down a narrow road. The road is lined by an enthusiastic crowd in party mood. A group of three men in their early twenties, wearing identical women's clothes and wigs are running together. One sights a young woman in the crowd and as he passes gives loud voice to the following observation: "Put them away madam! Cor, there must have been a good two-thousand quids-worth of silicone there! I bet they don't roll into her armpits when she lies down!" The other men with him supportively chortle but no one else, especially the women running nearby, pay him or his comment any attention. It's hit-and-run insult time.'

References

Agar, M. 1980. *The Professional Stranger. An Informal Introduction to Ethnography*. New York: Academic Press.

Cahill, S.E. 1987. 'Children and Civility: Ceremonial Deviance and the Acquisition of Ritual Competence', *Social Psychology Quarterly*, 50: 312–21.

Crossley, N. 1995. 'Body Techniques, Agency and Intercorporeality: On Goffman's "Relations in Public"', *Sociology*, 29(1): 133–49.

Gardner, C.B. 1980. 'Passing by: Street Remarks, Address Rights and the Urban Female', *Sociological Inquiry*, 50: 328–56.

Gardner, C.B. 1995. *Passing By: Gender and Public Harassment*. Berkeley and Los Angeles: University of California Press.

Goffman, E. 1963. *Behavior in Public Places: Notes on the Social Organization of Gatherings*. New York: Free Press.

Goffman, E. 1967. *Interaction Ritual: Essays on Face-to-Face Behavior*. Chicago: Aldine.

Goffman, E. 1971. *Relations in Public: Microstudies of the Public Order*. London: Allen Lane.

Matza, D. 1964. *Delinquency and Drift*. New York: Wiley.

Mauss, M. 1979. 'Body Techniques', in *Sociology and Psychology: Essays*, trans. Ben Brewster. London: Routledge & Kegan Paul.

Mills, C.W. 1940. 'Situated Actions and Vocabularies of Motive'. *American Sociological Review*, 5: 904–13.

Monaghan, L.F. 2001. *Bodybuilding, Drugs and Risk*. London: Routledge.

Scott, M. and Lyman, S.M. 1968. 'Accounts', *American Sociological Review*, 33: 46–62.

Shilling, C. 1993. *The Body in Social Theory*. London: Sage.

Smith, G. 1997. 'Incivil Attention and Everyday Intolerance: Vicissitudes of Exercising in Public Places', *Perspectives on Social Problems*, 9: 59–79.

Sykes, G.M. and Matza, D. 1957. 'Techniques of Neutralization: A Theory of Delinquency', *American Sociological Review*, 22: 664–70.

Turner, B.S. 1984. *The Body and Society*. Oxford: Blackwell.

Young, I.M. 1980. 'Throwing Like a Girl: A Phenomenology of Feminine Body Comportment, Motility and Spatiality', *Human Studies*, 3: 137–156; reprinted in I.M. Young 1990. *Throwing like a Girl and Other Essays in Feminist Philosophy and Social Theory*. Bloomington: Indiana University Press.

10
Stop Making Sense? The Problem of the Body in Youth/Sub/Counter-Culture[1]

Paul Sweetman

> People think it's all about misery and desperation and death and all that shite. Which is not to be ignored. But what they forget is, is the pleasure of it. Otherwise we wouldn't do it. After all, we're not fucking stupid. Or at least we're not that fucking stupid. Take the best orgasm you ever had, multiply it by a thousand and you're still nowhere near it.
>
> 'Renton', in *Trainspotting*, Boyle 1996

Introduction

Much of the existing writing on youth, sub, or counter-culture has adopted a predominantly textual or semiotic approach, focusing on subcultural style, in particular, and the resistant or confrontational meanings that such styles are said to convey. In so doing, however, this literature has tended to neglect the lived experiences of those involved, or, as Ken Gelder puts it, 'what they actually *do*' (Gelder 1997b: 145). This point has been frequently noted elsewhere (see, for example: Cohen 1997 [1980]; Gelder 1997b; Muggleton 1997). What this chapter seeks to address is a more specific aspect of this overall neglect: the tendency to overlook, or accord insufficient attention to, the way in which subcultural practices are articulated through or on the bodies of the actors concerned.

This is arguably of particular concern given the centrality of the corporeal and/or affective dimension to the bulk of the activities in question. In other words, 'what they actually *do*', where subcultures are concerned, tends to centre on the body, and if we want to do more than simply interpret subcultures as signifying systems – if we want to understand what motivates subcultural involvement and *what people get out of it* – then it is to the corporeal or affective dimension that we need to turn.

The following, then, looks first at the classic subcultural accounts associated with the Birmingham Centre for Contemporary Cultural Studies (CCCS) in order to illustrate the problems with the textual or semiotic approach. The chapter then goes on to draw on my own research into contemporary body modification, illustrating the various ways in which the process of becoming tattooed or pierced is central, rather than peripheral, to the motivations and experiences of many of those concerned. In the third section I briefly address some of the more recent subcultural studies, noting the ways in which studies of club culture, in particular, *have* addressed certain of the issues in question, but not always in a sufficiently rigorous manner. The fourth and fifth sections deal with some of the wider theoretical and methodological issues raised in the foregoing discussion. In section five, for example, I consider some of the practical implications of my position, and some of the problems it might raise for the researcher in the field.

In part, then, the chapter seeks to address certain of the wider implications of an insistence on engaging with the *felt* dimensions of subcultural involvement. The chapter's primary purpose, however, is to emphasize the importance of focusing on this area if one wishes to fully understand the phenomenon in question. To paraphrase Jack Katz, it is suggested that 'only through awareness and analysis of the phenomenological foreground of' subcultural activity, 'of the intricacies of its "lived sensuality"' can we understand not only its 'moral and sensual attractions', but also its wider cultural significance (Katz, in Ferrell 1993: 167).

Subculture as sign

As was noted above, the classic work on British subcultures associated with the CCCS tended to adopt a textual or semiotic approach, for the most part treating subcultural formations as signifying systems, and neglecting the lived experience of subculturalists themselves. As Gelder points out, in these studies, 'the focus on style comes at the expense of other subcultural features: modes of pleasure and fun, for example' (Gelder 1997a: 88), and the 'effects of a style' are frequently 'emphasized at the expense of the nature and behaviour of the participants who put it there' (Gelder 1997c: 378). In spite of Phil Cohen's insistence that there are three levels to sub-cultural analysis: historical, structural or semiotic, and 'the phenomenological analysis of the way the subculture is actually 'lived out' by those who are its bearers and supports' (Cohen 1997 [1972]: 95), little of this 'third level' analysis actually appears in the classic accounts (Muggleton 1997: 201).

In his own analysis of skinhead subculture, for example, Cohen himself focuses on the 'second level' – structural or semiotic analysis – suggesting that in their attempts to symbolically resolve the tensions inherent in the loss of the traditional working-class community, the skinheads' 'uniform[s] ... could be interpreted as a kind of caricature of the model worker' (Cohen 1997 [1972]: 95). John Clarke et al. (1976) similarly focus on style or signification, concentrating specifically on the way 'subcultures used the materials and commodities of the 'youth market' to construct meaningful styles and appearances for themselves', and suggesting that the 'adoption by Skinheads of boots ... and shaved hair was "meaningful" ... because these external manifestations resonated with ... Skinhead conceptions of masculinity' (Clarke et al. 1976: 56). In neither Cohen's (1997 [1972]), nor Clarke et al.'s (1976) accounts, however, do we find any discussion of the *practicalities* of such stylistic devices, or of the way in which such devices might themselves *construct*, rather than simply express, particular forms of (embodied) subjectivity.

Perhaps the most explicit (or exclusive?) focus on style is in Dick Hebdige's *Subculture: The Meaning of Style* (1979), whose very title indicates the author's arguably reductionist approach to his object of study. Hebdige refers, for instance, to 'the spectacular subculture' as a 'mechanism of semantic disorder: a kind of temporary blockage in the system of representation' (Hebdige 1979: 90), and adopting Umberto Eco's term 'semiotic guerilla warfare' (Hebdige 1979: 105), conflates the following two questions: 'how does a subculture make sense to its members? [And] [h]ow is it made to *signify* disorder?' (Hebdige 1979: 100, my emphasis). In relation to punk, in particular, Hebdige argues that:

> Certain semiotic facts are undeniable. The punk subculture, like every other youth culture, was constituted in a series of spectacular transformations of a whole range of commodities, values, commonsense attitudes, etc. It was through these adopted forms that certain sections of predominantly working-class youth were able to restate their opposition to dominant values and institutions. (Hebdige 1979: 116)

He later goes on to suggest that punk 'did not so much magically resolve experienced contradictions as *represent* the experience of contradiction ... in the form of visual puns' (Hebdige 1979: 121). Now, I am not arguing against such an interpretation (though it is questionable in certain respects), so much as suggesting that this leaves a great deal out: is this how the sub-culture made sense to its members? Is this what motivated their involvement? What of the activities associated with punk – pogoing, speeding, listening to punk music – were these engaged in solely for their semiotic potential?

Some of the writing associated with the CCCS does bring the body and its pleasures into the frame, albeit implicitly and only at odd points. Hebdige's own early study – *The Meaning of Mod* – for example, notes that '[a]mphetamines made life tolerable, "blocked" one's sensory channels so that action and risk and excitement were possible ... and confined one's attention to the search, the ideal, the goal, rather than the attainment of the goal' (Hebdige 1976: 91). It is not certain that the Mods themselves experienced speeding in precisely these terms, however. Even Paul Willis's (1976) piece in *Resistance through Rituals*, which contrasts with most of the other studies in its adoption of an ethnographic rather than semiotic approach, is problematic in its refusal to engage fully with the evidence presented. To be more specific, in adopting a 'Beckeresque' or constructionist framework in relation to his hippy respondents' drug consumption – and thus arguing against their direct physiological effects in favour of the social construction of meaning – Willis fails to consider the dialectical relationship between the cultural and the physiological apparent in certain of his informants' comments.[2] Talking about sex on LSD, for example, one of the interviewees notes:

> it was the most incredible experience I think I have ever had, because the whole orgasm becomes total, ... not only in the neurological centre of the brain that gives you a sensation of pleasure, not only in the tip of the penis, but over the whole of the body, man, in the tips of my fingers, I had orgasm after orgasm. Now that was a state of as near bliss that I think I shall ever get to. (quoted in Willis 1976: 110)

It would seem from this quotation that even amongst these more laid-back subcultural respondents, the pleasures associated with subcultural involvement were more than symbolic. Although apparently aimed at the more semiotic accounts, Stanley Cohen's critique of the CCCS approach is thus also applicable to Willis:

> The intellectual pyrotechnics behind many of these theories are ... too cerebral, in the sense that a remote, historically derived

motivational account (such as 'recapturing community') hardly conveys the immediate emotional tone and satisfaction of the actors themselves. (Cohen 1997 [1980]: 161)

Contemporary body modification and physical affect

While not, perhaps, strictly comparable with the activities or practices considered above,[3] I shall now present a few points drawn from my own research on tattooing and body piercing in order to further illustrate the dangers of a purely semiotic approach. These points form part of a wider study on contemporary body modification, for which in-depth, semi-structured interviews were conducted with 35 tattooed and/or pierced informants, as well as with several professional tattooists, body piercers and other key respondents.[4] Data were also generated through observation conducted at a number of tattoo conventions and tattoo and/or piercing studios, as well as analysis of the popular literature devoted to the forms of body modification in question.

The study as a whole married my theoretical interests in questions relating to the body, identity, fashion and consumption with a more personal interest in tattooing and related forms of body modification. Though not pierced, I was tattooed twice during the course of my research, once by appointment with a tattooist I had already interviewed, and once immediately after an interview with another key informant. In the latter case, I had asked the tattooist in question to discuss his method of tattooing with hand-made implements rather than by machine, and was told that perhaps the best way to understand the difference was to gain some first-hand experience.[5]

Certain of the implications of my own involvement with the forms of body modification in question are to be addressed below, as is the wider issue of access to the experiential or phenomenological aspects of subcultural involvement through standard methods of data collection. As indicated above, however, the present discussion is intended to indicate that, whilst amenable to textual analysis (see, for example, Sweetman 1999a), the tattooed or pierced body cannot, or should not, be reduced to pure text, and that the *process* of becoming tattooed or pierced – or *writing* the self-as-text – is central rather than peripheral to many contemporary body modifiers' motivations and experience. Physical or corporeal affect, in other words, is key to the lived experience of many such 'subculturalists', and while socially or culturally mediated, the affectual cannot, in this case, be reduced to a purely discursive effect.[6]

In the first place, many tattooees and piercees *enjoy* the process of becoming tattooed or pierced. As one young male tattooee told me: 'I loved it.... I just didn't want him to stop. You know, the longer it took the better.' Having found that there was 'something quite sexual' about the process, the informant in question 'went back and had [his tattoos] filled in again' soon after their initial application, in spite of the fact that 'they didn't really need' doing: 'I just wanted to have it done, 'cause it was enjoyable'. Another, heavily tattooed female interviewee told me that she too 'gets off' on getting tattooed: 'I think the whole process is gorgeous.... I mean even if I can't get a new one, ... I'll go in and get them touched up ... just 'cause I like the needle on the skin.'

Even those who don't relish the modificatory process itself frequently refer to the 'buzz' associated with the acquisition of a new tattoo or piercing. When asked how he felt immediately after being tattooed, one interviewee replied:

> Totally euphoric. I mean ... you're releasing tons of endorphins into your blood, and it's rushing around at God knows what speed ... and all of a sudden your body's not hurting any more, ... and it's like, 'Shit!', and it just hits you. And most of the time ... I ... could run around all over the place, and ... jump up and down and stuff when I have 'em done, I just feel that good.

And whether as a result of the initial process or the subsequent high, certain body modifiers find the acquisition of a new tattoo or piercing to be a cathartic experience, again illustrating that, for some, the necessary physicality of the process is key to their overall motivation. As one, heavily tattooed interviewee put it:

> I usually get tattooed if I'm bored or depressed, and that ... wakes your system back up again. ... I like the finished [tattoo], the fact that ... you're making a permanent marking at the end of it, but the actual process seems to kick your system back in a bit, if you're feeling down. (See also G. P-Orridge, in Vale and Juno 1989: 255)

The process is also seen by some as leading to new forms of experiential knowledge. As one young, male interviewee with a single nipple-piercing told me:

> It sort of open[ed] ... up an entirely new sort of world to me, something that I hadn't, although I'd seen before, it's nothing that

> I could have experienced before. ... I'm still learning ... what it feels like, erm, taking care of it, that kind of thing. What I can and can't do with it.

And another young tattooee told me that his enjoyment of the tattoo process had caused him to rethink certain fundamental attitudes towards pain, blood, emotion, and his own interiority:

> You know, the whole being bled process as well, the bleeding, and the pain, which I'd never really associated with a beneficial experience before. You know, blood and being cut, and pain had always been falling over when you're a kid in the street, or getting smacked on the way home from the pub. That was never like, something you'd look forward to. But this is quite an enjoyable, creative process, that involved, like, the pain. I think that brought me to the realization that every emotion in life is just the same, whether it's the emotions hate [and] love, pain and happiness, it's all the same. It's just an emotion and they can be used for beneficial purposes, and pain can be controlled, and blood shouldn't be looked upon as something to be scared of, do you know what I mean? It's just what's pumping around your body all day, and we just don't get to see it till it comes out, then you're scared of it.

A further effect of the necessary physicality of the modificatory process is that it can allow for the forging of intimate links between both artist and client (or piercer and piercee), and between the client and others in the studio. Noting that his girlfriend had been present while he had his nipple pierced, one interviewee told me:

> and I do feel it's sort of bonded us a bit ... because it was me sort of, exposing [myself], and being ... fully vulnerable at that point. You know, me sitting there letting myself have this dirty great needle put through me.

The necessarily invasive, physical and frequently painful nature of the modificatory process means that many tattooees and piercees also feel linked to others who have so modified their bodies. As one interviewee told me: 'I think you know what they ... felt when they had it done, and you know [the] reasons why they had it done. Erm, and ... you do feel part of, like, a community I suppose.' And as another, heavily tattooed and formerly heavily pierced interviewee put it: 'even if you're really rich, if you can't stand the pain, you can't get tattooed. So it's like something that everyone's been through, whether you've got loads of money or not.'

Finally, for some, this was seen explicitly as a form of 'tribal' membership:

> I do ... find there's a similar consciousness among people ... who've got a tattoo. ... it's like anybody who has a love of something, ... they all get together in the end, and that's modern day tribes. ... even if you break it down to what people do when they go out, you've got, you know, like, you've got the rockers, and you've got ravers, they all go out and do the same thing ... and there's a shared consciousness among them.

The process of becoming tattooed or pierced – the lived, corporeal reality of the modificatory process – is thus central to the motivations and experience of many contemporary body modifiers. As noted above, this is not to deny the validity of an analysis of the tattooed or pierced body as text. What it does suggest, however, is that a purely symbolic/semiotic/textual approach will fail to engage with much of what is significant, both from the point of view of the subcultural members themselves, and from a sociological or cultural studies perspective. Certain of the wider sociological implications of the points made above will be considered below. First, however, I intend to look briefly at some of the more recent subcultural literature that *has* engaged, to greater or lesser degrees, with the affectual dimensions of the subcultural experience.

Subculture as affect

Perhaps the most adequate account of the affectual aspects of subcultural involvement that I have yet encountered is Jeff Ferrell's (1993) study of the graffiti scene as a lived subculture, which focuses on the *act* of writing rather than simply the finished text, and stresses the need to pay attention to the 'lived experience of [subcultural] resistance' (Ferrell 1993: 177). Ferrell notes, for example, the 'adrenalin rush' associated with 'tagging and piercing' (Ferrell 1993: 172), and argues that such acts 'become meaningful for the writers not as moments of generic graffiti writing, but in the immediacy of distinctly shared experience. ... the meaning of graffiti writing is embedded in the details of its execution' (Ferrell 1993: 167).

Most of the work I will discuss in this section is less directly grounded in the actual experiences of those involved. Nevertheless, a considerable body of work has emerged in recent years that does address the affective dimension of subcultural involvement, much of it focused on music and, more particularly, the dance or club scene. Lawrence Grossberg (1997 [1984]), for instance, goes some way towards solving the problems associated with more semiotic analyses in focusing on the immediate pleasures and effects of rock and roll. Rejecting the textual analyses of figures like Simon Frith and Dick Hebdige (Grossberg 1997 [1984]: 477), Grossberg argues that:

> We might begin to understand how rock and roll works by affirming that it is, above all, fun – the production of pleasure. ... Its power lies not in what it says or means but in what it does in the textures and contexts of its uses. For in fact, different audiences interpret the same texts differently, and there seems to be little correlation between semantic readings and uses/pleasures ... Rock and roll ... is a performance whose 'significance' cannot be read off the 'text'. It is not that rock and roll does not produce and manipulate meaning, but rather that meaning itself functions in rock and roll affectively, that is, to produce and organise desires and pleasures. (Grossberg 1997 [1984]: 482)

For Grossberg, '[t]he politics of rock and roll arises from its articulation of affective alliances as modes of survival within the post-modern world' (Grossberg 1997 [1984]: 483).

Susan McClary (1994) presents a similar 'anti-textual' argument, suggesting that, where popular musical forms are concerned, 'the music itself – especially as it intersects with the body and destabilizes accepted norms of subjectivity, gender and sexuality – is precisely where the politics of music often resides' (McClary 1994: 32). For McClary, 'music is foremost among cultural "technologies of the body", that is a site where we learn how to experience socially mediated patterns of kinetic energy, being in time, emotions, desire, pleasure and much more' (McClary 1994: 37). Despite its physical or corporeal implications then, the power of music, for McClary, remains socially or culturally mediated: '[t]hese patterns inevitably arrive already marked with histories – histories involving class, gender, ethnicity' (McClary 1994: 37).

Within the more general writing on musical affect, then, there are differing degrees of emphasis on the extent to which such effects are socially or culturally mediated. This is also true of the more specific analyses of the dance or club scene. Certain accounts stress only the apparently extra-discursive nature of the clubbing experience. Chris Stanley (1997), for example, suggests that, 'the raver surrenders to the void in a Dionysian hedonism of an internal satisfaction of desire through the sacrifice of self to the dance' (Stanley 1997: 47). And this is purely about affect: '[t]his is a desire not to demonstrate deviancy, but to attain a knowledge at the limit of experience' (Stanley 1997: 48), '[t]here is no possibility of discussion-relationships, only movement in and out between an internal realm in a displacement of identity and an external realm in the collective atmosphere of the rave' (Stanley 1997: 51). Similarly, Simon Reynolds (1997) argues that rave, as a postmodern experience of 'culture without content', can be seen as 'a Bataille-like-sacrifice cult of expenditure-without-return' (Reynolds 1997: 106).

For Hillegonda Rietveld (1997) contemporary dance culture is centred on both physical affect and the 'collective effervescence' generated by the clubbing crowd. Talking about the early house scene in Chicago, she notes that '[t]his was not a political movement with manifestos in print. It was an ephemeral cultural event which was experienced through the movements of the body, its sexuality and its emotional reserves' (Rietveld 1997: 128). And the clubbers were drawn 'together in a sense of community, as though they were attending a religious gathering' (Rietveld 1997: 128. See also, Ross 1994: 11).

By way of contrast, Will Straw (1997 [1991]) suggests that contemporary dance is far more reflexive: less a case of 'lost in music' than a competition for sub-cultural kudos. '[D]istinction [amongst clubbers] takes shape around the degree to which people dance within disciplined parameters (as opposed to cutting loose)', and '[t]he significance invested in these differences obviously works against one familiar reading of the experience of dance: as a transcendent experience of the body in motion' (Straw 1997 [1991]: 500). Walter Hughes, in a related vein, also stresses the culturally mediated nature of 'disco affect': 'disco is less a decadent indulgence than a disciplinary, regulatory discourse that paradoxically permits, even creates a form of freedom' (Hughes 1994: 148). 'By submitting to its insistent, disciplinary beat, one learns...how to be one kind of gay man; one accepts, with pleasure rather than suffering, the imposition of a version of gay identity' (Hughes 1994: 148).

There is some tension, then, between accounts of contemporary music, and the clubbing scene in particular, which emphasize the transcendent and extra-discursive or the socially and culturally mediated nature of corporeal affect. What unites these studies from my own perspective, however, is the way in which they focus, at least in part, on subculture as lived-experience, and thus go a long way towards overcoming the difficulties associated with the more textual analyses considered above. That said, I would also argue that few of these studies go far enough in relating to actual reported experience: many of the assertions remain theoretical or speculative (or are presented as such) even if they do *address* the subculture as lived-experience side of the debate. As David Muggleton notes, there is still a 'lack of…studies which privilege the actual practices, meanings and experiences of [subculturalists] themselves' (Muggleton 1997: 185). Despite these difficulties, however, such work at least *suggests* that affect is central, rather than peripheral, to subcultural experience: that whether or not such pleasures are socially or culturally mediated, corporeal affect is key to an understanding of the pleasures, intimacies, subjectivities and socialities that inhere around subcultural experience. In this respect, such studies link up with my own work on contemporary body modification in suggesting that one cannot focus on subcultures as a whole, or subcultural bodies, purely and simply as texts. It is to some of the wider implications of this position that I will now turn.

Theoretical implications

Despite the problems raised above, the accounts of contemporary dance culture, combined with the comments of the various tattooees and piercees referred to earlier, lend support to the view that in order to fully grasp action of this sort we need to do more than focus on the cognitive or reflexive: we need, as Chris Shilling and Philip Mellor put it, to 'grasp [the] effervescent and fleshy aspects of human existence' (Shilling and Mellor 1996: 10). In emphasizing the corporeal and/or affective dimension of subcultural action, this chapter thus lends support to an ontological view of the body as something more than a discursive phenomenon: implicitly, at least, the argument presented concurs with Alex Hughes and Anne Witz's critique of the '[r]adical discursivization of bodies, at the heart of which lies a denial of bodily corporeality' (Hughes and Witz 1997: 58). The corporeal affect which informs and underpins subcultural activity may be mediated by discourse, but it is not reducible to it. Indeed, to the extent that physical affect is key to the construction of subcultural subjectivities, and thus to the construction of subculture(s) as a whole, one might argue that there is a dialectical relationship between the affectual and discursive realms: subcultural discourse mediates the experience of affect, but experience structures subcultural subjectivities. As Susan McClary notes in respect of one of the primary subcultural technologies:

> Music depends on our experiences as embodied beings for its constructions and its impact; but our experiences of our own bodies ... are themselves often constituted ... through musical imagery. (McClary 1994: 35)

In relation to the textual or semiotic analyses of subcultural formations referred to above, one might argue that the subcultural body is amenable to textual analysis, but again is not reducible to it: the subcultural body as text is *written* through action, and from the perspective of this chapter, the writing itself is key.

To acknowledge and explore the corporeal realities underpinning the affective pleasures of subcultural involvement is not to deny the importance of the social, however. Indeed, the current popularity of subcultural activities such as tattooing, piercing and clubbing, may on the basis of the evidence sketched out above, be said to reflect the resurgent sensuality which, in its opposition to 'the formal rationality characteristic of modernity' (Shilling and Mellor 1996: 10), is central to emergent patterns of sociality (see Jung 1996; Maffesoli 1996; Mellor and Shilling 1997; Hetherington 1998). In other words, the emphasis that many subcultural figures place on the intimate physicality of the procedures and practices involved suggests that their popularity may be seen, in part, as a manifestation of moves towards 'neo-tribal' forms of sociality, where a sense of belonging and togetherness is engendered more by affective proxemics than by any formal or contractual relationship between the parties involved. This is, perhaps, particularly true of the dance or club scene, with its intimations of collective effervescence and the 'temporary fusion of selves' (Shilling and Mellor 1996: 9).

Turning now from such relatively specific points to some of the more general implications of the material considered, the emphasis on the affectual or corporeal aspects of subcultural involvement also hints, perhaps, at the need for a more fully elaborated theory of the subcultural body. In addition to the points already raised, such an approach might also consider the following sorts of questions. First, given Norbert Elias's characterization of the 'civilizing process' as involving the progressive socialization, rationalization and individualization of the body (Shilling 1993: 150), how far might subcultural activity be understood to involve the more or less temporary *de*-socialization, *de*-rationalization and *de*-individualization of the corporeal selves concerned? Second, and in light of the increasing emphasis that certain writers have placed on the 'material acculturation' of the body into 'habitual practices of "femininity" and "masculinity"' (Bordo 1992: 167; see also Bartky 1988; Balsamo 1995; Lloyd 1996), to what extent might subcultural involvement be said to lead to the creation of new and potentially transgressive forms of embodied subjectivity? Third, could an emphasis on the above contribute to a more broadly based analysis of subcultural activity as transgressive *practice* rather than textual resistance, thereby overcoming some of the difficulties and/or ambiguities associated with the notion of 'semiotic guerrilla warfare' beloved of both the CCCS theorists considered above and certain more contemporary figures such as Judith Butler? (See, for example, Butler 1994.) Fourth, does the embodied nature of subcultural subjectivity, combined with Sarah Thornton's (1997) elaboration of the concept of subcultural capital, suggest problems with the notion of contemporary fashion as an eclectic free-for-all, where everything is up for grabs in the 'supermarket of style' (Polhemus 1997)? After all, if subcultural capital is embodied, then surely one can't fake it simply by purchasing the appropriate commodities?

Conclusion/methodological issues

Having presented some of the issues that might be considered in a more fully elaborated theoretical approach to the subcultural body, I would like to finish by raising one of the key methodological difficulties associated with a focus on the affective dimensions of subcultural involvement. Essentially, the difficulty is as follows: can one hope to approach the extra-discursive realities of embodied experience through standard methods of data collection, or does this position imply that only those involved can ever really understand the practices with which they are engaged?

I think I would like to argue the former. However, in relation to my own research, the fact that I am not pierced certainly limits my understanding and empathy, while my own experiences of being tattooed have not only acted as a passport into certain data-rich situations, but have also provided me with an insight into the experiential or affective dimension that would otherwise be unattainable. To some extent, of course, this point is simply another variant on the age-old question; 'Does one have to "be it" to research it?', and there are, as has been noted elsewhere, considerable dangers in privileging experience over interpretation (Frith and Savage 1997: 13). Nevertheless, my informants have repeatedly emphasized both the experiential quality of *their* understanding of the modificatory process, and the *difficulties* of explaining its meaning and significance to those who have not so altered their bodies, and I would argue that where physical affect is concerned, there are greater barriers to communication than in other fields of inquiry.

Of course, one can *ask* other people what their experiences are like, and what significance they hold, and I believe that my own research, in adopting a variety of methods of data collection, including a fairly open-ended interviewing approach (where I tried, as far as possible, to adopt a friendly and interested, rather than 'researcherly' persona), got as close as I could reasonably have hoped to the sort of data I required. Few people, however, whether researchers or researched, have the ability to effectively articulate such experiences in a verbal or written form. An accomplished writer, Kathy Acker, noted before her recent death the difficulties she herself faced in writing about her experiences of bodybuilding (Acker 1997: 143), and few have the eloquence displayed by Hunter S. Thompson in his short article relating the pleasures and affect, *and the difficulties of writing about*, riding a motorcycle at speed:

> with the throttle screwed on there is only the barest margin, and no room at all for mistakes. It has to be done right ... and that's when the strange music starts, when you stretch your luck so far that fear becomes exhilaration and vibrates along your arms. You can barely see at a hundred; the tears blow back so fast that they vaporize before they get to your ears. The only sounds are wind and a dull roar floating back from the mufflers. You watch the white line and try to lean with it ... howling through a turn to the right, then to the left and down the long hill to Pacifica ... letting off now, watching for cops, but only until the next dark stretch and another few seconds on the edge. ... The Edge. ... There is no honest way to explain it because the only people who really know where it is are the ones who have gone over. The others ... are those who pushed their control as far as they felt they could handle it, and then pulled back, or slowed down, or did whatever they had to when it came to choose between Now and Later. (Thompson 1991 [1965]: 111)

Acknowledgements

I would like to thank Sarah Cunningham-Burley for her helpful editorial comments, Graham Allan and Chris Shilling for their encouragement and advice in the longer term, and the Department of Sociology and Social Policy at the University of Southampton for supporting the wider study to which parts of this article refer. Thanks are also due to the interviewees quoted above, and to all those others who have helped with my research in some way, shape or form. I am also grateful to Pip Jones for helping me to get into this sort of thing in the first place, even if it did take me a while to see the light. The usual disclaimers, of course, apply.

Notes

1. The combined term 'youth/sub/counter-culture' is employed in part because of its inclusivity, but also because of the various problems associated with each of the individual terms in isolation. It indicates both an acknowledgement that such terms retain some value in referring, however obliquely, to particular cultural formations, and an uneasiness in settling on any one term given the questionable status of each. 'Youth culture' is problematic not simply because it can prove misleading – implying some form of age restriction which may well be empirically inaccurate – but also because of its somewhat derogatory connotations. 'Subculture', on the other hand, can be taken to imply some form of dominant or hegemonic culture against which it is articulated, and the latter is itself questionable from a postmodern perspective (see Muggleton 1997). Finally, 'counter-culture' sets up a potentially false distinction between middle-class and working-class cultural forms, with the latter – 'subcultures' – potentially valued as more 'authentic', and is also subject to the same objections as the latter term, i.e. the assumption of a dominant or hegemonic parent culture.
2. This charge cannot, incidentally, be laid at Geoffrey Pearson and John Twohig's (1976) critique of the 'Beckeresque' perspective on drug consumption. The authors point out, for example, that 'several [of their informants] joked that if Becker's subjects needed to learn to spot the effects, then they had been given a "bum deal"' (1976: 122), or as one particular respondent put it: 'that guy Becker should change his dealer!' (quoted in Pearson and Twohig 1976: 122).
3. Although the classic sub-cultures of the 1960s and 1970s may themselves have been more fragmented and less homogeneous than subcultural theories tend to suggest (Muggleton 1997: 200–1), contemporary body modification perhaps warrants the term 'subculture' (with its specific, theoretical connotations) even less. In the first place, few of my informants linked their tattoos or piercings to 'membership' of *specific* subcultural groups, and those who did express an affiliative impact or intention behind their adoption of such forms of body modification tended to refer to this in loosely 'tribal'

terms. Second, that both tattooing and piercing are popular amongst a range of 'subcultural' types, *and amongst many who appear not to identify with any particular subcultural group,* was confirmed by attendance at several tattoo conventions during the course of this research. Events such as *Tattoo Expo* and *Bodyshow* attract a varied crowd, apparently united only by a shared interest in tattooing, piercing or related modificatory practices. *Tattoo Expo,* in particular – as the largest and longest running annual UK convention – is remarkable for the way in which Hells Angels rub shoulders with rubber-skirted SMers, glamorous fetishists, punks, goths, skinheads and clubbers, not to mention the rest of the international crowd of attendees, most of whom are heavily tattooed or pierced, but the majority of whom are not easily slotted into a particular subcultural group (see Sweetman 1999c).

4. The 35 core interviewees were recruited in roughly equal numbers at tattoo conventions, through advertisements in a UK-based tattoo magazine and local student publications, and through introductions provided by existing informants, though three were already known to the author. A variety of methods were employed in order to allow contact with a range of contemporary body modifiers. The bulk of the interviews were conducted face-to-face, though seven took place by phone. Interviews were recorded, and ranged in duration from 20 minutes to approximately three hours.

   Fifteen of the 35 tattooees and/or piercees interviewed were women, and ages ranged from 19 to 40 amongst the women, and 20 to 60 amongst the men. The mean ages for each group were 24 and 32 respectively. Occupations ranged from the unemployed and students to credit analysts, local government officers and company directors. Around 40 per cent of the women and 70 per cent of the men were heavily tattooed and/or pierced, which generally implies that they had three or more of either form of body modification. This is a fairly loose definition, however: several standard ear-piercings, for example, would not place someone in the heavily pierced category, while someone with a full backpiece as their sole tattoo would certainly be counted as heavily tattooed.

5. This point is mentioned not in order to illustrate some sort of peculiar dedication to the research process, but rather because it links up with certain of the methodological issues raised below. Given that I already admired my informant's work, I was happy to accept such a generous offer, and would certainly not have gone through such a process simply for the sake of my research.

6. The following by no means exhausts the points relevant to this discussion: for a fuller account of the significance of corporeal affect and effect to many contemporary body modifiers, see Sweetman (1999b), and for a related discussion of the relationship between body modification and fashion, see Sweetman (1999c). For a consideration of the 'reclamation discourse' that frames the modificatory process for many contemporary female body modifiers, see Pitts (1998).

References

Acker, K. 1997. *Bodies of Work: Essays*. London & New York: Serpent's Tail.

Balsamo, A. 1995. 'Forms of Technological Embodiment: Reading the Body in Contemporary Culture', *Body & Society*, 1 (3–4): 215–37.

Bartky, S.L. 1988. 'Foucault, Femininity and the Modernization of Patriarchal Power', in I. Diamond and L. Quinby (eds) *Feminism and Foucault: Reflections on Resistance*. Boston: Northeastern University Press.

Bordo, S. 1992. 'Postmodern Subjects, Postmodern Bodies' (Review Essay), *Feminist Studies*, 18 (1): 159–75.

Boyle, D. 1996. *Trainspotting*. Channel Four Film Corporation.

Butler, J. 1994. 'Gender as Performance: An Interview with Judith Butler', *Radical Philosophy*, 67: 32–9.

Clarke, J. et al. 1976. 'Subcultures, Cultures and Class', in S. Hall and T. Jefferson (eds) *Resistance through Rituals: Youth Subcultures in Post-war Britain*. London: HarperCollins.

Cohen, P. 1997 [1972]. 'Subcultural Conflict and Working-Class Community', in K. Gelder and S. Thornton (eds) *The Subcultures Reader*. London: Routledge.

Cohen, S. 1997 [1980]. 'Symbols of Trouble', in K. Gelder and S. Thornton (eds) *The Subcultures Reader*. London: Routledge.

Ferrell, J. 1993. *Crimes of Style: Urban Graffiti and the Politics of Criminality*. New York & London: Garland Publishing.

Frith, S. and Savage, J. 1997. 'Pearls and Swine: Intellectuals and the Mass Media', in S. Redhead et al. (eds) *The Clubcultures Reader: Readings in Popular Cultural Studies*. Oxford: Blackwell.

Gelder, K. 1997a. 'Introduction to Part Two', in K. Gelder and S. Thornton (eds) *The Subcultures Reader*. London: Routledge.

Gelder, K. 1997b. 'Introduction to Part Three', in K. Gelder and S. Thornton (eds) *The Subcultures Reader*. London: Routledge.

Gelder, K. 1997c. 'Introduction to Part Seven', in K. Gelder and S. Thornton (eds) *The Subcultures Reader*. London: Routledge.

Grossberg, L. 1997 [1984]. 'Another Boring Day in Paradise: Rock and Roll and the Empowerment of Everyday Life', in K. Gelder and S. Thornton (eds) *The Subcultures Reader*. London: Routledge.

Hebdige, D. 1976. 'The Meaning of Mod', in S. Hall and T. Jefferson (eds) *Resistance through Rituals: Youth Subcultures in Post-war Britain*. London: HarperCollins.

Hebdige, D. 1979. *Subculture: The Meaning of Style*. London: Routledge.

Hetherington, K. 1998. *Expressions of Identity: Space, Performance, Politics*. London: Sage.

Hughes, A. and Witz, A. 1997. 'Feminism and the Matter of Bodies: From De Beauvoir to Butler', *Body & Society*, 3 (1): 47–60.

Hughes, W. 1994. 'In the Empire of the Beat: Discipline and Disco', in A. Ross and T. Rose (eds) *Microphone Fiends: Youth Music & Youth Culture*. New York and London: Routledge.

Jung, H.Y. 1996. 'Phenomenology and Body Politics', *Body & Society*, 2 (2): 1–22.

Lloyd, M. 1996. 'Feminism, Aerobics and the Politics of the Body', *Body & Society*, 2 (2): 79–98.

Maffesoli, M. 1996. *The Time of the Tribes: The Decline of Individualism in Mass Society*. London: Sage.

Mellor, P.A. and Shilling, C. 1997. *Re-forming the Body: Religion, Community and Modernity*. London: Sage.

McClary, S. 1994. 'Same as it Ever Was: Youth Culture and Music', in A. Ross and T. Rose (eds) *Microphone Fiends: Youth Music & Youth Culture*. New York and London: Routledge.

Muggleton, D. 1997. 'The Post-subculturalist', in S. Redhead et al. (eds) *The Clubcultures Reader: Readings in Popular Cultural Studies*. Oxford: Blackwell.

Pearson G. and Twohig, J. 1976. 'Ethnography through the Looking-Glass: The Case of Howard Becker', in S. Hall and T. Jefferson (eds) *Resistance through Rituals: Youth Subcultures in Post-war Britain*. London: HarperCollins.

Pitts, V. 1998. '"Reclaiming" the Female Body: Embodied Identity Work, Resistance and the Grotesque', *Body & Society*, 4 (3): 67–84.

Polhemus, T. 1997. 'In the Supermarket of Style', in S. Redhead et al. (eds) *The Clubcultures Reader: Readings in Popular Cultural Studies*. Oxford: Blackwell.

Reynolds, S. 1997. 'Rave Culture: Living Dream or Living Death?', in S. Redhead et al. (eds) *The Clubcultures Reader: Readings in Popular Cultural Studies*. Oxford: Blackwell.

Rietveld, H. 1997. 'The House Sound of Chicago', in S. Redhead et al. (eds) *The Clubcultures Reader: Readings in Popular Cultural Studies*. Oxford: Blackwell.

Ross, A. 1994. 'Introduction', in A. Ross and T. Rose (eds) *Microphone Fiends: Youth Music & Youth Culture*. New York and London: Routledge.

Shilling, C. 1993. *The Body and Social Theory*. London: Sage.

Shilling, C. and Mellor, P.A. 1996. 'Embodiment, Structuration Theory and Modernity: Mind/Body Dualism and the Representation of Sensuality', *Body & Society*, 2 (4): 1–15.

Stanley, C. 1997. 'Not Drowning but Waving: Urban Narratives of Dissent in the Wild Zone', in S. Redhead et al. (eds) *The Clubcultures Reader: Readings in Popular Cultural Studies*. Oxford: Blackwell.

Straw, W. 1997 [1991]. 'Communities and Scenes in Popular Music', in K. Gelder and S. Thornton (eds) *The Subcultures Reader*. London: Routledge.

Sweetman, P. 1999a. 'Marked Bodies, Oppositional Identities? Tattooing, Piercing and the Ambiguity of Resistance', in S. Roseneil and J. Seymour (eds) *Practising Identities: Power and Resistance*. Basingstoke: Macmillan.

Sweetman, P. 1999b. 'Only Skin Deep? Tattooing, Piercing and the Transgressive Body', in M. Aaron (ed.) *The Body's Perilous Pleasures*. Edinburgh: Edinburgh University Press.

Sweetman, P. 1999c. 'Anchoring the (Postmodern) Self? Body Modification, Fashion and Identity', *Body & Society*, 5 (2–3): 51–76.

Thompson, H.S. 1991. *Songs of the Doomed: Gonzo Papers Vol. 3,* London: Picador.

Thornton, S. 1997. 'The Social Logic of Subcultural Capital', in K. Gelder and S. Thornton (eds) *The Subcultures Reader*. London: Routledge.

Vale, V. and Juno, A. 1989. *Re/Search #12: Modern Primitives – An Investigation of Contemporary Adornment & Ritual*. San Francisco: Re/Search Publications.

Willis, P. 1976. 'The Cultural Meaning of Drug Use', in S. Hall and T. Jefferson (eds) *Resistance through Rituals: Youth Subcultures in Post-war Britain*. London: HarperCollins.

11
'All We Needed to do was Blow the Whistle': Children's Embodiment of Time

Pia Christensen, Allison James and Chris Jenks

Introduction: children, bodies and time

Children's experience of time as a social category is, as this chapter will show, mediated through a series of cultural narratives that are focused upon the self and body in terms of appearance and behavioural practices. However, these narratives are not peculiar to children but are derived from the historical progress of modern cultures and, in particular, from both conceptualizations of time passing and understandings of the self as embodied and placeable (Csordas 1994).

Time as understood in contemporary society is known through a mechanistic and quantitative model provided initially by Kant and his immanent categories of understanding. This philosophical perspective is writ large within European and North American cultures through conspiring with scientific notions of linear causality, with moral imperatives of progress and improvement, and with elements of a pressing political economy. Through the capitalist requirement of costing all being, and therefore all bodies, time itself was rendered a significant variable in the productive process and a cost in relation to space and labour (Shilling 1993: 127–49). Bodies were thus rendered a mobile resource in the logistics of productivity such that, for example, with the onset of the factory system disabled bodies became stigmatized for their inability to compete within the changing conditions of the labour market (Oliver 1989). In this chapter we propose that it is as children, and in growing up, that we gradually come to know that time is tangible and valuable, that time is a scarce resource not to be wasted but rather wisely invested. Thus, significantly, children come to understand that time lays out the ground-rules for present and future behaviours. And in this childhood learning, as we set out below, it is through the body that we come to owe a primary obedience to such temporal constraints.

This temporal understanding is further impressed onto our consciousness by another determining moral imperative of modernity: mortality. Death represents the very interface of time and embodiment: 'the unfinishedness of human embodiment means that the death of the self is presented to the mind as a particular problem' (Shilling 1993: 179). The death of children – those who have lived but a short time – is literally untimely. We cannot afford, therefore, to compromise on life; and indeed, it is in notions of time passing that we measure and evaluate our time spent. However, it was not until Bergson in the nineteenth century that the topic was approached through the conception of time as *durée*. That is, time is to be seen as duration, a series of qualitative changes interweaving and permeating one another. *Durée* is the very essence of reality, a constant becoming, never a static achievement for, according to Bergson, time seen in this latter, mathematical Kantian way, represents another kind of space, not a passage of being.

This shift in conceptions of time has meant that the narrative experience of time is now focused on quality, rather than quantity. Understandings of childhood, and indeed a major part of our childrearing ideologies, emphasize the temporal texture and the quality of being and embodiment, rather than simply an understanding of the quantity of time passing, which is registered and sequenced as the 'ageing' body. Indeed, as Featherstone (1982) has argued, the aged body is increasingly being disguised in contemporary consumer cultures through routines of body maintenance and repair for it is upon the ageing body that the passing of time is so visibly inscribed as an unwelcome reminder of approaching death.

As we shall go on to show, through a series of ethnographic examples, these twin perspectives of 'time' and 'being' in relation to the body can already be seen to predominate in children's everyday lives at primary school. They provide a fixed and inflexible juxtaposition through which children come to grips with cultural conceptions of 'continuity' in the understanding that mastery in shaping one's own future, short as well as long term, takes place through present embodiment. In December 1997, for example, the pupils of Northwich school performed Charles Dickens' *A Christmas Carol* as a show for their parents, teachers and school governors. This is not an uncommon choice of school play and, no doubt, pupils in many other schools in England were, at the same time, also acting out this classic tale. *A Christmas*

Carol is, in essence, a moral tale about the importance of generosity for the maintenance of social relations – generosity of spirit, pleasure, compassion and money – but it is through the metaphorical play around the themes of time itself that the transformation of miserly, vicious Scrooge is achieved. The end of the play sees Scrooge rescued from the compulsions of his character through the literal embodiment of time past, present and future. Via frightening bodily encounters with the different ghosts of Christmas, Scrooge begins to see the part that the passing of time and past experiences have played in the shaping of his own biography and, finally, he is shown a vision of the future which, if he does not mend his ways, will prove tragic. In sum, therefore, the moral causality of *A Christmas Carol* lies in its espousal of the Protestant ethic – that 'time is money' – linked to the demands of the biological clock – that 'time is short'. Thus, the play acts as a reminder that social action is temporalized through its location in individual biographies and that, in this sense, its consequences reverberate across the life course through the lived bodily experiences of individuals. The play also exposes the potential conflicts or even contradictions between time as quantity ('time is short'/'time is money') and the quality of time in terms of that which cannot be quantified, namely pleasure and the enjoyment of generosity in close social relations, thus exposing the image macabre of saving versus spending.

That children are so frequently involved in acting out such a temporal and moral tale at school is perhaps not surprising for, as we go on to argue, it is precisely this embodiment of time passing which children learn in their everyday lives. They do so in two interlinked ways. First, children are, as we shall show, defined through their bodies, bodies which are seen to develop and mature in relation to externally derived conceptions of their social, intellectual, physical and moral competencies. Second, through a temporal disciplining of the body in the everyday social practices of the classroom – a discipline wrought upon the body by the self or by others – time becomes understood by children as a commodity which is subject to an exchange relationship based on both discipline and/or liberation. Children are taught, and some of them more painfully learn, that present behaviour shapes future outcomes and that pleasurable futures may be denied on account of present misdemeanours. Presented in this way it was made clear to each child actor in *A Christmas Carol*, by the teacher at Northwich school, that if they did not concentrate on their school work, including behaving well in class (see below), they could envisage being forbidden to attend the very show in which, for such a long time, they had invested so much of their time and efforts. What is, perhaps, of more import is that such misbehaviours are themselves temporally circumscribed. As Corrigan (1979) has noted, disputes between staff and pupils at school are often, and principally, disputes about time use – what forms of behaviour are appropriate at which kinds of time.

In this chapter, we distinguish between 'curriculum time' – time that is controlled by teachers – and those times, such as playtime, which are seen by children as being under their own control.[1] We show how the paramountcy of 'curriculum time' is achieved and sustained in the classroom through the controls and demands placed upon children's bodies by staff. However, as we also explore, through the adoption of particular bodily styles some children can manage to extend their control over time at school to liberate a little time for themselves by wresting free from the restrictive demands which 'curriculum time' places upon them. Children are, in this way, revealed as embodied beings; they are not simply the outcome of socialization and pedagogic processes but active participants in the social world, 'persons [who] experience themselves simultaneously *in* and *as* their bodies' (Lyon and Barbalet 1994: 54). This chapter explores the temporality of that embodiment as the successful development of an acceptable vocabulary of body techniques and bodily placement, both as the locus of self but also as the normalising symbol of incorporation, that is, of being 'in one's place'.

The study in context

This chapter draws on data from an ethnographic study of children's understanding and use of time. The study focused on 10–12-year-olds and their experiences of the transition from primary school to secondary school and took place in three primary schools and two secondary schools in an urban and a rural setting in the North of England. We draw on data produced in the three primary schools. One was a small village primary school with 57 pupils, six of whom were in Year 6. The two other primary schools comprised one in the city centre of a large town and another in a bigger village. These schools were of comparable size, each with about 225 pupils, 35 of whom in each school were in Year 6. The study followed a self-selected group of these children through the transition to secondary school.

A wide range of methods was used to capture children's conceptions and practices of time and temporality, methods that explored different aspects of children's time: everyday time at home and at school; social relations at home with regard to time use; the time of school transition; time values and social organization; biographical time, including issues of age and development. The methods included individual and peer group interviews, together with participant observation in schools and, later, a large-scale quantitative survey.

However, in addition to these more conventional research techniques, a set of participatory research tools was developed to explore how children come to embody the temporal practices and rhythms through which their everyday lives unfold (Christensen and James 2000). These tools were developed out of the basic ideas or models that have been used by development workers in carrying out rural appraisals (Chambers 1992, 1994). Data were produced using a set of simple paper charts, inscribed with circles, boxes or lines which the children filled in as they chose. These charts mediated the communication between the researcher and the children and provided them with a way to concretize what are often rather abstract or implicit ideas about time passing. For example, through creating their own pie charts to depict the way time is spent in the week (the 'my week' tool) or filling in a graphic chart about decision-making at home and at school, the children were able to reflect on the experiential differences between these different kinds of times and their own control over time use and the social relations involved. That which is simply experienced as everyday social practice, and as we shall show becomes inscribed onto and into the bodies of children, was through the use of the tools thus granted an unusually explicit solidity and its familiarity and routine was temporarily objectified and estranged.

Temporal perspectives and analytic locations

Our understanding of the ways in which the spatio-temporal divisions and bodily locations are experienced by and represented to children is informed by two competitive sociological traditions which here we term 'liberating' and 'controlling' in relation to the ways in which time is seen to act upon and empower or constrain the individual and the body. The former is located within the Durkheimian tradition and arises from Durkheim's concern to delineate the basic 'categories of understanding', the ultimate principles which underlie all our knowledge and which give order and arrangement to our perceptions and sensations – including, for example, the concept of time. Reviewing the dominant epistemological explanations, Durkheim dismisses the types of idealism which depict the ultimate reality behind the world as being spiritual, informed by an Absolute; or those which account for the categories as being inherent in the nature of human consciousness. Such an 'a priorist' position, he says, is refuted by the incessant variability of the categories of human thought from society to society; and further it lacks experimental control, it is not empirically verifiable. In thus rejecting a Kantian position which demands that such categories exist somehow beyond the individual consciousness, as prior conditions of experience, Durkheim prefers to constitute time as a representation, rather than as something which is immutable and universal:

> Men frequently speak of space and time as if they were only concrete in extent and duration, such as the individual consciousness can feel, but enfeebled by abstraction. In reality, they are representations of a wholly different sort, made out of other elements, according to a different plan, and with equally different ends in view. (Durkheim 1915: 441 fn)

Thus, although the categories of thought vary from society to society, within any one society, they are characterised by universality and necessity. In relation to concepts of time, therefore, he writes:

> It is not my time that is thus arranged; it is time in general, such as it is objectively thought of by everybody in a single civilisation. (Durkheim 1915: 10)

For Durkheim, therefore, society is the fundamental and primary reality; without it there is no humankind – but this is a reciprocal dependency. Society can only become realized, can only become conscious of itself and thus make its influence felt through the collective behaviour of its members – that is, through their capacity to communicate symbolically. Out of this concerted conduct springs the collective representations and sentiments of society and, further, the fundamental categories of thought – including, of course, that of time.

So for Durkheim the classifications of time are social in origin. They arise from and reflect the patterns and rhythms of social life. Such a soft determinism, or what has been called a social Kantianism, implies that sociality itself precedes both mind and matter and the latter two realms are shaped according to the ways of the social. Seasons reflect socio-temporal dispositions; calendars are manifestations of symbolic and ritualistic patterns; all appearance of fixity and naturalness is derived, historical and ultimately conventional.

> The divisions into days, weeks, months, years etc., correspond to the periodical recurrence of rites, feasts, and public ceremonies. A calendar expresses the rhythm of the collective activities, while at the same time its function is to assure their regularity. (Durkheim 1915: 10–11)

Such a view of time implies, therefore, an almost symbiotic, if not sympathetic, relationship between the individual and time. In relation to the child, such a view implies a temporal context that is liberal if not liberating in as much as it enables the child to become at one with the meter of the historical process. The child's body, and indeed the child's identity, become microcosmically analogous to the total body of the social (an idea later taken to cybernetic hyperbole by Talcott Parsons through the 'stable unitary isomorphism' of his *Social System*). In the following sections we show how such a 'liberating' temporal narrative is inscribed upon children's bodies or is hindered during their experience of schooling.

Our second perspective is somewhat different in the gloss it places on children's embodiment of time and we have termed this as 'controlling'; time is seen and experienced as a disciplining constraint. And here the work of Foucault stands out as emblematic. For Foucault, just as he regards knowledge as power, so too he understands time as a primary device and strategy in the exercise of modernity's power. Foucault inevitably fits temporality into his thesis on disciplinary regimes and the constraint of the free will with the most singular time-power device of modernity being the timetable – its object being the body. Indeed, the timetable can be regarded as a metaphor for modernity itself. Rather than an instance of social rhythms expressing themselves in regularised patterns *à la* Durkheim, timetables are, for Foucault, combinations of moves within the politics of experience. Specifically, Foucault (1979) speaks of the history of the timetable as follows:

> The time-table is an old inheritance. The strict model was no doubt suggested by the monastic communities. It soon spread. Its three great methods – establish rhythms, impose particular occupations, regulate the cycles of repetition – were soon to be found in schools, workshops and hospitals. The new disciplines had no difficulty in taking up their place in the old forms; the schools and poorhouses extended the life and the regularity of the monastic communities to which they were often attached. The rigours of the industrial period long retained a religious air; in the seventeenth century, the

> regulations of the great manufactories laid down the exercises that would divide up the working day, but even in the nineteenth century, when the rural populations were needed in industry, they were sometimes formed into 'congregations', in an attempt to inure them to work in the workshops; the framework of the 'factory-monastery' was imposed upon the workers. (Foucault 1979: 149–50)

Discipline, it would seem, involves the control of a body, or more specifically an activity, and does so, most effectively, through a timetable. This device, for Foucault, is of monastic origin and relates to the regular divisions in the monk's day which was organized around the seven canonical hours. Through the systematic extension of this fundamental device, the timetable, a regularity and a rhythm became instilled in all activities and tasks; productivity and predictability were assured. Such rhythms became applied to the individual through, significantly, the individual's body such that, eventually, they became integral to the individual's performance of duty and style of life. So, for example, soldiers are drilled persistently even beyond basic training, and children are required to eat, sleep, wash and excrete, mostly, at specific and regular times. For the child, then, even the most elementary bodily functions are scheduled; and, at school, play, which we superficially regard as free and perhaps creative, occurs in designated temporal spaces within a timetabled curriculum. Within the modern conditions for discipline there is, however, a further internal temporal segmentation for each activity. That is to say, each activity is periodized and subdivided into steps or stages and, for the individual, the learning of tasks is similarly subject to a spatial and temporal division of labour. Just as an appropriate combination of exercises makes for the fit and healthy body, so also a series of component activities contributes to a more specialized and efficient function in relation to task, a fact well known to Adam Smith in his theory of the division of labour. Foucault uses the example of children and their mastery of handwriting, and here some of us (those old enough) might recall the achievement of a perfect page of handwriting, the laborious process of breaking each letter of the alphabet down into a series of technical strokes with the hand/pen. The symbolic reward for such technical perfection would be the issue of personal exercise books and thus an inability to disport such books would signify a pre-disciplined body. What such bodily conditioning instils at a different level are life-governing imperatives such as being on time or 'always being in the right place at the right time'!

What Foucault's discussion of the conditions of discipline brings us to with respect to our study is, therefore, the realization that such control functions through a combination of devices; what he refers to as tactics. The whole premise of adult interaction with the child, even often in pleasure, is control and instruction. All conditions combine and conspire to that end. The individual, it appears, emerges therefore through the modern form of control, exercised through regimes of discipline as Sheridan (1980) describes:

> This power is not triumphant, excessive, omnipotent, but modest, suspicious, calculating. It operates through hierarchical observation, normalizing judgement, and their combination in the examination. (Sheridan 1980: 152)

Foucault's time is thus no benign medium in which to be and grow. This 'time' is always intended and planned, it governs and it manages, and, most serious of all, it is internalized to become the regulator and arbiter of all experience (all the time we think that we are exercising free will). Foucault's child is therefore captured through time and captured by it and, in a radical interpretation, the body becomes the very instrument of time.

The 'liberating' and 'controlling' perspectives on time, outlined above, represent two points of analytic departure for us in exploring children's experience and embodiment of time. They must not be read, however, as being all that there is, for such a view would render the classroom an austere political arena indeed! The dichotomy between freedom and constraint is thus informative but not exhaustive of our need to understand (Jenks 1998); these perspectives are, with regard to children, themselves subject to and have to engage with a third, more dominant, perspective on time which derives from the very temporality of children's bodies. Both everyday and, to a large extent, professional conceptions of the child are dominated by an almost hegemonic grasp of the child's aged body in relation to developmental theories.

Most seriously crystallized in the work of Piaget, but others also, the child has come to be understood as an unfolding project, a natural trajectory, a staged becoming and an inevitably incremental progress into adulthood. Such understandings have received more recent challenge (Jenks 1982; Morse 1990; Burman 1994) and deconstruction but the roots of such a belief run deep and integrate seamlessly with the physiological demands of medicine and the logistical demands of a society based on hierarchical stratification and hierarchical distribution of provision. Developmental time is thus a powerful discourse which routinely structures children's experience, their time and how their bodies are read, managed and monitored. Children are, indeed, read as if they were pausing on the path to reason, but their pauses are both determined and determining. And these pauses, suspensions or interruptions in the developmental journey are marked out for children in terms of the achievement of competence, full adult competence being journey's end – the modernist project writ small! (Hockey and James 1993). This temporal 'journey', which in part we detail below, may be both shaped and experienced by children as alternately liberating and disciplining.

The entrenched status of such developmental models is nowhere better witnessed than in the everyday interactions of the school classroom. Here a stratification and disciplining of the child population is achieved through the marking out of levels and stages of competence and achievements, essentially measured in relation to the steady progress of chronological age and achievement of developmental tasks. In their everyday life at school children are suspended in social groups constituted through an almost taken-for-granted theory about a 'natural' concordance between age and physical maturation. Children's peers, friends, associates, competitors and playmates are, therefore, to a large extent determined and assembled according to bodily-based age cohorts, 'year groups', which are meant to equate pragmatically with their interests, achievements and abilities.

Furthermore, even though modern schooling seems to provide some flexibility within this model through horizontal streaming – that is that children within a single year group may work on different levels towards different key stages – this may inadvertently place upon children a greater burden in relation to demonstrating achievements of social competence and physical maturity. The potential liberation which such 'levels' and 'stages' may bring through its disassociation from the developmental demands of the aged body may be replaced, instead, by an over-emphasis and increasing specificity about the achievement of competencies through a disciplined body. It is difficult enough for a child to achieve normatively, and compete, *within* an age cohort; for a member of a specialist set assembled because of particular common excellences or techniques of the body there is nowhere to hide.

In the everyday social practices of the classroom, as the following sections explore, ideas about the use and social organization of time are narrated through the process of schooling and become inscribed upon children's bodies. In this sense it is, literally, a schooled body which effective education aims to produce, one which is ordered in time and space. In this sense, our chapter uncovers what Bourdieu has called an embodied memory which is entrusted with 'in abbreviated and practical i.e. mnemonic form, the fundamental principles of the arbitrary content of the culture' (1977: 94). This embodied temporality we explore below through a series of ethnographic examples.

The body in curriculum time

The insistent demands wrought by the embeddedness of developmental models of childhood have, until recently, meant that children's bodies – seen as aged bodies in terms of years lived through – have been used as the primary ordering principle through which the social organisation of the school is achieved. Children enter primary school aged five and leave for secondary school aged eleven, irrespective of the social and educational competencies which they may, or may not, have acquired en route. However, while these entries and exits remain for the three primary schools participating in the study, and the children are divided into year groups or age classes, in the daily organization of lessons, they may be reorganized and reordered. Instead of using age as a classifier, the body's competencies and skills are used to cluster children in relation to levels of achievement. Thus children, as well as the teachers, did not only identify themselves as being ten or eleven years old, but they also used the terminology of 'level' and 'stage'. These levels are defined in relation to the demands of the National Curriculum or, for example, the key stages of a reading scheme, and it should be noted that children themselves are highly skilled in using this categorical system to position themselves relative to one another.

For example, for most children in the village school their prospective move to secondary school has highlighted for them the importance of this system – the children understand that the 'level' they achieve at their final tests at primary school will determine the group they will be placed in at secondary school. These points were illustrated in a conversation with Hannah and Julie, ten-year-olds from the village school, Wellthorpe, as they discussed the practices for the SATS tests in May and, what it means for them:

Hannah: When you go to Molton school, I think it tells you what class you have to be in. Like if you are really, really brainy or if you are not that good.

Julie: In my practices I have got three levels four, one level five and a level six.

Hannah: I have got one five and all the rest are fours.

Pia: Why is it important for you the tests?

Hannah: I think it's quite good. Because it tells you what class you'll be in and everything like that and the levels tells you what position you are in. Like if you get a five you are in a good level aren't you? – and if you get a four, you're all right. The ones that are a bit dumb in our class get like threes and stuff, like Tom, Peter and Lily.

Pia: But, why is it important to you whether you get a level three or not?

Julie: Well, my mum would be quite disappointed, because I am quite brainy, aren't I? – and if I get a six which is the highest I think, I'll be top class at Molton wouldn't I?

In this manner the children make sense, therefore, of the way the teacher has required them to sit in class during the school year, that is with which group and at which table and, in particular lessons, which colour book they are working with. Through these clues children are not only able to orient themselves in the present time and space, but they also become aware that these tests form an important marker and punctuation of how their present performance can work to shape, and to effect, an ordered disciplining of their prospective futures. In the children's own vocabulary the class was divided into subgroups of 'the dumb', 'the boffs' or 'the brainy table', thereby spatially demarcating an alternative horizontal stratification which placed the bodies of children either nearer or further away from the teacher.[2] In this complex way, therefore, the tests become understood by children literally as embodied practices, not abstract and external exercises. The test, as performance, and the outcome of the test, as competence, both legitimizes and shapes their place and position in the future: 'Because it tells you what class you'll have to be in and everything like that' (Hannah above).

In Northwich school, which is a large inner city school, pupils' ability is, in the same vein, seen as highly differentiated (that is, understood as 'mixed') in relation to the aged body. At each change of lesson in the mornings the children routinely regroup themselves, moving from classroom to classroom, or sitting at different desks in their 'form' room, in accordance with their level of attainment in Maths or English. It constitutes a well-rehearsed orchestration of 'ability', visibly demonstrated by the movement of the bodies. Thus in any teaching group, at any particular point in the day, in the city school children aged nine, ten and eleven may be receiving tuition alongside one another, a situation magnified in the smallest of the village schools where children aged 7–11 routinely occupy the same classroom for all their lessons. Although their classroom maintains an invisible spatial division of the room into three age groups, 'curriculum time' operates here also in such a way that children throughout the school day are engaged in grouping and regrouping according to their levels of work and achievement.

Thus from these examples it would appear that, despite the apparent hegemony of bodily based developmental models of childhood, the age of the body is made a deliberately fragile indicator of children's identities at particular points during the school day. Within the national structuring of educational provision, levels of achievement take precedence over age, specifically in relation to the core curriculum subjects of Maths and English which are viewed as fundamental to all other learning. This is in stark contrast to those other subjects – art, physical education, sports and music – which more apparently focus on the techniques and abilities of the body (skills such as manual dexterity, artistic ability, physical agility, even musicality). In these lessons children find themselves, once more, regrouped, but here according to the chronological age of their bodies and, in respect to PE and sports, to gender. Such a distinction and fluctuation in the use of the aged body as an identifier underlines, we suggest, children's gradual embodiment of the wider cultural narrative of 'time as investment' during their growing-up at school. As one child in the city school noted, it is 'Maths and English that you will need all your life'; they will get you a 'a good job'.

However, it was not just in relation to the organization of formal teaching that conceptions of the age, maturity and competence of the child's body were variously and variably employed to regulate and quite literally timetable children's lives at school. The more casual judgements made by teachers to assess, monitor and control the behaviour of children routinely drew upon these different, external and temporal ranking systems to assess children's behaviour during 'curriculum time'.

Significantly, for example, one of the ways in which children's social competence and intellectual 'maturity', as opposed to the age of the physical body, is judged by teachers is in relation to children's abilities to manage their time effectively. Thus, as one teacher remarked, observing what she regarded as the 'silly' behaviour of two girls: 'Year 6 girls should know better.' They should be 'sensible', that is, literally use their senses so as to better regulate or discipline their bodies in accordance with the externally set propriety denoted by developmental age. On another occasion a ten-year-old boy was made to attend Key Stage 1 – singing lessons – those performed by younger children – as a form of ritualized bodily degradation. Among the group of 5–7-year-olds his tall body and deep voice was visually exposed and the penalty for his age-inappropriate conduct in class on the previous day was highlighted.

Whole groups of children can be identified and disciplined in this manner. One teacher in the city school offered the opinion that her current Year 6 were 'immature'. A long-serving and experienced teacher, she felt this particular class fell below an implicit behavioural expectation for 10–11-year-olds and, by way of explanation, pointed out that a key indicator of this immaturity was the children's failure to use their time properly. They lacked self-discipline over time use and organization. At the start of each school day the attendance and dinner registers were taken, during which time the children were supposed to sit still and read silently. That this group of children needed reminding and reprimanding each day was seen by the teacher as a sure sign of their immaturity. In previous years children of this age would not have needed such close monitoring of their behaviour.

That the children themselves may, however, simply be choosing not to comply with this rule was not an explanation offered by the teacher for their failure to conform. However, had it been, this would simply have served, in her eyes, to underline their immaturity. For this teacher, and in Foucauldian terms, it is in learning to accept the controlling demands of curriculum time that children can demonstrate their maturity through proffering a docile and compliant body, yet concentrate on their work tasks.

However, close observation of this period of relatively free time in the school day revealed that many children *were* in fact making an active choice about how to spend their time. They were managing it on their own, rather than the teacher's, terms, and thereby were able partially to liberate themselves from its rigid discipline. And, it was through drawing on particular techniques of the body – specifically those of posture – that children were able to gain this relative freedom from constraint (Mauss 1950). In a day that is heavily structured for children in terms of how their time is spent – indeed, finding time to do the research proved difficult – this 30-minute period at the start of the day represents a valuable 'breathing' space. It is relatively unstructured and unsupervised, not quite a lesson and yet not play time. What this time could actually be spent doing was open to multiple interpretations by the children: some children did read; others, however, got out their reading books, opened them and then sat lost in thought or whispered to their friends; others gathered around the book shelves in a huddle with their pals, ostensibly to choose a new book, but never taking one down from the shelf; others sat and fiddled with their pencil cases, or with their hair, their books open in front of them but never turned a page; still others wandered around the room, looking busy, as they ferreted in their trays or searched the resources table. A small number of children, however, sat at their tables with no books visible or talked openly with their friends. Thus, out of a class of 35 maybe only ten children might be 'sitting and reading' for the whole period of time. But it was only those children who failed to adopt the body posture and style of 'sitting and reading' who would be daily judged by the teacher to be behaving in an 'inappropriate' and thus 'immature' manner.

Thus, the bodily constraints which 'curriculum time' can place on children can also permit them some liberation. Field notes record ten-year-old Gemma who sat quietly for an hour in a practice test for the SATS. She kept her head down, neither speaking to her classmates nor yet putting pen to paper. Through such bodily deportment she gained time for herself. Her bodily posture, a body bent over the table with sheets of paper in front of her, reflected a body at work at school – studying – and did not therefore attract the attention of the teacher who oversaw the children's performance.

Although through such examples it is possible, using our three analytic perspectives, to generate accounts of children's 'resistance' through ritual as if they conspired in a subversive political insurgence albeit through passivity or dumb insolence, this would, we suggest, be to exaggerate and consciously politicize such instances. Although regulatory and constraining, the disciplining of children's bodies through the schooling process is also, at another level, to be seen as pastoral and benign. That children are controlled is indeed an instance of power and hierarchy, but to stop them running or rocking on their chairs may also be a way of ensuring their safety and exercising a duty of care. In addition, that many children engage in the form of 'passing' displayed by Gemma may be interpreted as a way of gaining control, it may also be a way of 'getting by' or, what de Certeau (1984) refers to as 'making do'. He argues that:

> The operational modes of popular culture ... exist in the heart of the strongholds of the contemporary economy. *[see here the school]* Take,

> for example, what in France is called *la perruque*, 'the wig'. *La perruque* is the worker's own work designed as work for his employer. It differs from pilfering in that nothing of material value is stolen. It differs from absenteeism in that the worker is officially on the job. *La perruque* may be as simple as a secretary's writing a love letter on 'company time' or as complex as a cabinetmaker's 'borrowing' a lathe to make a piece of furniture for his living room ... this phenomenon is becoming more and more general, even if managers penalize it or 'turn a blind eye' on it in order not to know about it. (1984: 25)

Gemma's device is thus both a control mechanism *and* an 'artistic trick' through which she conspires and manages her body and is able to manage the situation. This, according to de Certeau, helps to

> traverse the frontiers dividing time, place and types of action ... these transverse *tactics* do not obey the law of the place, for they are not defined or identified by it. In this respect, they are not any more localizable than the technocratic (and scriptural) *strategies* that seek to create places in conformity with abstract models. (1988: 29)

It is therefore children's knowing attention to bodily posture and appearance which may enable them strategically to take some control over their own time at school, to pass off leisure as work. Through adopting behaviours and bodily postures associated with, for example, the act of reading, children passed the time *as if* they were reading (James 2000) and were thus able to escape the watchful eye of the teacher.

Such a practical mastery of bodily knowledge is important for children in many of their negotiations with teachers over time use at school. For example, a common practice among all the teachers involved in the study was, at playtime, to let those children leave the classroom first who presented an organized and tidy exterior appearance. Thus, children learn that, immediately when the bell rings or the teacher announces the time, they must sit up straight, be silent, with their arms folded with a clear desk space in front of them. Such children will be selected as the first to escape from the classroom. Coming in from play also requires a certain bodily knowledge. Wellthorpe school was the only primary school in the study that had abandoned lining children up after playtime, as one of the senior teachers explained:

> When I came here the teacher on duty would blow the whistle, the children would line up on the field, they would then walk from the

> field into the playground and line up in the playground. The teacher would then tell them to go from the the playground into school and they'd walk into school and they would then line up outside their classroom. I felt that in the fifteen-minute playtime they were lining up three times and it was just a waste of time and it took some time for me to persuade the head teacher who was in force that all we needed to do was to blow the whistle, tell the children in advance that once the whistle was blown, they stopped what they were doing and they walked into school. And this solved, in my opinion, much of any discipline problems, 'cos you blew a whistle to get them to line up on the field, they were all lining up in lines and they're pushing and shoving and half of the children would be lining up correctly, others would be being silly and trying to push into lines, you'd spend ages getting them into lines you'd then get them up, lined up on the playground and the same thing again, they'd be pushing to see who could get first in the line and all the rest of it, then into the school and they'd be standing outside classrooms and pushing and shoving again and all the rest of that and I felt that you just blow a whistle and you say walk sensibly into school and they do it. When I'm on duty I go out blow the whistle and stand in a position where I can see the children from the furthest point and then I start to walk into school almost like the shepherd taking the sheep in really ... they're all in front and you can just, you know, cajole the stragglers into coming in.

In the day-to-day encounters that children have in school with pedagogical practices it is clear, therefore, that it is the body which is a primary medium through which cultural essentials such as effective time use – 'time is money', 'time is short' and must not therefore be wasted – are experienced. Teachers both discipline and empower or, as it were, liberate children, through temporal narratives focused on the minutiae of the body's behaviour and, as noted in the examples below, it is often disputes about effective or correct time use which provoke such temporal lessons to be played out upon the body.

The importance of such body style in relation to children's learning has been noted by Bourdieu in his account of the workings of the *habitus*:

> 'The principles [of culture] em-bodied in this way are placed beyond the grasp of consciousness, and hence cannot be touched by voluntary, deliberate transformation, cannot even be made explicit; nothing seems more ineffable, more incommunicable, more inimitable, and

> therefore more precious than the values given body, made body by the transubstantiation achieved by a hidden persuasion of an implicit pedagogy, capable of instilling a whole cosmology, an ethic, a metaphysic, a political philosophy, through injunctions as insignificant as 'stand up straight' or 'don't hold your knife in your left hand'... The whole trick of pedagogic reason lies precisely in the way it extorts the essential while seeming to demand the insignificant' (1977: 94–5)

At two of the schools in the study the children were required to keep relatively quiet and to work consistently throughout the lessons. However, if the level of noise and talk among the children rose or if the teacher wanted the children to attend better to their work the children would be temporarily halted in their progress with the demand: 'Hands on your heads.' Up would go 35 pair of hands to land on the head. Or the children might hear the order: 'Sit up straight, fold your arms on the table.' Through the literal 'freezing' of the body in time, the uniformity of children is established. Children are reminded of all being the same – 'a schooled child' – under the controlling gaze of the teacher and thus the control of the teacher over the temporal patterning of 'curriculum time' is restated.

Although through such instruction children's activities are momentarily punctuated in time – they are made to stop work and sit still – the intention of such commands is to teach them about the way to proceed more effectively, that is, to make more efficient use of their time through adopting more disciplined behaviours. This was emphasized by the teacher who, in a low-key voice, continued giving instructions to the class about how to proceed appropriately with their work. It is thus – through punctualizing children's time by imposing a particular bodily order – that the connections and continuity of 'curriculum time' are restored and enabled.

However, one teacher at Wellthorpe village school refrained from using the above strategy. He addressed the collectivity of the children with more subtlety while still drawing the children's attention to the importance of correct bodily posture and conduct. He explained how he would use a particular tone of voice:

> I tend to focus in, perhaps, on one individual and say something along the lines of: 'I like the way Roger is sitting up and he's ready to go.' That generally is enough to get the rest of the children... I think they want to please you, so if you say that to one child and praise some positive behaviour then... the rest of them follow.

Though adhering to this principle of not raising his voice in the classroom the teacher would occasionally hold what he termed a 'telling off assembly' through which all children at the school could be admonished:

> So you go into the hall... I don't wish to see this unacceptable behaviour...: they see that side of me as well, where I'm pushing forward the views that the school must be like this and we must show pride in ourselves, show pride in our school, we must be great ambassadors of our school and all the rest of that kind of a *spiel*....

Time shifting and body discipline

A further embodied cultural narrative to which children become subject is that which teaches children that 'time is a commodity'. Through systems of both reward and punishment, played out through the body, children learn that present behaviour has consequences for the future and in teaching children such lessons the daily school assembly is an eloquent vehicle.

Thus, for example, in Northwich, the city school, a pupil's past academic achievement was publicly acknowledged in the weekly '*Curly Wurly* assembly'. Each pupil had a record-of-achievement card and, throughout the weeks at school, the children might collect a star for good work. These stars were recorded on the card and once a child had amassed 15 stars their achievement was made public in the '*Curly Wurly* assembly'. The whole school was gathered together for this event and the children in each year group were asked, in turn, 'who had achieved 15 merits'. Any child who had 15 stamps on their card would go to the front of the hall, and stand before their peers. They were then given a *Curly Wurly* (a chocolate toffee bar), a sticker to wear on their bodies and they shook hands with the deputy head of school. Rarely, a child might manage 30 stars in which case they would receive two chocolate bars. This ritual was thus focused on the individual body of the child and took place among the corporate body of the school. The child's body was individualized, paraded, decorated and rewarded through a very public exposure of the body.

Bad behaviour was, however, also exposed and made visible through the symbolic body of the school assembly. If children fidgeted, talked or failed to pay attention in assembly they too would be removed from the collective body of children and would be made to sit alone, at the front, where the age hierarchy of the school is most keenly felt. The youngest children always sat at the front, with the eldest lining the back walls of the assembly hall. This meant therefore that frequently a ten- or eleven-year-old child would be forced to spend their assembly time sitting isolated in front of a line of four- and five-year-olds, their large size contrasting with the smaller bodies of the younger children, providing a very visible and corporeal reminder of their offence.

A teacher, at one of the village schools, used the same system to temper troublesome pupils during assembly and on one occasion she had moved Martin, one of the boys from year 5, to sit in the front row as he had been bothering the boys next to him. She accounted for her action as follows: 'It means I can keep an eye on him.' But the comments from his age mates and those older and slightly younger than himself demonstrate the less explicit consequences of this movement. Eight-year-old Tim said: 'Yes, that's good! – Let him sit with the babies.'

Thus, in these examples, time-shifting as a corporeal disciplinary device can be seen to occur in two ways: the temporary reassignment of developmental age is achieved via the physical movement of bodies and the child pays the penalty for the incorrect use of curriculum time through receiving a temporary but very visible public bodily exposure. Should such measures, however, prove insufficient to instil in children the local sense of temporal order which constitutes 'curriculum time', then further temporal and spatial restrictions may be placed on children and again enforced through the body. Not infrequently this entailed additional demands being made on children's own time at school such that the privilege of 'play time' (that part of the school day which is relatively free of external constraints) would be withdrawn. In two of the schools, children who have been badly behaved in assembly or in class were told that the next playtime, or, the next few play-times, would have to be spent standing outside the staff room for the duration. The symbolism of this is stark. Bodies which normally at this time of day are running around the playground for pleasure are rendered immobile. Faces are turned to the wall so that the children cannot see their friends or participate in their games. All they can hear, at a distance, is the noise of other children running free. Their individual identities are hidden from view, except to the teachers who come and go from the staff room. That this disciplining of the body takes place outside the staff room simply serves, for the miscreant, to underscore the gravity of their offence. Time is made to literally stand still for the child – the welcome punctualization of curriculum time which playtime brings is forgone and children's control of time at school becomes elided, an experience and a lesson narrated through the immobility of the body. Through bodily discipline children learn that time is a valuable commodity.

Conclusion

This chapter has explored the different ways in which children come to understand the qualitative passage of time both in relation to their everyday lives at school and in relation to their growing into adulthood. The central feature of our argument is that in this process of learning the body plays a critical and orienting role. The body does not simply define or locate the child at a particular point in the life course, but through its physical representation of that development stage, it permits the overlay of concepts of social competence and maturity. The competencies and capacities of the body are themselves, in turn, made the focus of the particular temporal regimes associated with the punctuations of 'curriculum time' at school; time, therefore, comes to be literally embodied by children through the twin processes of discipline and liberation which shape their everyday time at school. Bodily discipline is most strongly asserted by teachers, as we have shown, and thus, ironically, it is through using the very bodily practices, postures and behaviours that curriculum time imposes, that children are able to liberate themselves from its constraints.

Acknowledgement

This paper derives from research conducted within the project 'Changing Times' as part of the ESRC programme 'Children 5–16'. All three authors have equivalent status in the preparation of work for publication.

Notes

1. Although children do see playtime as being under their own control they are none the less also keenly aware that 'playtime' and 'lunchtime' take place within 'school time' and are thus subject to the wider structures of control operative within the school. Thus behaviour at 'playtime' is regulated by the teachers on duty, and at lunchtimes by the dinner ladies in whom authority to punish children for their behaviour is, for that moment in time, invested. For example, dinner ladies as teachers can make children go 'on the wall' as a punishment for bad behaviour (see later).
2. This, as we show later, is similarly exemplified in the assembly where moving up and away from the teacher indicates both age and achievement literally embodied in growth by a bigger body.

References

Bourdieu, P. 1977. *Outline of a Theory of Practice*. Cambridge: Cambridge University Press.

Burman, E. 1994. *Deconstructing Developmental Psychology*. London: Routledge.

Certeau, de M. 1984. *The Practice of Everyday Life*. Berkeley: University of California Press.

Chambers, R. 1992. 'Rural Appraisal: Rapid, Relaxed and Participatory', IDS *Discussion Paper 311*. IDS: University of Sussex.

Chambers, R. 1994. *Participatory Rural Appraisal: Challenges, Potentials and Paradigms*. IDS: University of Sussex.

Christensen, P. and James, A. 2000. 'Childhood Diversity and Commonality: Some Methodological Insights', in P. Christensen and A. James (eds) *Research with Children*. London: Falmer Press.

Corrigan, P. 1979. *Schooling the Smash Street Kids*. London: Macmillan.

Csordas, T.J. 1994. *Embodiment and Experience: The Existential Ground of Culture and Self*. Cambridge: Cambridge University Press.

Durkheim, E. 1915. *Elementary Forms of Religious Life*. London: George Allen & Unwin.

Featherstone, M. 1982. 'The Body in Consumer Culture', *Theory, Culture and Society*, 1: 18–33.

Foucault, M. 1979. *Discipline and Punish: The Birth of the Prison*. Harmondsworth: Peregrine.

Hockey, J. and James, A. 1993. *Growing Up and Growing Old*. London: Sage.

James, A. (2000). 'Embodied Being(s): Understanding the Self and the Body in Childhood', in A. Prout (ed.) *The Body, Childhood and Society*. London: Macmillan.

Jenks, C. 1982. *The Sociology of Childhood: Essential Readings*. London: Batsford.

Jenks, C. 1998. (ed.) *Core Sociological Dichotomies*. London: Sage.

Lyon, M.L. and Barbalet, J.M. 1994. 'Society's Body: Emotion and the "Somatization" of Social Theory', in T.J. Csordas (ed.) *Embodiment and Experience: The Existential Ground of Culture and Self*. Cambridge: Cambridge University Press.

Mauss, M. 1950. 'Les téchniques du corps', *Sociologie et Anthropologie*. Paris: Presses Universitaires de France.

Morse, J. 1990. *The Biologising of Childhood: Developmental Psychology and the Darwinian Myth*. London: Lawrence Erlbaum.

Oliver, M. 1989. 'Disability and Dependency: A Creation of Industrial Societies', in L. Barton (ed.) *Disability and Dependency*. Lewes: Falmer Press.

Sheridan, A. 1980. *Foucault: The Will to Truth*. London: Tavistock.

Shilling, C. 1993. *The Body and Social Theory*. London: Sage.

12
Dreams of Disembodiment: The Secret History of the Remote Control

Mike Michael

Introduction

As is well known, recent sociological thought has turned to the role of the body and embodiment in social processes (e.g. Shilling 1993; Synnott 1993; Turner 1996). However, less attention has been paid to the way that bodies are heterogeneously distributed – how the functions of bodies are, as Latour (1992) puts it, delegated to technologies. Further, we can think of these delegations as, within modernity, attached to what we might call 'dreams of disembodiment'. By this I mean to connote the ways in which various activities are concerned with removing the body, making it redundant, delegating its functions, wholesale or in parts, to other entities. And, it might be suggested, this dream of bypassing the body is about attaching human will to the world without the interventions, the mediations, of the body.

Once we begin to think of the body as distributed in this way, we come face to face with what Latour (1993a) has called 'hybrids', that is, mixtures of humans and non-humans. As we shall see, Latour has argued that we moderns have been somewhat backward in addressing these hybrids, even though, all the while, they proliferate. In contrast, I shall argue, drawing upon the examples of the remote control and the couch potato, that in popular culture such hybrids can be scrutinized and judged. But further, I want to suggest that such 'scrutiny' is not the domain of pure humans – it is practised by hybrids themselves in complex, distributed ways. An upshot of this is that our 'dreams of disembodiment' are punctured by 'the return of the body'.

In what follows, then, I shall begin with a condensed overview of Latour's account of the delegation of body functions to technological non-humans, linking this to modern 'dreams of disembodiment'. I will then consider Latour's analysis of how we moderns have purified the human from the non-human; even as delegation proceeds apace, we have routinely failed to attend to these mixings – hybridizations – of human and the technological. However, I will also problematize Latour's narrative by discussing the television remote control, especially in its association with humans to produce the 'couch potato'. I will suggest that the couch potato has been the object of considerable discourse. However, I will additionally propose that this 'scrutiny' or surveillance of the couch potato is conducted not only in normalizing discourse, but also through various heterogeneous relations within the home. In particular, I will examine how the loss of the TV remote control illustrates not only the 'return of the body', but also processes of 'surveillance' that are distributed across the *arrangements* of technologies and humans. In the process, I explore some of the implications of this analysis for our understanding of the body and agency.

Delegation and disembodiment

For Bruno Latour (1991, 1992; Latour and Johnson 1988) technological nonhumans are routinely used in the replacement of human actors who, in so far as they are potentially unreliable in performing their allotted tasks, would require disciplining, training, supervision, surveillance, and so on. Such continuous monitoring is, Latour suggests, inconvenient and inefficient. Currently, a more convenient and efficient means of ensuring that certain things get done is to delegate to relatively 'reliable' nonhumans (technological artefacts). Latour illustrates this point with an analysis of the operation of the door-closer (or groom – the mechanism which slowly closes the door without slamming). This serves as a replacement for such relatively inefficient and potentially subversive human functionaries as the concierge, the porter or the bellhop. In this story, the will of the user of the door, which previously had to pass through the unreliable body of the porter, now bypasses that human body altogether and hinges instead upon the door groom.

Notice, however, the 'return of the body', for now the technology, as Latour points out, operates upon and shapes the user of the door. To quote (Latour 1992: 234):

> neither my little nephews nor my grandmother could get in unaided because our groom needed the force of an able-bodied

person to accumulate enough energy to close the door later... these doors discriminate against very little and very old persons.

Such persons, the objects of technological discrimination, must enrol others, humans or nonhumans or both, to help them negotiate the groomed door.

This story applies not only to the bodies of others, but also to our own bodies. Our body parts have their functions delegated to technologies. For example, the zip is a convenience because it saves on the complex and repetitive manipulation of fingers and thumbs that was necessary to use hook and eye fastenings. These body-part routines could be removed with the invention of a mechanism that fastened two separate pieces of material together as the zip does. That is, these movements are delegated to the zip. Of course, there are a number of conditions that need to hold for the zip to operate in this way. First, the zip must hold the material sections together until the need arises to separate them. As Friedel (1994) documents, the early versions of the zip certainly did not fulfil this criterion. But a zip can be made to 'work' along other criteria, say, by lowering the expectations of users – trading 'convenience' for 'function'. Such a trade-off might entail more cautious movement in an attempt to ensure that the zip did not come undone. In the modern zip, the shaping of our comportment is concerned with, for example, ensuring that surrounding material does not get caught up in the teeth of the zip: we have developed new routines that serve the zip's function. If certain body-parts and their movements were removed, consigned to the workings of a technology, other body-parts and their movements have developed to ensure the workings of that technology. As Nikolas Rose (1996: 184) writes: 'Rather than speak of "the body", we need to analyze just how a particular body-regime has been produced, the channelling of processes, organs, flows, connections, the alignment of one aspect with another.'

As the foregoing suggests, criteria such as 'efficiency' or 'convenience' against which the 'functionality' or 'working-ness' of a technology are assessed are highly complex. 'Inconvenience' and 'inefficiency' are themselves historically contingent qualities – under the appropriate economic conditions, forms of human servitude are 'more efficient and convenient' than the development and application of technological artefacts capable of fulfilling the same function. Furthermore, these criteria are likely to reflect broader cultural values concerned with disembodiment, the attainment of insubstantiality that frees the will from the body.[1] Virilio (1995: 80) puts it thus: 'To expand, to dissolve, become weightless, burst, leave one's heavy body behind: our whole destiny could now be read in terms of escape, evasion' (see also Morse, 1994, for a critical discussion of such dreams in relation to the cyborg). But as we have seen in relation to the door groom and the zip, the 'body returns' – subject to new discriminations, obliged to learn new routines.

The purified hybrid

In developing the notions of 'dreams of disembodiment' and the 'return of the body', all I have done is simply exemplify one of Latour's (1993a) theses in *We Have Never Been Modern*. According to Latour, humans are necessarily hybrid: admixtures of the human and nonhuman, the social and the nonsocial. But so too are nature and technology. What is to count as a 'human', an 'agent', 'nature', 'technology' is an effect of a network of heterogeneous entities involved in heterogeneous relations. Moreover, while I have talked about 'the return of the body', this is not just the upshot of the re-assertion of the social over and against the object. By this I mean that it is not that these technologies – the door groom and the zip – confront a set of social circumstances that do not quite match the routines inscribed in the technology. Rather, the technologies themselves, however much their designers attempt to circumscribe their possibilities or potentialities, always seem, much like humans, (or so Latour 1996, tells us) to escape these circumscriptions: the preceding designs are outstripped by subsequent technology. As Latour puts it, 'we are *exceeded* by what we create' (1996: 237, emphasis in original). As we shall see, this excessiveness can be partially traced in certain coincidences that enable unforeseen events to stem from a technology; in the process, this opens up new possibilities, resistances, 'surveillances', shifts around the doings of the body.

Now, Latour (1993a) argues that, in contrast to premodern cultures, modernity has been fundamentally concerned to purify these hybrids, to disaggregate them into their ostensibly component parts. Thus, we moderns have routinely indulged in dualism; for example, we have represented nature as transcendent, while society is seen to be our free construction. Yet beneath all this activity of purification, the hybrids have been multiplying at alarming rates. For example, Latour (1993b: 6) posits the hybrid of the gun-person. For Latour, contrary to both the view that 'it is guns that kill' and it is 'people that kill' , it is the 'citizen-gun'. Rather than ascribing essences to the 'gun' and the 'citizen' – each being either good, or bad, or neutral, what Latour aims to do is show how the new hybrid entails new associations, new goals, new translations and so on. As one enters into an association with a gun, both citizen and gun become different. As Latour puts it (1993b: 6):

> The dual mistake of the materialists and of the sociologists is to start with essences, either those of subjects or those of objects... Either you give too much to the gun or too much to the gun-holder. Neither the subject, nor the object, nor their goals are fixed for ever. We have to shift our attention to this unknown X, this hybrid which can truly be said to act.

So, here, what should be policed is not the gun or the person – not subject or object alone – but the combination – the hybrid. But, according to Latour, we moderns have been singularly inept at such policing, even as we are ever more deeply embroiled in – indeed, the effect of – hybrid networks.

I will later dispute this vision of modernity. But for the moment, I want to elaborate on some of the media through which the relations between humans and nonhumans, bodies, minds and technologies, are conducted. According to Callon and Law (1995: 486), such relations are necessarily heterogeneous. For them, all actors are hybrids in so far as they are effects of networks made up of heterogeneous entities, or rather as they phrase it in their characterization of *hybrid colléctifs*, 'Relations. Links. Interpenetrations. Processes. Of any kind'. Whatever a hybrid's 'overt size' it can be decomposed into multiple heterogeneous components – or preferably relations. In relation to this process, Akrich and Latour (1992: 259) provide a valuable, expanded definition of semiotics: 'The study of how meaning is built, [where] the word "meaning" is taken in its original nontextual and nonlinguistic interpretation: how a privileged trajectory is built, out of an indefinite number of possibilities; in that sense, semiotics is the study of order building or path building and may be applied to settings, machines, bodies and programming languages as well as texts ...'. So, in additon to intertextuality, we can talk of intermateriality (or interobjectivity; cf. Latour 1996).

Drawing out the implications for the body of this discussion, we can say that the body is distributed – hybridized – across a heterogeneous set of entities and relations that entail both the semiotic and material. What I now want to do is consider one such mode of distribution: the relation of the body to the television remote control. In contrast to Latour who argues that such a hybrid is made invisible by virtue of our modernist investments in purification, I want to suggest that this human body remote control hybrid is subject to multiple scrutiny. Sometimes, there are complaints that it is a dangerous entity; sometimes that its full potential has yet to be realized. Sometimes, there is a concern to limit the engagements between body and the technology; sometimes there are activities that aim to enhance contacts. The point is that there are numerous discourses and practices out of which this hybrid emerges sometimes stabilized, sometimes destabilized.

The television remote control

Remote control is a very broad term that essentially describes the control of a device at a distance. Important here is the medium of communication between the control device and the reactive device (or receiver). There are numerous types of media. Sometimes these are physical connections – wires or cables; mostly, electromagnetic waves are used – radio or infrared (see http://hometeam.com/lighting/remotes.htm – 28/1/98). The remotes with which most of us are familiar usually control the television and/or the video, and the hi-fi. In June 1996, the TV remote control was 40 years old. First introduced by Zenith as the Space Command Remote TV Control, it was marketed under the slogan: 'Nothing between you and the set but space!' The Space Command was a replacement for an earlier version that was connected to the television by a wire – the 'Lazy Bones' model (*Daily Telegraph*, 25 June 1996). Nowadays, the most common TV remote controls use infrared light. The remote control device flashes a rapid series of signals (like Morse code), each signal code designed for a particular function. The signals are determined by a microprocessor in the remote control, and are translated into infrared flashes produced by a diode located at the front of the remote. These different signals, repeated five times a second to ensure the receiver in the TV has read them, serve numerous functions – changing channel, colour, volume, operating the VCR and so on (http://www.zenith.com/main/about/howremot.html – 28/1/98).

Needless to say, the development of the remote control has not stood still. So, for instance, coming onto the market are combined controls. For example, US Electronics (self-proclaimed as the world's largest independent manufacturer and distributor of cable television remote controls) has marketed a four-function remote that offers 'complete control over your cable box, TV, VCR and either a Digital Music terminal, or a second cable box, TV or VCR' (http://www.shopnetmal.com/use/use – 28/1/98). More radically, Zenith has noted that many controls have become overcomplicated and have developed a Z-Trak, a PC mouse-like device that uses a track ball-controlled cursor to bring up various function menus on the TV screen (http://www.zenith.com/main/about/howremot.html – 28/1/98).

Now, in terms of the Latourian model of the relation between human and technology, the standard remote control can be regarded as the technology to which the functions of certain body parts are delegated. The body parts are the legs, the back, the arms – all those that together operate in moving the fingers from the sofa to the television. The remote control is, in such an account, the functional equivalent of this body-part complex. The potentially unreliable body parts, that would otherwise have to be disciplined, surveilled, are replaced by a machine that does their work for them more reliably, more efficiently. Of course, as mentioned above and elaborated below, notions such as reliability and efficiency are themselves contextual, resting, at the very least, on a conception of the viewer as someone 'interested' in minimizing the energy expended in the process of television watching.

However, this analysis presupposes a conception of technology as a medium which fulfils (and shapes) practical ends. In contrast, we can note that the remote control, and indeed, all technologies, serve expressive ends. In other words, technology mediates cultural and social investments as they are expressed through the body. The very obvious point is that nothing simply 'works' – a machine always speaks to a range of 'function-expressions'. By 'function-expressions' I mean that technologies do not just perform practical functions – they are not simply instrumental, as is often portrayed in actor-network (and sociology of technology) studies of technology. Latour's (1992) door groom is not simply a means of shutting doors, minimizing drafts and halting any chance of slamming. For users (perhaps, the better term is consumers – see Lury 1996 for an excellent review of some of these issues) it enables the expression of who one is. If one is muscle-bound, one can open the door, stiffened with a door groom, with a muscle-bound flourish, or with the greatest delicacy – each serves expressive ends. If one cannot open the door, one can discreetly recruit relatives or loudly complain to passers-by. Technologies, as things of consumption and use (and also non-consumption and non-use), are 'opportunities' for the performance of taste and self-identity (Bourdieu 1984; Mauss 1985). To reiterate, the promises offered by technologies address not only the practical but also the expressive, indissolubly so indeed, and some of these expressive dimensions are enabled (if never determined) by the design of the technology itself.

For example, the function-expression of the remote control is intimately tied up to the domestic context of its use. Morley (1992) has analysed these contexts in terms of relations of power. He documents the role of the remote control in the conflict over television viewing choices. Amongst his participants, it was the 'man of the house' who, when present, had monopoly of the remote control. Moreover, some of the women complained that the husband used the device 'obsessively, channel flicking across programmes when their wives were trying to watch something else' (Morley 1992: 147). The remote tended to sit on the arm of the father's chair, used almost exclusively by him. As Morley puts it, the remote control 'is a highly visible symbol of condensed power relations' (ibid.). But, importantly, this view of the remote control misses out on the functionality of the remote control. It is not just a symbol, but because of the sorts of actions it enables, it serves as a mediator and shaper of such family relations of power. (Morley 1995 also elaborates on this point in relation to the way that the physical television set serves the complex social, symbolic and physical adjustments of the household.)

With the mention of channel surfing (or hopping), we can also address how the ease of access to multiple, fractured, fragmented images structures (post)modern consciousness. So, the remote control serves as one technological tool (out of very many – see, for example, Gergen 1991) through which we are exposed to a disorderly parade of signs. Our selves might become 'saturated' as Gergen has phrased it – 'a multiphrenic condition ... in which one swims in ever-shifting concatenating and contentious currents of being' (Gergen 1991: 79–80). But, this can also be viewed as a consumption of signs that refer only one to another, with no especial connection to referents – reals – beyond (e.g. Baudrillard 1983). Our attention span diminishes, what we become used to, what we desire, is the flow of signs – the surface, the spectacle of their rapid procession is what pleasures us. However, we can also suggest that the man of the family, through the very monopoly of the remote control's channel hopping facility comes to reproduce the relations of power within the family. That is to say, in order to enjoy this luxuriant consumption of fragmented signs there needs to be in place a set of social, political, economic and cultural circumstances that enable such consumption. Thus, if there is something like a saturated self, this coexists with another social self that is endowed with 'capacity' to become saturated: the identity of the post-modern is couched within the practices and privileges of an indulgent consumer (e.g. Lury 1996) sustained in a network of relations of power.

If this expressive dimension is bound up in the relations of power that are exercised within the household, it is also enabled (though certainly not determined) by the functions fulfilled by the remote control – its ability to translate the inconvenient, complex manoeuvres necessitated by old-fashioned channel-switching into the simple movements of a few fingers. However, it should also be noted that such functionality is only possible if the appropriate network is in place. Most basically, we might say, is the requirement that fingers are dextrous, not too large or shaky or immobile. Moreover, the remote control must ensure that it is used in an appropriate way in relation to the television – it must give certain clues that enable functional use. Over-specification on remote controls has led to the design of a new generation with a much simplified button layout (e.g. large colour-coded buttons). And occasionally, there is the problem under-specification which can also confuse users (see Norman 1988).

So, for proper functioning of the remote control, there needs to be in place a certain bodily comportment which, ideally, is invoked by the remote control (design). However, the body is also socially distributed, and for the remote to 'function' it also requires a certain social configuration. So, the domestic relations of power mentioned above need to be in place for the remote to work. But, this simple statement ignores the multiplicity of cultural resources through which the 'working remote control' is constituted. If the members of a family fought physically over the control of the remote control, can it be said to 'work'. Conversely, if the 'man of the house' monopolizes the remote control, it might 'work' for him, but does it work for the other members of the family? In other words, the 'workingness' of this technology rests on relations of power between a number of (potential) users-in-interaction. Yet, the remote control is not an innocent in this struggle, it also mediates – symbolizes, crystallizes *and* materially affects – these relations.

In this section, I have, albeit superficially, traced some of the complexities entailed in the delegation of body functions to the remote control. Not unexpectedly we find, instead of simple delegation, complex distributions of functions and expressions, goals and relations of power that operate on a terrain of contestation. The body parts that were disembodied, delegated to, re-embodied in the remote control return in the form of others' more or less docile bodies, and one's own, more or less, redisciplined, reconfigured, body. No longer do we see separated body and technology, no longer purification but the hybrid, or the *hybrid colléctif*.

But, the hybrid that is TV remote control and human is not exclusive to academic discourse. It features, *contra* Latour, in popular culture in the guise of the couch potato. In what follows, I will consider how this figure is constructed and evaluated.

The couch potato

What is the couch potato? Here is one definition:

> Couch potato n. One who is addicted to watching television and does this while lying on the couch, as inert and braindead as a potato. (Green 1995: 78)

Now, the link between the couch potato and the remote control is not hard to exemplify. Here is a typical example: 'The TV remote control is 40 years old this month. The couch potato's friend made its first appearance in June 1956...' (*Daily Telegraph*, 25 June 1996). Given this popular connection between the remote control and the couch potato, what are the discourses that construct the couch potato? To what extent do they attempt to separate human and remote control, and to what extent do they attempt to reinforce their association, bind them closer together?

There seem to be two broad discursive complexes that constitute the couch potato. On the one hand, the emphasis is very much placed on the 'badness' of the couch potato. An ironic statement of this status of couch potatoes can be found in the adult comic *Viz*:

> TV viewers. Avoid laziness by screwing your TV remote control to a wall or piece of furniture at least ten feet away from your chair. (Donald, 1994: 67).

On the other, the couch potato is accepted, even celebrated, as another quote from *Viz* illustrates:

> Attach a 'bayonet' to your TV remote control by taping a fork to it. This way you can keep control of the television whilst eating TV snacks. (Donald 1995: 60)

Let me now more fully exemplify each of the 'good' and 'bad' discursive complexes.

The couch potato is bad

First there are those accounts which document the terrible price in terms of health that must be paid for the indulgence of the couch potato. Individuals will personally suffer because they have not engaged in what is deemed to be appropriate levels of physical activity. Further, there will be consequent strains placed upon the public purse – the couch potato, and couch potato culture, works directly against national good housekeeping. For example: 'A three-year, £9 million government health education campaign was launched yesterday aimed at changing "couch potato" Britain by encouraging everyone to take at least 30 minutes moderate exercise five times a week…' (*The Guardian*, 20 March 1996).

To be a couch potato means not only that one places unnecessary strains on one's body, but one is also economically unproductive. This same argument applies to one's cultural productivity: the couch potato slips into a sort of animality where false bodily pleasures are preferred to true cultural self-development. As the following quote suggests, there is relief that the frontiers of couch potato culture are being rolled back – that children and adults are still able to engage in 'proper' cultural activities: 'The couch potato is a threatened species, because the British are becoming more cultured and more active. We are reading books more, visiting the theatre and museums more and watching television less, according to the latest Cultural Trends study by the Policy Studies Institute' (*The Independent*, 27 March 1997).

Finally, the couch potato can be represented as a body that is politically sequestrated – sybaritically lost in the pleasures of television, as opposed to exercising political will in the public sphere. Here is one example of this discourse: 'This week Mrs Bottomley had a fit of the principles and called for more stringent controls on sex and violence on television. But her initiative to woo the couch-potato electorate with a hit list of televisual ills made some crucial omissions…' (*The Independent*, 12 December 1996).

The couch potato is good

These 'bad couch potato' discourses are concerned with disciplining the couch potato; or rather, they have been essentially oriented toward a disaggregation of the couch potato into its constituents parts, so that the human body is recovered, re-endowed with such proper qualities as health, and a productivity that can be economic, cultural or political. However, there are also those discourses that presuppose the couch potato, that celebrate it, that nurture it. In this first example, we see the couch potato represented as being underdeveloped – that potato-ness is constrained by the available technology. In other words, the couch potato is seen as a potential market identity to which appeals can be made in the promotion of new technological or service products (e.g. the new Parker Knoll recliner armchair designed for TV watchers, with a holder for the remote on one; Couch Potato investment portfolio).

However, in contrast to these marketing niche readings of the couch potato, there are less instrumental accounts that celebrate it, that use it as a commonplace in the articulation of subcultural identity. Here we have couch potatoes talking to one another, expressing their common couch potato-ness. Sometimes, a couch potato is the sedentary sports watcher. A webpage entitled 'Proud to be a couch potato' lists the homepages of various US sports teams. More often, the celebration of the couch potato hinges on the enjoyment of television watching. For example, one webpage entitled 'Why we like bad TV' devotes a story to TV Land, a channel 'dedicated entirely to reruns'. It is 'to the delight of Couch Potatoes everywhere'. (http://www.bostonphoenix.com/alt 1/archive/tv/badtv/NICK_TV_LAND.html – 21/10/97).

The secret life of the remote control

To the extent that some of the preceding examples illustrate discourses that constitute the couch potato as 'bad', they are concerned to extricate the body and the person: to make it less wasteful of self and state; to make it more productive – economically, culturally, politically. *Contra* Latour, what we have here, I think, is not a modernist disinterest in the hybrid. Rather, through characteristic modernist discourses of rationalization and government, there is a scrutiny of this hybrid, which, in essence, advocates the dismemberment of the couch potato, a removal of the remote control from its grasp, a recovery of the technologically corrupted body that can once again be put to work. Conversely, we have discourses of the 'good' couch potato that assume and celebrate the couch potato. Again, the hybrid is addressed, this time through the modernist discourses of consumption.

Now, the surveillance manifested in the discourses of the 'bad' couch potato is only one form of surveillance that is possible. When thinking about the heterogeneous network in which the couch potato is embedded, and which includes the discursive complexes outlined above, we can also point to certain material contingencies which serve in the uncoupling of human and technology, person and remote control. As such, we would want to show that the 'wasted' body that is distributed through a network can occasionally be 'recovered' not only through discursive means, but also through material ones.

In their discussion of *hybrids colléctifs*, Callon and Law (1995) argue that it is very difficult to think about agency where the locus of the agent is distributed. The Western tradition has fundamentally assumed agency to be attached to 'singularized' entities. Hybrids and their agencies are both distributed. In some cases, it is possible to generate an account of these, but, as Callon and Law conclude, perhaps we cannot 'know' all these hybrids and their agencies. Here, what I want briefly and speculatively to consider is a sort of contingent agency, where certain events are enabled (but not determined) by the conjunction of certain heterogeneous arrangements and designs. The event I am interested in the 'loss of the remote control' – a traumatic event that, albeit momentarily, disrupts the ostensibly smooth agency of the couch potato. Or rather, put more accurately, it reflects the contingencies of the heterogeneous network out of which the couch potato emerges. I have already hinted above that such disaggregation might stem from the social dynamics of the family. Here, however, I want to explore some of the technological conditions that shape this disruption.

But first, how might we think the 'loss of the remote control'? That it is a commonplace event is not in much doubt, as advice from *Viz*'s Top Tips demonstrates: 'Avoid the frustration of repeatedly losing your TV remote control by keeping it in a "cowboy" holster fashioned out of a child's sock and an old belt' (Donald 1994: 65).

The 'loss of the remote control' clearly stirs up great emotions. The Opinion Research Corporation's survey of Americans' relationship with the remote control found that:

> Over half (55%) of the respondents said they lose the remote control up to five times a week. And 11% of those surveyed said they lose the remote between six and ten times a week. 'After they've lost their remote controls, 63% of Americans say that they spend up to five minutes a day looking for it. Sixteen percent say that they spend 10 minutes a day looking for it. The most frequent places that Americans find their remotes include in and under the furniture (38%), in the kitchen or bathroom (20%), and in the refrigerator

> (6%). (http://www.empire.net/~psl/Fun_People/1994AWM.html – 2/10/97).[2]

The *Viz* solution, and that derived from the survey (see note 2) are technological. In contrast, the Megadodo homepage promotes a human solution: 'The remote control can suddenly be missing. If this happens, try to be calm and do a rational search of the surroundings. Most often the remote is tired of your continuously zapping and can be found hiding on the floor' (http://megadodo.com/articles/ 6R18.html – 2/10/97).

These two contrasting solutions to the reunification of remote control and human map directly onto the human/nonhuman dichotomy. But – and this is the important point here – we need to ask how it is that this local, practical dissolution of the couch potato came about. Well, clearly there are social dynamics that predispose the loss of the remote control – young children playing is one possible factor. Yet the loseability of the remote is something that can also be said to reflect a number of material ironies, in particular, what we might call the accidental coalition of technological designs, or technological coincidentalism. Thus, in coming to grips with the remote control's affinity for the back of the sofa, we can note that the continuity of the couch potato is partly influenced by the seemingly irrelevant fact that sofas are designed with removable seat cushions (that enable seat covers to be taken off for cleaning). One structuring assumption here is the nature of the hand: the remote control nestles neatly in the palm; the pliable gap between seat cushion and sofa back is perfect for fingers aiming to remove the former. The size of the remote control matches, more or less ideally, the space between sofa cushion and back.

The central point is that the distribution of the body across a heterogeneous network is something that is constantly performed. That performance can be undermined by the enablements or allowances generated by the coincidence or coalition of technological design features. The coincidence of the dimensions of remote control and the sofa-cushion gap, along with whatever other social dynamics are in play, comprise a *hybrid colléctif* that serves in the disaggregation of the couch potato. Perhaps what is being witnessed here are some of the strange distributed agencies that are performed by *hybrid colléctifs*.

Concluding remarks

It might seem odd to call the process of 'losing the remote control' – born of the conjunction of technologies, the coincidentalization of design (as well as social factors) – a form of surveillance. In concluding, I want, albeit speculatively, to develop this line of thought.

If we recall from Foucault (1979) Bentham's panopticon, surveillance is conducted by an unseen agent – the continuing possibility that one is being watched by a hidden, conceivably present agent shapes the comportment of the body. Here, then, there is a potential human agent that, through an architectural configuration, scrutinizes the comportment of the prisoner: these arrangements are, of course, moral. Now, let us recall Latour's door groom. It too discriminates against certain bodies, demands certain capacities from the body. It is another moral agent that disciplines the door user – as Latour would have it, the door groom is morality objectified.

In both cases the body is distributed across arrangements of technologies and humans – it is emergent in these heterogeneous networks. More broadly, what the loss of the remote control suggests is an arrangement, a configuration, an assemblage that is coincidental; such chance-like, unintended associations generate new potential causal pathways. The body that should be indolent, unexercised when embedded within that configuration known as the 'couch potato' is unexpectedly exercised, manoeuvred, manipulated in the regular search for the remote control.

These new associations and their related pathways are, I suggested, some of the hidden, unknown, agencies that Callon and Law mention. They are agencies distributed across accidental material and, of course, social coalitions and collusions: heterogeneous, distributed, unintended, contingent, stochastic. If *contra* Latour, moderns do, sometimes at least, assess and police hybrids as evidenced in the discourses of the good and bad couch potato, it is not just modern *humans* who do this. Rather, it is also hybrids themselves. We need to begin to theorize how hybrids themselves practice this 'surveillance' – hybrids that are comprized of accidental conjunctions and distributions, what we might call coincidentalisations, of the social, the corporeal and the technological.

Acknowledgement

I would like to thank Susan Condor and Gavin Kendall for their helpful comments while this chapter was in preparation.

Notes

1. Turner (1992) also mentions 'disembodiment' in relation to anorexia nervosa, linking it to western asceticism and gendered consumerism (the

slim body). By comparison, I am interested in disembodiment as a mode of luxuriance, where will is attached to the world without the unruly mediations of the body. Of course, as I note, this process is gendered too.

2. We need to be a little cautious about this survey, for, it should be noted, over and above the usual reasons, the survey was sponsored by Philips Consumer Electronics Company which produces the Magnavox Remote Locator (TM) colour televisions which help TV viewers swiftly locate their lost remote controls by pressing the TV's 'power-on' button.

References

Akrich, M. and Latour, B. 1992. 'A Summary of a Convenient Vocabulary for the Semiotics of Human and Nonhuman Assemblies', in W.E. Bijker and J. Law (eds.) *Shaping Technology/Building Society*. Cambridge, MA: MIT Press.

Baudrillard, J. 1983. 'The Ecstasy of Communication', in H. Foster (ed.) *The Anti-aesthetic: Essays in Postmodern Culture*. Port Townsend: Bay Press.

Bourdieu, P. 1984. *Distinction*. London: Routledge and Kegan Paul.

Callon, M. and Law, J. 1995. 'Agency and the *Hybrid Colléctif*', *The South Atlantic Quarterly*, 94: 481–507.

Donald, C. (ed.) 1994. *Top Tips: From the 'Letterbocks' pages of Viz*. London: John Brown Publishing Limited.

Donald, C. (ed.) 1995. *Top Tips 2: From the 'Letterbocks' pages of Viz*. London: John Brown Publishing Limited.

Foucault, M. 1979. *Discipline and Punish*. Harmondsworth: Penguin.

Friedel, R. 1994. *Zipper: An Exploration in Novelty*. New York: Norton.

Gergen, K.J. 1991. *The Saturated Self*. New York: Basic Books.

Green, J. 1995. *The Macmillan Dictionary of Contemporary Slang*, 3rd edition. London: Macmillan.

Latour, B. 1991. 'Technology is Society Made Durable', in J. Law (ed.) *A Sociology of Monsters*. London: Routledge.

Latour, B. 1992. 'Where are the Missing Masses? A Sociology of a Few Mundane Artefacts', in W.E. Bijker and J. Law (eds.) *Shaping Technology/Building Society*. Cambridge, MA: MIT Press.

Latour, B. 1993a. *We Have Never been Modern*. Hemel Hempstead: Harvester Wheatsheaf.

Latour, B. 1993b. *On Technical Mediation: The Messenger Lectures on the Evolution of Civilization*. Cornell University, Institute of Economic Research: Working Papers Series.

Latour, B. 1996. 'On Interobjectivity', *Mind, Culture and Activity*, 3: 228–45.

Latour, B. and Johnson, J. 1988. 'Mixing Humans with Non-Humans? Sociology of a Few Mundane Artefacts' *Social Problems*, 35: 298–310.

Lury, C. 1996. *Consumer Culture*. Cambridge: Polity Press.

Mauss, M. 1985. 'A Category of the Person: the Notion of Person; the Notion of Self', in M. Carrithers, S. Collins and S. Lukes (eds.) *The Category of the Person*. Cambridge: Cambridge University Press.

Morley, D. 1992. *Television, Audiences and Cultural Studies*. London: Routledge.

Morley, D. 1995. 'Television: Not so Much a Visual Medium, More a Visible Object', in C. Jenks (ed.) *Visual Culture*. London: Routledge.

Morse, M. 1994. 'What do Cyborgs Eat? Oral Logic in an Information Society', in G. Bender and T. Druckrey (eds) *Culture on the Brink: Ideologies of Technology*. Seattle: Bay Press.
Norman, D. 1988. *The Psychology of Everyday Things*. New York: Basic Books.
Rose, N. 1996. *Inventing Our Selves: Psychology, Power and Personhood*. Cambridge: Cambridge University Press.
Shilling, C. 1993. *The Body and Social Theory*. London: Sage.
Synnott, A. 1993. *The Body Social*. London: Routledge.
Turner, B. 1992. *Regulating Bodies*. London: Routledge.
Turner, B. 1996. *The Body and Society*, 2nd edition. London: Sage.
Virilio, P. 1995. *The Art of the Motor*. Minneapolis: University of Minnesota Press.

Index